DEEP POWDER & STEEP ROCK

DEEP
POWDER & STEEP
ROCK
THE LIFE OF MOUNTAIN GUIDE
HANS GMOSER

BY CHIC SCOTT

RMB

RMB | Rocky Mountain Books Ltd.
rmbooks.com
@rmbooks
facebook.com/rmbooks

Cataloguing data available from Library and Archives Canada
ISBN 978-1-77160-112-2 (paperback)
Also available in electronic formats

Book design by Linda Petras

Printed and bound in Canada by Marquis

Distributed in Canada by Heritage Group Distribution and in the U.S. by
Publishers Group West

For information on purchasing bulk quantities of this book, or to obtain media
excerpts or invite the author to speak at an event, please visit rmbooks.com and
select the "Contact Us" tab.

RMB | Rocky Mountain Books is dedicated to the environment and committed
to reducing the destruction of old-growth forests. Our books are produced with
respect for the future and consideration for the past.

We acknowledge the financial support of the Government of Canada through
the Canada Book Fund and the Canada Council for the Arts, and of the province
of British Columbia through the British Columbia Arts Council and the Book
Publishing Tax Credit.

Nous reconnaissons l'aide financière du gouvernement du Canada par
l'entremise du Fonds du livre du Canada et le Conseil des arts du Canada, et de
la province de la Colombie-Britannique par le Conseil des arts de la Colombie-
Britannique et le Crédit d'impôt pour l'édition de livres.

Contents

Just Another Day

Monday, July 3, 2006, was a beautiful day in the Canadian Rocky Mountains, with blue morning skies promising a hot afternoon. Hans Gmoser, the 73-year-old elder states-man of the Canadian mountain community, rose early at his home in Harvie Heights, near Canmore, Alberta, as was his habit. After the usual morning ritual—shower, shave, coffee, juice and granola—he sat down at his computer to check the day's email.

On the desk beside his computer sat a small, framed photo of a man walking across a broad, snow-covered mountaintop. The man was Hans and the date was April 1963. He had just led a group of ski mountaineers to the summit of Mount Columbia, the highest peak in Alberta. A member of the group, Lloyd Nixon, looked down through his viewfinder camera and snapped the image. When he looked up, Hans was gone! The overhanging snow cornice had broken and Hans had begun a 2000-metre plunge to the Athabasca valley.

Peter Fuhrmann, another guide in the group, pulled a rope from his pack and, safely belayed by the others, crawled to the jagged edge. Peering over, he was astonished to see Hans, 20 metres below, balanced like a cat on a snow-covered ledge that had arrested his fall. Hans was able to traverse carefully across the shelf, around a corner and to climb, shaken but alive, back onto the summit.

For more than 40 years Hans had kept this image on his desk—perhaps to keep himself humble and acknowledge his fallibility, but more likely to remind himself how tenuous life is and how quickly things can change.

His morning affairs completed, Hans turned off the computer and went to change. After putting on his cycling shorts and a light shirt, he said goodbye to his wife, Margaret, and loaded his road bike into the car. Cycling was one of his favourite activities and he had travelled the world in pursuit of his passion.

Leaving Harvie Heights, he drove through the entrance gates of Banff National Park, past the town of Banff and parked at the Fireside Picnic Area. After unloading the bike, he put on his helmet and began riding west along the Bow Valley Parkway (or 1A Highway). Narrow and hilly and with a speed limit of 60 km/h, there is little traffic on the road and it is a favourite with cyclists. Hans felt good as the cool mountain air washed over his skin. Cycling was the one way he could relieve the chronic back pain he suffered.

The mountains of the Bow Valley flew by—the west face of Mount Cory, where he had climbed a new route in 1960; The Finger, which he had climbed in 1956; and Castle Mountain, where he had made a film in 1962. These peaks were all old friends; they all had memories and many stories to tell.

*Hans, walking across the summit of Mt. Columbia
just before the cornice broke*

Rosa Gmoser and her young son Hans

PART ONE

Hard Years in Austria

(1932–1951)

*"There is nothing like a little hunger
and despair to clear your vision."*
—Hans Gmoser, speaking to the Banff Rotary Club,
September 17, 1986

Johann Wolfgang Gmoser was born July 7, 1932, in Braunau am Inn, a quiet rural town in the province of Upper Austria. Braunau is a border town, and across the strong-flowing waters of the Inn River is Simbach am Inn, in German Bavaria. At the south end of Braunau's cobblestone main square is a medieval gate tower dating from the 13th century. Above it all towers the spire of St. Stephen's Church, almost 100 metres high. But Braunau's unenviable claim to fame is that 43 years earlier, on April 20, 1889, it was also the birthplace of Adolf Hitler. Over the rich farmland surrounding the town there is not a mountain in sight.

Hans's mother was 18-year-old Rosa Juliana Gmoser, who was working as a domestic at the time. His father, Hans Resch, a 21-year-old soldier, took no interest in or responsibility for the child, who was given his mother's family name. Little is known about the first year of Hans's life, but his mother must have struggled with the financial problems and social stigma that have always plagued unwed mothers.

Soon after Hans's birth, Rosa took her young son and moved to Traun, another small rural town in Upper Austria near the city of Linz. Located along the Traun River, the

The Resch family. Standing: (left) Hans Resch [Hans Gmoser's father] and his brother Karl (right). Sitting: Anna and Karl Resch [Hans's grandparents] and their daughter Anna (right).

town at that time was not much more than a few homes gathered around the elegant St. Dionysius Church. It was hard to tell where the town ended and the country began and many folk kept animals in their backyards. Here Rosa found work manufacturing cigarette paper at the Feuerstein factory, where her father, Hans Ranetbauer, was a foreman. At the Feuerstein factory she also found a husband, and a father for Hans. Erasmus Hintringer was 23 years old and was everything that Hans Resch was not—quiet, patient and caring. Rosa and Erasmus were married January 6, 1934.

The Gmoser/Hintringer family lived in a two-room apartment near the centre of town, upstairs at what is today called Badergasse #10. Water came from a pump in the garden, and the family slept together in an unheated room. Life, though spartan, was comfortable: they even had an inside toilet, which was appreciated on cold winter days.

The Gmoser/Hintringer family.
Rosa (holding Walter), Erasmus and Hans.

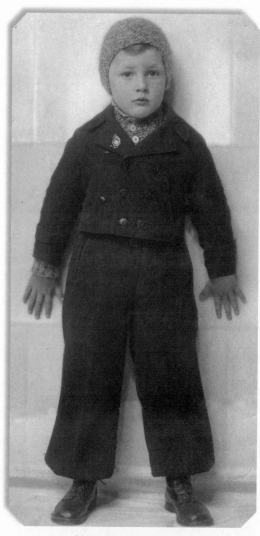
Young Hans Gmoser

On February 13, 1937, Walter Hintringer was born, and Hans now had a younger brother. Room was made for the baby in a corner of the small apartment, and Hans adjusted to the new addition.

That summer, Hans had his first exposure to mountaineering. Many years later, he told the story: "When I was five years old, my mother took me on a train trip through the Austrian mountains from Linz to Graz. The impressions of this journey are still alive and vivid in my memory. The mountains seemed to rise straight and clean from the railroad tracks into the sky. The streams were pure and foaming as they rushed out of the hills and the lakes were indescribably beautiful. At one point we saw two mountaineers get off the train. With a rope slung across the shoulder of one of them, they walked from the station, and it seemed to me then, climbed straight up a mountain. These impressions may well have kindled and nourished a desire to climb mountains myself."

The Dark Night of the Austrian State

The 1930s were troubled times in Austria. The worldwide depression had had a devastating effect, unemployment was widespread and political stability in the struggling First Republic was tenuous. To the north, the German Reich, now under Adolf Hitler, had eyes on Austria. On July 24, 1934, the Nazis attempted to overthrow the Austrian government; however, although Chancellor Dolfuss was murdered, the coup was unsuccessful. Hans was, of course, oblivious to all this, playing in the fruit trees of the small farm just across the street from where he lived.

Then came the *Anschluss*. In March of 1938, Hitler's Nazi Germany engulfed Austria, and this nation, with 1,000 years of history, ceased to exist. On March 12, Hitler drove across the Austro-German border and received a rapturous reception in the Hauptplatz in Linz. "The jubilation of the crowds convinced him to completely integrate Austria into Germany."[1] The dark night of the Austrian state had begun.

Hitler had great ambitions for Linz (which he considered his hometown) and planned to make it one of the great cities of the Third Reich. He dismantled factories in Czechoslovakia and moved them to Linz. He rebuilt the historic Nibelungen Bridge over the Danube River and he created the Hermann Göring Werke, a giant factory dedicated to the manufacture of iron and steel for the military. Of course, the economy of Linz improved and Hitler was welcomed.

At the same time as they improved the economy, the Nazis completely purged the government, police and courts of anyone who was not sympathetic to their philosophy. According to one source, "It became patriotic to denounce neighbours who made incautious remarks or lacked the proper enthusiasm for the Fuhrer.... The atmosphere of vigilantism and suspicion also spread to the schools, where students were sometimes encouraged by fanatical Nazis to spy on their own parents."[2]

In September 1938, Hans went to elementary school, located only 150 metres away, around the corner from his home. Next to the school was St. Dionysius Church, where he was soon an altar boy. Tall, white and stately, the church had an interior that was elaborate and ornate, and the services were heavy with ritual and incense. No doubt Hans was impressed, and for more than a decade the Catholic Church would have a profound influence on his life and thought.

On September 1, 1939, Hitler's tanks roared into Poland and the Second World War began. Britain, in turn, declared war on Germany, and a colossal fight to the finish was set in motion. The first few years of the war had little effect on Hans's life. Living in a small, circumscribed world, he went to school, served as an altar boy, played in the fields and swam in the local Traun River. And he discovered skiing! "I got my first pair of skis at age nine and also broke my leg for the first time. This didn't stop me, though, from becoming a real terror on the local ski slopes. For us there was only one way to go down a hill—straight! There was no point in turning unless you had to.... With old work boots tied to a pair of slats with leather straps, with pants made out of woollen blankets flopping in the wind and with a heavy overcoat we tore up and down those hills with an unbound enthusiasm."

One of the first consequences of the war was an elaborate food rationing system whereby food coupons became a necessity of life. Eventually, shoes, textiles, fuel and other goods were also subject to rationing. Life in a war-oriented economy also had other unpleasant effects: prices and taxes rose while wages remained static; workers were

Hans's first communion at St. Dionysius Church.
Hans is in the middle row, fourth from left.

forcibly removed from their hometowns; the workweek was raised to 60 hours and it became impossible to change jobs without a permit. The social rights that had been so patiently won over the years gradually disappeared.

In 1942, Hans was sent for four weeks to Bad Reichenhall in Bavaria, not far from Salzburg, for some good food, fresh air and exercise. Years later, he recalled, "This was the most glorious time for me. We went on hikes to easy peaks and played in the woods." Another brother, Karl, was born in 1942, but he lived only a short while, dying in 1944. At about this time, Hans played hooky from school for several days, the authorities thinking that he was sick at home. Hans swam in the Traun River and lay, daydreaming, on the grass. Eventually, his teacher contacted Rosa, enquiring about Hans's health, and his ruse was discovered. Franz Dopf, a childhood friend of Hans, remembers Hans's male teacher "pinning him against the wall and giving him a dressing-down in front of the whole class."

During 1940 – 1942, most families still led relatively normal lives. The war was far away, casualties were few,

*Hans on his first pair of skis
in front of the family home in Traun*

and news was not readily available. On weekends, the trains were crowded. Trips to the countryside offered a pleasant outing, as well as an opportunity to purchase food from the farmers. Most people still thought that the Nazis would win the war.

In November 1942, Rommel's Afrika Korps was defeated at El Alamein and the German Sixth Army was encircled by the Russians between the Volga and Don rivers. Casualties began to mount and confidence in a German victory began to wane. But it was the battle of Stalingrad that changed the face of the war. In February 1943, the last remnants of 22 German divisions surrendered to the Russians and public support in Austria for the Nazis was lost. "Daily life became more strenuous. Food rations were decreased and many small enterprises had to close because of a lack of raw materials. Church bells were confiscated as metal became scarce."[3]

Until this time, Austria had been out of the range of the Allied bombers, but on August 13, 1944, "In all of Lower Austria the wailing of sirens announced the arrival of a new enemy from the skies, the US Air Force. In Vienna only a distant grumbling was heard, but 33 miles to the south 187 tons of bombs fell on the industrial town of Wiener Neustadt, home of a large aircraft factory. When the bombers left, the plant was in a shambles, about 200 persons lay dead in the ruins, and a full passenger train was ablaze at the railway station. The air war had finally reached Austria."[4]

British, American and Canadian troops had invaded the Italian mainland in September 1943, and by December there were about 35,000 US Air Force personnel stationed in the country. Linz now became an important target—particularly the Hermann Göring Werke. During 1944 and 1945 there were 22 bombing raids on Linz, resulting in large-scale destruction and many casualties.

Through all of this, Erasmus was away from home, conscripted into the German army, and Rosa raised her boys alone with a stern moral authority. She is reported to have got herself in trouble with the authorities for smuggling food to starving Gypsies working as slave labour. When the head of the local Hitler Youth requested she send Hans to their gatherings, she reportedly refused. These acts were small but dangerous at a time when those who offered resistance to the Nazis risked being sent to the Mauthausen concentration camp, located just 20 kilometres east of Linz. And there were spies everywhere.

By 1945, Hans "had to report for various duties like building tank barricades and filling in bomb craters." In the final few months of the war, Hans and Walter were sent to relative safety with their grandfather, Karl Hintringer, in Gaspoltshofen, 60 kilometres west of Linz. Hintringer worked as a stockman, dealing in livestock for butchers, so he had access to additional food.

In the spring of 1945, the American bombers operated with little resistance almost every day over Austria. The food supply had even further deteriorated and people began to trade their possessions for anything edible. Sixteen-year-old boys and old men were drafted into the German army. During these months, Vienna filled with deserting soldiers and thousands of refugees fleeing the advancing Russians, now in Hungary. In only a few months, Vienna suffered 51 air raids that destroyed many historic monuments. Through it all there was a deceptive mood of normalcy. Often there were weekend soccer matches and evening concerts. The Germans, however, sent four SS divisions to Vienna for a last-ditch defense.

On March 20, 1945, the Red Army crossed the Austro-Hungarian border and, after three weeks of fighting, reached Vienna. For about ten days in early April, a fierce battle between the Russians and the German SS raged in

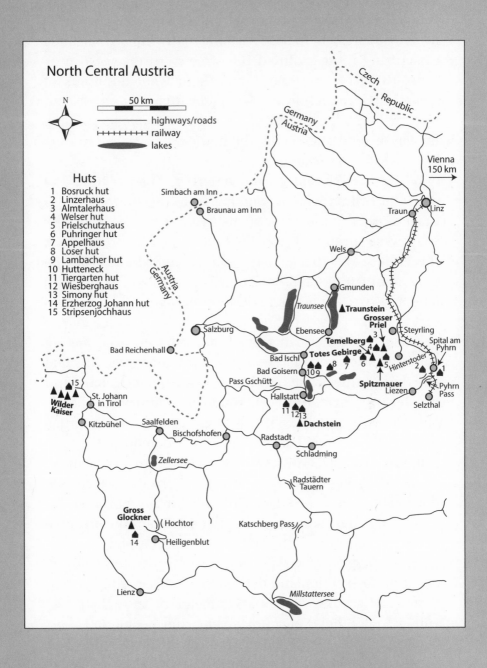

North Central Austria

N

50 km

——— highways/roads
+++++ railway
⬭ lakes

Huts
1 Bosruck hut
2 Linzerhaus
3 Almtalerhaus
4 Welser hut
5 Prielschutzhaus
6 Puhringer hut
7 Appelhaus
8 Loser hut
9 Lambacher hut
10 Hutteneck
11 Tiergarten hut
12 Wiesberghaus
13 Simony hut
14 Erzherzog Johann hut
15 Stripsenjochhaus

Czech Republic

Germany / Austria

Vienna 150 km

Austria / Germany

Simbach am Inn
Braunau am Inn

Traun
Linz

Wels

Gmunden

Traunsee

Salzburg

Bad Reichenhall

Traunstein
Grosser Priel
Steyrling
Spital am Pyhrn

Ebensee
Temelberg
3
Totes Gebirge 4
8   7   6   5   Hinterstoder
Bad Ischl
10 9
Bad Goisern
Spitzmauer
Liezen
2   1
Pyhrn Pass
Selzthal

Wilder Kaiser 15

St. Johann in Tirol

Kitzbühel

Saalfelden

Bischofshofen

Pass Gschütt
Hallstatt
11 12 13
Dachstein

Radstadt

Schladming

Zellersee

Radstädter Tauern

Gross Glockner
Hochtor
14
Heiligenblut

Katschberg Pass

Lienz

Millstattersee

the streets. The city was chaotic with lootings and rape, and many old accounts were settled. The electricity was not functioning, there was no coal for heating, and there was no fire department to deal with the many fires. Thousands of starving refugees filled the streets. To the west, near Linz, things were quieter, but there were hundreds of deserting German soldiers fleeing the Russians. Years later, Hans would tell the story of being sent out one morning to forage for food and seeing the bodies of several deserters hanging in the trees.

While the Russians were entering Austria from the east, the British were advancing from the south through Carinthia and the Americans were coming from the southwest through Tyrol. Encountering little resistance, the Americans turned east and advanced towards the approaching Russians, entering Linz on May 5. Three days later, the two armies met at the Enns River, 20 kilometres east of Linz.

When the American troops entered Linz, the feeling amongst the citizens was relief that the fighting was finished and thankfulness that they had survived. But the hardship was far from over. In the surrounding countryside, bands of marauders attacked villages and pillaged lonely farms. In the cities, a great many crimes were committed.

It is remarkable, however, that the Austrian love of music survived through all of this. On April 27, in Vienna, despite the streets being full of rubble and many corpses, the Vienna Philharmonic gave its first postwar concert. Five days later, on May 1, the State Opera performed Mozart's *The Marriage of Figaro*. "Amidst political uncertainty, material destruction and deprivation," observed historian Richard Hiscocks, "actors and musicians gave their best with strong official encouragement, and people left their damaged homes and empty larders to enjoy the good things that life still had to offer."[5]

The Long Occupation

After seven years under Hitler and the Third Reich, Austria endured another ten years of occupation by foreign troops. The country was divided into four zones— Russian, American, British and French. This made the job of rebuilding the country much more difficult, as the Russians were continually obstructive and relations between the Soviets and the Western Allies steadily declined. This was a further humiliation for the Austrian people, whose self-confidence was at an all-time low. Not particularly proud of their war record, they wanted to forget their involvement with Hitler's great tragedy and move on.

Although Austria was ultimately under the control of what was called the Allied Commission, it had a democratically elected federal government of its own that was responsible for the day-to-day running of the country. The first elections were held on November 25, 1945, and there was a 93 per cent turnout. Leopold Figl, a leading resistance figure during the war, was elected chancellor. At Christmas, he spoke to the Austrian people: "For your Christmas tree, if you even have one, I can give you no candles, no crust of bread, no coal for heating, and no glass for your windows. We have nothing. I can only beg of you one thing; believe in this Austria of ours."[6]

The economy of Europe was in ruins, and soon most Austrians were starving. According to historian Gordon Brook-Shepard, "At its worst the official food ration in Vienna was a bare 600 calories a day, less than many a concentration camp level. Thanks mainly to emergency deliveries of flour and other supplies from American army reserves, it rose during the winter of 1945–46, to a more sustaining 1550 calories a day, only to be cut back again in the spring to 1200."[7] Hard winters in 1946 and 1947 exacerbated the suffering. Hans remembered years later, "We were always hungry, but it didn't bother me. That's just the way things were."

Traun was in the American zone of occupied Austria, and a number of troops were stationed nearby. According to both Walter Hintringer and Franz Dopf, the Americans treated them well. Walter remembers the thrill of seeing black men in uniform. Franz remembers seeing US soldiers on guard duty, sitting back with their feet up on the table. Recalling the discipline of the German soldiers, he wondered how they had lost the war.

Slowly, the country began to function again as the radio stations, cinemas, courts, trains and postal system resumed operation. Everyone did what he or she could to survive. Hans showed his innate survival skills in the harsh grey world and soon became a wheeler-dealer on the street. Years later, he would recall, "I was quite a black marketeer. I dealt in cigarettes and anything I could get my hands on. I think I could have become a first rate gangster." He made friends with several American soldiers who would leave a little food in their mess kits for him to eat, and in return he would wash the kits for them. He would collect washing and sewing from the US soldiers to bring home for his mother. Cigarettes were like gold, and the soldiers would play games with the kids as to where they would flick their smoking butts. Hans was, no doubt, a little quicker than most.

For fun the boys would swim in the ruins of the Traun River Bridge, which the retreating Germans had blown up, hoping to hinder the advance of the American troops. The giant blocks of stone and cement with protruding jagged steel reinforcing bars made an exciting and dangerous play spot for the ragged street kids.

The defining event in Hans Gmoser's life came in early 1947. Konrad Dorfner, a young priest at St. Dionysus Church, noticed these boys playing in the streets and joined in, making friends with them. From January 2 to 7, he organized a ski trip for 20 of the boys to the Lambacher hut, located high above Bad Goisern at the west end of the Totes Gebirge, a mountain range south of Traun.

Food for the trip was a problem, but Dorfner had a solution. He had relatives living on farms in the area called Mühlviertel, on the north side of the Danube in the Russian zone. He arranged that the food would be gathered at a church in Linz in the Russian zone of the divided city; then, on a rainy Sunday, the boys walked across the Nibelungen Bridge from the American side to the Russian side, filled the pockets of their bulky coats with potatoes, carrots, onions, bread and meat, and walked back across the bridge under the unsuspecting gaze of the Russian guards. After several trips, the food was across and the boys were on their way to the mountains.

> From where we got off the train it was to take three hours to the hut. After three hours one other boy and myself weren't even half way and nobody of the group was in sight. Finding the packs too heavy, we put them on our skis, which we dragged behind us. It was a steep trail and every once in a while a big sled laden with heavy logs would come roaring around a corner and we had to jump quickly up on the bank not to get run over. Every time we saw a farmer or a logger, we'd ask how far it was to the hut. The answer was "not far" and after looking at us for a few moments they would add, "but long".
>
> When we reached the end of the logging trail the snow became very deep. Still trying to walk

At the Lambacher hut in January 1947

we got stuck in the snow. We had to put our skis on, shoulder the pack and start side stepping up a steep slope. There were few in our group who had climbing skins. This was just hopeless. We had to make our skis stick if we wanted to reach the hut before nightfall. If we could somehow ice the skis up. But there was no water anywhere and spitting on them didn't do much either. There was only one other solution! After some embarrassing moments, we said, "So what."

Suddenly climbing was a cinch. We even passed a few other stragglers and three hours later reached the hut. The tiredness was immediately forgotten and I was thoroughly enchanted by my first experience of "Huettenzauber", literally translated as "hutmagic".

Now 20 of us were in this small two room hut. Our only material wealth was a crate full of food. We were all little devils, potential troublemakers. But somehow the remoteness of this place, the wintry mountain night outside, the coziness of this hut, had put a shine in our eyes and a strange feeling inside us. Even when you tripped the other guy, so he fell flat on his face with a bowl of hot soup, you didn't do it with the same feeling of sadism as usual, in fact, you almost felt sorry about it. We sang, listened to the stories of the older boys who had been in mountain huts before and knew that something had penetrated our already hard and cynical shells.

Dorfner had opened the door to the mountains for Hans, and his life would never be the same. Hans started a journal, or *Tourenbuch*, after that trip. On the front page he wrote: "*In Todesgefahr, bitte einen kath. Priester verstandigen!*" ("When in a life-threatening situation, please call a Catholic Priest!")

Soon Hans was thinking of how he might get into the hills again. At Easter that same year, he and friend Karl Baumann made Palm branches, small traditional "bouquets" of pussy willow that are hung on the wall in the home, and sold them in front of the church to raise enough money to buy a train ticket to Spital am Pyhrn. From there they made their way to the Gowialm hut, where Hans tried unsuccessfully to ascend the Phyrgas on skis.

On July 19, 1947, Hans graduated at age 15 from grade 8. Owing to the disruption of the war, school had ceased to exist at Christmas 1944, and consequently Hans and his classmates were forced to repeat one year. According to a friend, Hans was one of the few boys who could speak a little English at graduation, a skill that served him well in those years of the American occupation. His report card credits him with the highest grade, *sehr gut* (very good), for behaviour (*Betragen*), and a very credible *gut* (good)

On the trail to the Dachstein in July 1947. Hans is second from left.

for *Fleiss* (diligence or ambition). His best subjects were religion, history, geography, mathematics and crafts, where he received *sehr gut*. He also did well in German language, writing, singing and gymnastics, receiving *gut*. His poorest subjects, where he only received *befriedigend* (satisfactory), were natural history, biology and English.

That summer, Hans was back in the mountains once again with the priest Dorfner and his group of unruly boys. This time the goal was the Dachstein, a beautiful, glaciated, limestone peak located about 50 kilometres southeast of Salzburg. After a steep, 1400-metre hike from Hallstatt to the Wiesberghaus, where they spent the night, they continued another 300 metres up to the Simony hut, then set off across the Hallstatter Glacier towards the peak. On a rope for the first time, the boys puffed higher and higher along the path in the snow. By the time they reached the Dachsteinwarte viewpoint on the east ridge, some of the boys were having second thoughts. But Hans and three other adventurous lads were keen on the summit and continued up broken chimneys and across exposed ledges to the top. Although there were a few steel posts and cables anchored to the rock, most of the way would have been unprotected climbing and the consequences of a slip would have been fatal. At the summit cross, the view was obscured by clouds, so after a brief halt, the boys descended to their companions waiting below.

By then the group that had stayed behind had decided that they, too, could climb to the top and would afterwards descend the west ridge on the far side of the mountain to the Gosau Glacier. Meanwhile, Hans's group descended a distance down the Hallstatter Glacier, then climbed to the Steinerscharte, a notch on the north ridge of the mountain. With the aid of some cables and ladders, they descended to the Gosau Glacier and from there continued down to the Adamek hut, where they were reunited with the other group.

At the Adamek hut. Hans is in the back row, second from right, and Franz is next to him, second from left.

The next morning, in the sunshine, Hans stripped and dove into a frigid glacial lake before setting off on the long march back to the road. After two days of hiking, with an overnight at the Theodor Korner hut, they reached the town of Gosau. Hans wrote in his *Tourenbuch*: "In Gosau the hostess took pity on me and I got a meal without food stamps."

In the middle of August, Hans and unknown companions visited, for the first time, the Prielschutzhaus, a hut at the northeast end of the Totes Gebirge. These mountains are the closest ones to Traun, and over the next few years they would become a favourite destination where he would make some of his best climbs. On this occasion he was unsuccessful in ascending even the easy route on the west side of the major summit, the Spitzmauer. Undoubtedly, he admired the steep ribs, walls and gullies of the north face, which must have seemed unclimbable.

In September, Hans began a three-year apprenticeship as an electrician. The Hermann Göring Werke, in nearby Linz, had been converted after the war to the manufacture of more peaceful iron and steel products and had been

The Prielschutzhaus in about 1950. Brotfall is the peak on the left and the Grosser Priel is on the right.

An aerial view of VÖEST (United Austrian Iron and Steelworks)

renamed Vereinigte Österreichische Eisen u. Stahlwerke (VÖEST), or the United Austrian Iron and Steelworks. It was here that Hans would spend the next four years, working with thousands of other men in the smoke and dust of the giant steel plant. It was not the most pleasant experience of his life. Years later, Hans would comment, "I was quite disappointed that I could not go to school. I would have liked to go to school but my parents couldn't afford it. While I was an apprentice I felt unhappy. I thought I was in a long tunnel with no way out."

There were no excursions to the mountains that winter. Hans was just too busy with work and courses, learning his trade. He also made an attempt to further his education by taking night classes, but after working a nine-and-a-half-hour day in the steel plant, he found that three or four hours of evening classes were too much. Some weekends, however, with his young brother Walter, he would take the train to Linz and ski on the slopes of the Postlingberg, a low mountain across the river in the Russian sector of the city. From the old baroque church on the summit, sitting in the sunshine, he would look across the city at the fuming smokestacks of VÖEST and beyond to the snow-covered peaks on the horizon and dream of adventure.

Hans made only one mountain excursion during the summer of 1948, but from the entries in his *Tourenbuch* it appears that it was very special for him. From July 19 to 23, he walked alone across the Totes Gebirge, admiring the beauty of the world and thinking about his place in the grand scheme of things.

Starting from Steyrling, he hiked beside the rushing stream to a high wooded pass, then descended to the Almtalerhaus, a delightful, two-storey log hut tucked away in the trees. The next morning, in the mist, he strolled, enchanted, through a beautiful forest. He wrote: "A hike through the Almtal is an invaluable gift from God. The marvellous forest is a true cathedral of God. Everything is specifically done to connect mankind with God."[8] Hans's religious feelings were very strong at this time, and heavily influenced by the charismatic priest Dorfner, he had aspirations to become a priest himself.

Climbing steeply for 1000 metres to the Welser hut, he surprised a family of chamois. "I was completely absorbed with my thoughts when suddenly I heard a whistling behind me and heard rocks falling. I turned and saw on the scree slope five chamois: a real family with three young ones. They jumped at breakneck speed down the slope and not far behind them came two more chamois. I followed their trail until they disappeared from view then I continued on my way. Hardly had I taken a few steps when a marvellous chamois stood on a boulder. I stopped in a trance. The big ram jumped from boulder to boulder then disappeared down the canyon."

After a night at the hut, he set off in the morning across the high, rocky plateau of the Totes Gebirge. Even at this late date there was still plenty of snow to provide a contrast with the jagged limestone spires. "The day was a gift from God; not one cloud in the sky and the mountains framed by dark azure blue." After hours of tramping across snowfields and rock slabs, where wildflowers lay scattered in grassy patches, he arrived at the Pühringer hut, exhausted. The lush surroundings of the hut, which were hidden in a little valley, beside a small lake, contrasted with the stark, grey, rocky peaks.

On the third day, under another cloudless sky, Hans traversed a "landscape interlaced with rocks, dwarf pine, larch trees and last but not least wonderful alpine flora.... The trail leads through peaceful pastures where innumerable springs seep down from the walls." Arriving at the Appelhaus, he wrote: "Up here, I am satisfied."

On his last day, Hans continued across meadows, the air full of the sound of tinkling cowbells, then along a rugged high trail to the Loser hut, perched far above the valley. Sitting on the terrace and admiring the view across to the Dachstein, he mused: "I feel very close to God up here. Up here one can cleanse one's soul. It is a true piece of paradise up here. Above the Auseer area are high clouds and the Dachstein Glacier is glowing majestically. Lucky is the person who can witness all of this."

In the spring and summer of 1948, the European Recovery Program, better known as the Marshall Plan, went into operation. Over a period of four years, the United States of America pumped 13 billion dollars' worth of aid into the war-damaged countries of Europe. It had a huge effect on their economies and was very important politically, as people in many countries were turning out of desperation to communism to improve their lot. Austria received 468 million dollars—on a per capita basis, the most money of any country. Millions of dollars were invested in VÖEST to increase the output of steel and sheet metal from its six blast furnaces. The Marshall aid resulted in a marked acceleration in the rate of Austrian recovery, put an end to the last days of food shortages and ended the black market.

Life in the small home in Traun remained simple but comfortable. In the evening, Hans and Walter would prac-

Hans and Walter in about 1948

tise playing the zither, a skill that would give both of them joy for many years. At times, Erasmus, who also played the zither, would join in. Hans would read books borrowed from Mr. Rumpold, who lived in the apartment downstairs, or listen to the radio. Although the living room was warm and cheery, the sleeping quarters were cold in winter.

On occasion, Hans and Franz would attend the cinema in Linz. Most of the films were American, and Franz remembers that the first one they saw after the

Hans (centre) performing in an amateur theatrical production

war was *Gold Rush* with Charlie Chaplin. The pair also enjoyed performances of Franz Lehár operettas from their seats in the upper balcony at the theatre. At about this time, Hans developed a love for theatre, and for the next few years he would often perform in amateur plays and operettas.

During the winter of 1948–1949, Hans managed to get out skiing only twice. In March, at the Wiesberghaus, after just a few hours on the slopes, he broke his ski, something that would become a regular occurrence. With characteristic resourcefulness, he fixed an old pair of skis with a few nails and descended the next day to the valley.

There was only one mountain trip for Hans in the summer of 1949, but once again it was a very special adventure. Over a period of two weeks, in late July and early August, he and Franz cycled from Traun to the Grossglockner (at 3798 metres, the highest mountain in Austria), climbed the mountain, then cycled back to Traun, a distance of about 600 kilometres, all on the heavy one-speed bicycles of the day.

Franz and Hans had known each other for a long time. They had grown up together on the streets of Traun, they were in the same grade at school and Franz had also been on the Dorfner adventures to the Lambacher hut and the Dachstein. Franz, too, was apprenticing, but as a cabinetmaker in a small shop in Traun. Now a close friendship would develop between the two boys, a partnership of the rope common amongst climbers all over the world.

Franz was the perfect complement to Hans. Slight of build, with dark wavy hair and gypsy eyes, he was soft-spoken and accommodating. Hans, on the other hand, had grown tall and thin, with sharp, chiselled features. Even at the young age of 16, he was always in charge and made the decisions. For a friend, Hans needed someone who would not argue too much and would acquiesce to his more dynamic personality. According to Franz, Hans's mother liked him because he was a "calming influence" on her son. She must not have realized that Franz was just as reckless and that together the boys would share some wild escapades.

The first day of their Grossglockner adventure was almost the last when, a short distance from Traun, Franz crashed his bicycle coming down a steep hill. Hans wrote that he "bandaged him up like Lazarus," although Franz remembers that it was a doctor in a nearby town who did the bandaging. After the first night at the Feichtau hut, near Molln, they pedalled steeply up to Pyhrn Pass, where they crawled into their tent under a starry sky. The following two days they covered about 80 kilometres each day. Luckily, the road was not busy, for few people in Austria owned a car in those days. From Pyhrn Pass they descended to Liezen, then continued along the Enns valley to Radstadt, where they turned south, finally stopping for the night at Untertauern. The next day, they crossed two passes: the Radstädter Tauern to Mauterndorf, then, in brutal midday heat, the 32 per cent grade of Katschberg Pass. From there it was downhill to the Millstaettersee, where they camped on the edge of the lake and rested for two days, swimming and eating. To supplement their rations, Franz milked a local goat (his mother kept a goat at home in Traun, so he knew how to do this).

After another 80-kilometre day ascending the Moell Valley in extreme heat, they arrived thoroughly exhausted at the town of Heiligenblut. Here they stayed in the youth hostel and in the evening admired the Grossglockner, towering 2500 metres above them.

Early the next morning, they were back on their bikes, pedalling 16 kilometres up the Grossglockner road to the Franz Josef Hotel and viewpoint. Leaving their bikes and excess baggage behind, they descended to the glacier,

Franz Dopf poses with his bicycle below the Grossglockner

crossed to the northeast slopes of the mountain, then slowly climbed the 1100 metres to the Erzherzog Johann hut, at the Adler's Ruhe. Once again exhausted after a big day, the boys sank into their blankets, while outside the mountains glowed silver in moonlight.

Their rest wasn't long, however, and the next morning the pair were on their way at sunrise. Hans later remembered, "We didn't have any equipment. We just walked up the glacier to the hut. In the hut we realized we had better get some equipment. You could rent an ice axe and crampons. So we put on crampons for the first time, got an ice axe and went to the top."

Feeling the effects of altitude and breathing deeply, they ascended snow and ice slopes to the base of the summit pyramid. The granitic rock was rough and solid, and the handholds square-cut and positive. For these young men, strong and confident and full of anticipation, treading the edge of the abyss was exquisite pleasure. After about 150 metres, they reached a subsidiary summit, the Kleinglockner, and gazed across at the true summit only a short distance away. It would be necessary to descend into an airy notch, balance across a thin, icy crest above a steep, snow couloir called the Palaviccinirinne, which swept into the depths, then climb a further 50 metres of steep rock to the top. Hans recalled, "We were very proud of ourselves because there were a number of people trying to climb the peak who didn't want to cross the gap at the top of the Palaviccinirinne, which is a scary place. But when you are that young you have more confidence than you should, and we just went across." In short order they were at the summit cross. Hans wrote in his *Tourenbuch*: "Stunning was the view from the summit—the 4000 m peaks of Switzerland, the sharp summits of the Dolomites and also our own mountains of home." Despite the intense sunlight, the air was cold and a cutting breeze swept

Franz (left) and Hans on the summit of the Grossglockner

across the peak. They soon became chilled, so "With a great experience in our hearts we started our descent."

Returning down the mountain to their bikes, the pair were not finished for the day. They descended the Grossglockner road for a few kilometres, turned left and pedalled uphill again to a high pass called Hochtor. Descending steep switchbacks on the other side, they were surprised by a thunderstorm that forced them to stop for the night at the Hochmais viewpoint. The next day, their tenth on the road, they continued the long descent to the valley. Down they went, switchback after switchback, pressing back hard on their pedals to brake the descent. At some point, Hans's brakes failed and he was forced to walk slowly down the road. At last the bottom was near and Hans, frustrated at his slow progress, hopped on his bike and just let it go, hoping that he would have a long run-out at the bottom. Franz watched in horror as Hans went faster and faster, straight towards the toll barrier across the road at the bottom of the hill.[9] Hans could do nothing but hang on and pray. At the last moment, the astonished woman in the tollbooth raised her head, saw Hans rapidly approaching and, just in time, raised the barrier. Hans raced past and continued far down the road until the angle relented and he could finally stop. From then on, Hans braked by sticking his foot in the front fork of the bicycle.

For three days they rode, in the rain, at a more leisurely pace: over Pass Gschütt to Bad Goisern, then on to Gmunden and Traun. Famished at the end of the trip, but out of money and almost out of food, they were reduced to eating bread and pressed lard that had been sent by Franz's Uncle Louis, who lived in Edmonton, Canada. It had been a fabulous adventure and completely successful. Now it was back to work at VÖEST—or, as Hans called it, "the grey grind of everyday life."

Hans managed to get out skiing on several occasions during the winter of 1949–1950, but he was now experiencing teenage growing pains. At Hutteneck in mid-February he enjoyed a very *gemütlich*[10] Saturday evening, filled with song and stories, likely joining in on the zither that he often brought up to the mountain huts. On Sunday morning, however, he descended to the valley to church. Like many teenage boys, he was torn between the desires of the flesh and the attraction of the pure life. He wrote in his *Tourenbuch*: "Here at the hut is a splendid girl; I am becoming whimsical," then continued: "Nature is now really beautiful. The snow on the trees looks marvellous. Pity that we have to go home soon."

That summer, Hans's interest in girls was further awakened. In early June he and several friends went tenting at Traunsee, a beautiful lake on the edge of the mountains about 60 kilometres southwest of Traun. There they swam, played *Völkerball*, sang songs around the fire and had a very gay time. Befriending a family by the name of Holzinger, they erected tents in their yard in Gmunden. Hans was attracted to the Holzinger daughters and wrote in his *Tourenbuch*: "For the Holzinger girls, including their mother, I have great admiration—splendid people." Back again at Traunsee a month later, Hans and his friends again set up their tents in the Holzinger yard. Once more he was attracted to the Holzinger daughters and wrote: "I can't get Friedl off my mind. I am crazy about her. It is good that I am here for the last time because I would be a too-bad chap for her."

At home in Traun, however, Rosa maintained strict control of Hans and watched his development with trepidation. One night, he came home after drinking too much and was severely beaten by his mother while Erasmus sat back and let Rosa be the disciplinarian.

Erasmus and Rosa Hintringer

Hans Resch

On occasion, Hans visited his biological father's home in Freinberg, about 100 kilometres up the Danube River from Linz. Photos from the era show an awkward Hans standing with Resch, his wife and their four children, one of whom Resch had also named Hans. According to Annemarie, Hans Gmoser's half-sister, discipline in the Resch home was severe and no talking was allowed at dinnertime. It is unlikely that these visits resulted in any bond forming between father and son.

In the late summer of 1950, Hans's interest in the mountains seems to have taken a serious turn, and for a week, from July 31 to August 6, he and Franz had a climbing adventure on the Dachstein. Having just purchased new bikes, they "felt like lords" as they cruised along the road. On their way through Gmunden, they stopped to pick up some climbing hardware from Mrs. Holzinger, who had promised them equipment that had belonged to her son who had been killed during the war. They now had some pitons and carabiners and a piton hammer.

On August 2, the weather was beautiful. High above the Simony hut, streams were flowing across the ice of the Dachstein Glacier and the dark summits stood out against the azure sky. First, they climbed the Dachstein; then, needing more, they climbed a subsidiary peak called the Dirndl. The weather broke the next morning as they crossed the Steinerscharte to the Adamek hut, and it began to snow. "The going was terrible. The fresh snow covered the blank ice. Painfully we had to get to the rock. Often we had to stray off course because of the hard ice and we could barely kick steps with our shoes.... I barely could feel my fingers." On August 4, after a long and arduous hike in pouring rain, they reached Hallstatt, mounted their bikes and pedalled to the Holzinger home in Gmunden, where they "surrounded the stove with our rags."

On Sunday, August 13, Hans and Franz once again returned to the Prielschutzhaus, this time with Walter Puchmayr and Karl Gossenreiter. Leaving Traun at 5 a.m. on their bicycles, they rode 50 kilometres to Kirchdorf, where they stopped for Mass. After the service, they continued another 20 kilometres, arriving at the trailhead near Hinterstoder at noon, and only two hours later were 800 metres higher at the hut. Fit and strong, these young men pushed themselves hard just to get to the mountains. Immediately, they set off for the south ridge of the Grosser Priel, but they had trouble finding the route and when Walter took a five-metre fall they decided to turn around.

The next morning the weather was socked in and the young men sat frustrated in the hut. Finally, Franz, Hans and Karl set off towards the Spitzmauer. At the Klinserscharte, a pass below the peak, their paths diverged. Franz and Hans scrambled in light rock shoes towards a route called the *Gruberrinne* on the north face, while Karl, who carried his friends' boots for the descent, headed for the summit via the easy west face. The fog was thick and soon it began to rain, so the pair returned to the hut. Karl, however, returned to the hut at 2 p.m., having reached the summit and deposited the boots. Hans wrote: "At 2:45 pm it suddenly started to clear, the sun almost broke through and one could see a bit of blue sky. Our decision was made and within a few minutes we were dressed, packed and off we went to the Klinserscharte." The hut custodian warned the boys that it was too late in the day to climb the Spitzmauer, but the bit was in their teeth and they ignored him. On top of that, they had to retrieve their boots.

At the start of the route, "a youth worker's prayer was said" and off they went. Hans led and Franz carried the rucksack. "Swiftly we climbed, rope length after rope length, exactly according to the guide book." As the *Gruberrinne* was running with water, they climbed to the right on the *Dambergerweg*, then higher up traversed back into the *Gruberrinne*. High up, a difficult spot stopped Hans momentarily, but after several tries he made it. Two pitches later, they took off the rope and in fading light soloed to the top. Standing on the summit, "The whole world seemed to belong to us. We felt the closeness of heaven and also very sheltered."

They put on their boots and began the descent via the west face, but in the dark they stumbled on the loose rocks and were soon completely lost. Unable to see where they were going, they could very easily wander over a cliff, so they returned to the summit and prepared for their first bivouac. After putting on all their spare clothing, mitts and hats, they emptied the rucksack and pulled it over their feet. At first it was quite comfortable sitting there under the stars and they enjoyed their dramatic position, but after an hour they started to chill and after two hours their teeth began chattering. It was going to be a long, unpleasant night. Franz remembered looking enviously down to the valley at the lights of Hinterstoder and watching the patrons leave the bar, get into their cars and drive away.

Franz and Hans

Cold and stiff, they began their descent at first light, arriving at the hut just before the rescue group set off to look for them. The hut custodian was, of course, annoyed, but Hans was very pleased. Despite the unplanned bivouac, he wrote in his *Tourenbuch*: "My first real climb. It went very well."

From then on, Hans was out most weekends in the mountains and on weekday evenings he was often rock climbing on the granite cliffs above the Danube River, just upstream from the Nibelungen Bridge in Linz. Sometimes older members of his climbing community were there and would instruct him in technique. At work, he would put in two weeks straight (shift work), then have a long, three- or four-day weekend. He had finished his apprenticeship, his pay had improved and he had a little more freedom. However, there was trouble brewing at his workplace.

Last Climbs in Austria

Austria was locked in an emerging Cold War between Russia and the Western democracies. The Russians were attempting to increase their control of the country, and in September of 1950, through their influence in the Austrian Communist Party, they tried to provoke a general strike. Linz was one of the worst trouble centres. On September 26, the workers at VÖEST went on strike and 15,000 men gathered in the Hauptplatz with their demands. Hans was likely caught up in all of this. It is unknown what effect this had on Hans's politics, but the future of Austria was obviously uncertain: the occupation had gone on for five years and perhaps would last indefinitely (the occupation finally ended in 1955). For a young man, it was hard to plan for the future, and Hans started looking about for opportunities around the world.

Meanwhile, Hans continued to ski hard and earned quite a reputation. One of his friends later remembered, "Hans was a crazy skier; he just went straight down." On

Skiing in Austria on a cold winter day.
Hans is second from left and Franz is on the far right.

January 27–28, Hans and Franz competed in the Upper Austrian Diocese Ski Race on the Feuerkogl, a ski resort near Ebensee. For the third time, Hans broke a ski, this time after only five minutes on the slope. Franz and Hans nailed it together so that Hans could compete in the downhill race. Unfamiliar with the course, Hans had to wait for the next racer to pass him, then followed him down the hill, finishing in 11th place.

That winter, Hans and his new girlfriend Gretl Hackl went to the Linzerhaus with Franz and Karl Klambauer. Gretl was not used to mountain skiing, so most of the time she waited in the hut while the three men went skiing. On the last day, the men had a superb run down the Loigistal, in a metre of fresh snow. The sun shone through and a few shreds of cloud chased over the summits. Hans wrote:

Spring ski touring near the Dachstein

"Very close to each other we went down and often we passed other skiers. The closer we got to the valley the braver we became. We schussed down wooded slopes, then as the crown of creation, made a neck-breaking dive through the Kannonenrohr [Cannon Barrel], and finally we drifted down into the valley. It was heavenly." There is no mention of how Gretl got back down to the valley.

On another occasion, Hans went to the Prielschutzhaus with Franz and Karl Klambauer. Much of the time they practised on a slalom course they had prepared on a slope near the hut, but they also managed to ascend two peaks, the Spitzmauer and Brotfall. They gave themselves a good scare on Brotfall, where they found themselves on steep avalanche terrain, and at the end of the week, Hans wrote in his *Tourenbuch*: "It was a wonderful week which will bring back many memories and which in certain regards made me smarter and more cautious. Maybe I found my way back to God a bit."

In fact, Hans was gradually losing his Christian feelings, replacing them with a romantic view of nature's magnificence as an alternative to the evils of the modern industrial world. And he was learning to express this love and respect for nature in his writings. The previous summer, camped in the valley below the Spitzmauer, he had written in his journal: "The summits of the Totes Gebirge surround us and from everywhere water descends to the valley. The meadows are a splendour of gentians and other flowers. As I sit alone on the watch, the fire flares unsteadily up and down and the roar of the waterfall fills my ears. My God, how wonderful is your world. Fear takes hold of me, but when I look at the heavens, I find peace again."

That winter, Hans made the decision to go to Canada. The oft-told story, according to Hans, goes as follows: "One day in February, 1951, I met Leo [Grillmair] in the main square of our home city of Linz in Austria. After exchanging hellos, Leo announced proudly that he was going to Canada. Leo motioned across the square and said, 'You can sign up at that travel agency.' Within two minutes we were there and I also filled out an application to immigrate to Canada. At that time the government loaned you, without interest, 90% of the cost of a one-way ticket. When the travel consultant asked where in Canada we wanted to go, we said, 'Wherever there is lots of skiing.' He told us that Toronto would be the right place for us!"[11]

Leo has a completely different story of how it all came about. According to him, he was working for the Klein Plumbing Company in Linz and was about to be laid off due to lack of work. His boss suggested that he sign up to go to Canada and even made a phone call to the travel agency on Leo's behalf. Leo borrowed his boss's bicycle, cycled over to the Hauptplatz and filled out an application to go to Canada. That evening in Traun, he was on his way to the *Gasthof* for an evening drink when he ran into

Hans and told him that he had signed up to go to Canada. "Why don't you come along," he said to Hans. Hans replied that he wanted to talk to his mother first before making a decision. About four days later, he came by Leo's house and announced that he had decided to go to Canada and was going to sign up. According to Leo, Hans's version was just a story made up for the media.

Hans and Leo had grown up together on the streets of Traun, but they were not close friends. Leo was two years older than Hans and was a member of a different climbing club, the Naturfreunde, which was associated with the Socialists, whereas Hans was a member of the Österreichischer Alpenverrein, which was associated with the Catholic Church. Although aware of each other, they had never actually climbed or skied together.

Hans's mother was very unhappy with his decision. According to Hans, "I had a good job with a big company. That's where you spend the rest of your life and to suggest anything else was sacrilege." Hans thought he would go to Canada, earn some money, continue to perfect his climbing skills, then return to Austria and take the mountain guide exam.

From a climbing point of view, Hans's last summer in Austria was his best. Teaming up primarily with Franz, he graduated from routes of modest difficulty to some serious rock climbs, edging into what is called the Sixth Grade. However, his first climb of the summer, on May 26, proved to be somewhat of an embarrassment. Years later, he told the story:

> The first time I used a carabiner I made a real ass of myself. Franz and I were climbing a route on the south ridge of the Grosser Priel. There are several towers on this ridge and at the first tower there was a little traverse and there were two pitons in

it.... At that point I thought you just used a piton like a handhold. So I put my finger through this piton and tried to swing out onto the slab. I didn't like that at all. I backed off and scratched my head. Then I clipped a carabiner into the piton and put my hand in the carabiner, which was a little better. But still it didn't feel all that hot to me. Looking over everything I had, I thought if I clip my rope into this carabiner it's going to go really slick. I did it and went across without any problem. I thought I had made a real discovery. We finished the climb and when I got back to the hut I couldn't wait to tell everybody what I had discovered. The guys just killed themselves laughing. I made a horrendous ass of myself.

The next day, the pair hoped to climb the south ridge of Brotfall, but as Hans wrote in his *Tourenbuch*: "At the start of the climb I was in such a bad mood that I felt like turning around. And I did after the first tower, as I could not do otherwise." No doubt Hans's sensitive young pride had been seriously damaged the previous day.

In mid-June, Hans, Franz and Karl Mitterlehner were back on the north face of the Spitzmauer. Following a series of cracks up the north face, Hans in the lead, they reached the northeast ridge, where they were surprised by a thunderstorm. Soaked and shivering, they decided to continue; but again the black skies opened, and large chunks of hail beat against their heads and shoulders. Despite fingers numb with cold and feet that slipped on the wet rock, they kept climbing, determined to succeed. The sun shone through briefly while they sat on the summit, but then it rained again on the descent. Back at the hut after nine hours on the move, "We did not have a dry thread on our bodies, but we had made it."

Returning to the Prielschutzhaus on July 8, Hans and Franz made the best climb of their careers to date. To this point they had been climbing routes graded II, III and IV,[12] but on this day they upped the ante, climbing the spectacular north pillar of the Spitzmauer, graded VI at the time.[13]

On their way at 4:15 a.m., they hiked to the Klinserscharte and scrambled up to the base of the cliff. "I distinctly remember the closer we got the more and more scared I got." After ascending the *Steyrweg* north face route for a short distance, they traversed right to the start of the north pillar, where "It looks rather forbidding, you see the underbellies of all those yellow overhangs. We sat on a ledge and Franz looked one way and I looked the other. We didn't say a word for an hour. Finally Franz said to me 'Well if you want to get up there you had better get going.' And I said to Franz 'If we are still alive tonight we'll never go climbing again.'"

The first two pitches were the hardest. With feet scrabbling on small holds and fingers and forearms aching with fatigue, Hans led the steep wall. The intensity of the action did not allow him to become frightened, and with brute strength and aggression rather than technique he willed himself up. Reaching easier ground, he tied himself to a piton and belayed Franz up.

The middle section of the route was nowhere near as difficult, but it was very exposed and there were few pitons in place. Franz and Hans were moving slowly when two climbers approached from below, talking, laughing and climbing fast. Soon they were up close and one of them suggested that Hans and Franz should move over and let them pass. Hans was a little annoyed and just kept climbing. So he was surprised when the pair moved out to the side and raced by them, climbing with great skill and technique.

Hans led the last two difficult pitches up a steep corner. Sometimes hanging from the crack by jammed fists and sometimes bridged, legs spread wide apart over the abyss, he worked out the puzzle, and just before 5 p.m. they reached the top of the climb. Exhausted and with bloody hands, they were elated. Hans wrote in his journal: "This was our finest tour so far." Years later, however, he would admit, "We made a terrible job of the climb. We massacred it."

Looking up at the Spitzmauer north pillar

Climbing on the Spitzmauer

When they return-
ed to the hut, they
learned who the two
other climbers had
been. One was Erich
Waschak; and the
other, Leo Forstenlech-
ner. The pair had just
the previous summer
made the fourth ascent
of the notorious Eiger
north face, the most
feared mountain wall
in all of Europe. Hans
and Franz were not put
off, however, for they,
too, had climbed a good
route and were now
sixth-grade climbers.

In mid-August Hans
and Franz journeyed
to the Wilder Kaiser,
northeast of Innsbruck,
for a climbing holiday.
After an all-night train
journey, they set off
up the Kaiser Valley
while birds sang in
the forest and the mist
lifted, slowly revealing
the jagged limestone
peaks. At the Stripsen-
jochhaus, where they
planned to base them-
selves, the view was

breathtaking and they must have felt an intense mixture of fear and anticipation.

First, they climbed the north face of the Totenkirchl, and this time Franz led. "It was quite extreme. It took us two hours for the first two pitches. After seven hours of exceedingly difficult climbing we stood on the first terrace and now kept going up the *Heroldsweg*. After a total of 11 hours we reached the summit." Back at the hut, they had a greater respect for these Wilder Kaiser climbs and noted that they seemed to be harder for their grades than those in the Totes Gebirge.

Two days later, they climbed the east face of the Fleischbank. While they were searching for the start of the route, another pair of climbers arrived, so the two groups joined forces for what would prove to be Hans's hardest lead to date. After climbing a pleasant crack and overhang, Hans was forced to make a 15-metre tension traverse to the left, something he had never done before. As the others shouted instructions, Hans struggled on the exposed wall, leaning back on the rope while his feet searched for minute holds. A second tension traverse higher up proved easier, then the climbing progressed over beautiful rock. Two overhangs in the exit cracks were difficult, but soon easy ground led to the summit. Descending the *Heerweg*, they made it back to the Stripsenjoch "very proud of the tour."

At the end of August, Hans went to Salzburg, where he passed his physical exam for Health and Wellness Canada and a Canadian visa was stamped in his passport. During the interview, the visa officer asked him why he wanted to go to Toronto, and Hans said for the skiing. The visa officer replied that the Canadian government wanted immigrants to go to western Canada, as plenty were signed up for Toronto. He suggested Hans go to Winnipeg. "By that time I knew enough about Canada and said no, I don't want to go to Winnipeg. I said I would like to go where there are mountains. So he said go to Edmonton and I said are there any mountains in Edmonton. And he said yes, it's right in the mountains." So Hans signed up for Edmonton, and when he came out and saw Leo in the hallway, waiting for his interview, he said to Leo, "Sign up for Edmonton."

In the short, cool days of September, Hans and four companions returned to the Prielschutzhaus. As usual, they rode their bikes from Traun, arrived at Hinterstoder after midnight, then in the small hours of the morning hiked up the trail to the Prielschutzhaus, arriving at 3:45 a.m. After only a few hours of sleep, they set off to climb the Temelberg north face. Hans had a pair of running shoes to which he had glued a special rope sole designed for rock climbing. The glue did not hold tight, and years later Franz recalled, "He was standing there and slowly he was creeping down, but the shoes were not moving." A handhold broke on a traverse and Hans took a hurtling fall over an overhang. Slamming into the end of the hemp rope, he was lucky not to be hurt, although with the rope tied around his chest, as it was in those days, he must have been winded. Climbing back up, this time he "went over the traverse in superior style," and the rest of the way was a "gorgeous airy climb to the summit."

Two days later, the group climbed the north pillar of the Spitzmauer. For Hans and Franz, it was the second time and they completed the route in only four and a half hours, a great improvement over the slow pace of their earlier ascent. An aggressive climber, Hans took another leader fall onto the rope. Years later, Franz described Hans's climbing style as "daring. He was not afraid to try something difficult even though he didn't know how to do it."

Late in the month, with Franz, Karl Klambauer and Karl Mitterlehner, his favourite companions, Hans climbed the Traunkirchnerkogl north pillar, above Traunsee, near

Gmunden. In an article entitled "VI Grade Climbing," in the 1956 *Canadian Alpine Journal* (*CAJ*), Hans described the climb:

It was still pretty chilly as we walked along the lakeshore; a light fog kept the peaks above us hidden. Turning off the road we followed a path through the forest for a while and then found ourselves above the mist. Right in front of us rose a steep and forbidding but- tress which was our goal. Looking past it, we saw all the "Goi- serer Berge" and the "Dachstein Massive" with its glaciers. We didn't look too long. We were nervous, may- be a little bit scared, but there was also an eagerness in us to get there and to begin the game on the rocks.

Hans Gmoser, mountaineer

A short scramble over some grassy ledges brought us right to the beginning of the climb. The sun was still in the fog and the surroundings looked very unfriendly just then. Our eagerness seemed to have reached a record low and our gang of four was as quiet as if we were in a church. Karl K. was my companion, and Franz was with Karl M. Above us there was overhanging rock, so smooth that there wasn't even a crack for a piton. With one foot we were standing on a 50 degree slab and the other foot we had in a horizontal crack between the wall and the slab. After about eight feet the slab

Karl Mitterlehner at far end of ledge, Franz Dopf in middle (hidden) and Karl Klambauer nearest camera

broke off and below it we saw nothing but fog. We took as much time as possible to prepare for the climb. Then we were ready, still too soon to have overcome our nervousness. As I was first out on the slab, I was supposed to be first over the overhang. In a crack too small for me, but too big for pitons, I inched myself upwards. Every now and then I looked down to see my three pals, one foot in the crack and one foot on the slab, just as if they were keeping the overhang from falling completely. There wasn't much to hang on to, and my feet had to be satisfied with the poorest of friction holds. Finally I found a little nose, just big enough to hang a stirrup on. (How far this was against the "rules", I don't know.) This was a lot of help. But my knees were trembling so much that I was afraid it might shake the stirrup off the nose. My other foot, resting on a tiny knob, looked more like part of a sewing machine than a human leg. I was now most of the way up on this first pitch, but things got worse the higher I went. Then, almost at the goal, I was at the end of my wisdom, as well as at the end of my strength. No more holds on this cold, grey bulge and the depth below me was pulling like mad on my fingertips—and on my nerves too.

It was high time for me to get down to the slab again. Karl M. had the next try, while I had a chance to observe this manoeuvre from a comparatively safe spot. But he didn't get any further. After he was down again, our spirits were very low. Nevertheless I decided to have another final try. Meanwhile, the sun had come out and even patches of the lake below were visible. From up there it looked as if it was just one straight drop down into the water. This time I made it. Don't ask me how. At one point I had wedged myself horizontally between two holds, and when I made a frantic dash upwards, I got a terrific hand-hold which was the key to the whole affair.

From then on the climbing was a little easier. A few pitons which were already placed gave us a lot of comfort, even though we could look down to the lakeshore between our feet. The satisfaction of having mastered the overhang, and the beautiful weather, gave me terrific moral support, so I was able to get the next couple of rope-lengths fast and clean behind me. As we were all four on the ropes for this first half of the climb, I always had a long rest while the last two moved up. The trees seemed far below us and I could already see a few houses of the town, which had been hidden behind a hump. It was peaceful and quiet, and an occasional short rope command was the only sound. Soon I had reached a little platform which was the end of the first and most difficult step on this buttress. A few patches of grass and some alpenroses made me almost forget the difficulties of our climb. After I had belayed Karl K. up, I stretched out on our little nose and literally let the sun shine on my stomach. It was warm and wonderful. Deep blue sky above us and down below on the lake we could see the little motorboat making its first trip over to the other side. Those gentle green hills over there made a very soothing contrast to our immediate surroundings. Before long I was sound asleep, and it wasn't until I could hear church bells from the village that I woke again. Holy smoke! 12 o'clock already. Where are my friends? I looked around and saw them several feet below me, trying to free the rope from a crack. They had been there for two hours, but now the rope came loose and it was high time for us to proceed.

We changed the lead and Franz went ahead. He had to get across a three foot crack onto a vertical and smooth slab. He just let himself fall over, got his rope and stirrup into a snaplink and there he was on the slab, like a fly on the windowpane. He made his way along a hardly-visible diagonal crack to the right and soon disappeared around the edge. Only by the rope could we follow his progress. After a few minutes he told Karl M. to follow. I went right on Karl's heels. The steepness and exposure was at its utmost, but the rock was very firm and so were the pitons which led up to a tiny ledge on which Franz was waiting for us. We called this little spot "Fliegenband" (Flyledge). Above it were two respectable overhangs, while below it there was only space, except for the lake 2000 feet farther down. Karl M. went up to the ledge and from there started to work on the first overhang. I took a place beside Franz and snapped my safety loop into our piton. Above us, poor Karl M. found himself confronted with quite a problem. Piton after piton went into the rock, and he sounded like an old steam engine. When he was up on top, he could not pull the ropes in. They were crossed so many times between the pitons that they just looked like a spider web. Now Franz had to climb up there, depending completely on himself. He dug his fingers into the rock. He labored from one piton to the other, finally having undone the whole "rope salad". This was the end of the major difficulties, and over much easier terrain we arrived on the big plateau just below the main summit.

The peak itself didn't interest us at all. It was one of those really fashionable ones, where you can find everything from two-week-old babies to cats, dogs and ladies with painted fingernails and high-heel shoes, which all get up there over well-prepared Alpenvereinsteige (Alpine Club trails). We cut across some meadows and scree to one of the mountain huts. There we sat down in the grass, and while we untangled our ropes and ate our schmalz-brot (lard sandwiches), we looked at all the mountain peaks around us. The caretaker of the hut brought us some lemonade which was a real treat after a day in the hot sun. We would have liked to stay longer and enjoy the warm sun and the beautiful view upon all those familiar mountains. Unfortunately, there was still a long way ahead of us. Very easy, but still long. We went down the trail and after a few hours we walked on a real road again. At the first inn we stopped, and looking back we saw the mountain and on it the forbidding rock-faces, on which we had found an adventurous but romantic way.

Well, what is there more to say; we sat down and celebrated the occasion with a glass of beer each, and our thoughts wandered off to new mountains, new climbs. Everybody sat quietly by himself. Only in our eyes could one see the happiness and satisfaction which we had brought down from the mountain.

In mid-October, with Hans Wasserbauer and Siegfried Kramlehner, Hans made a final visit to his beloved Prielschutzhaus. With Wasserbauer, he once more climbed the Spitzmauer north pillar, but the ascent didn't go so well, and it took five hours of struggles, falls and tight ropes to reach the top. The following day, they climbed the north face of the Spitzmauer by a route unidentified in Hans's *Tourenbuch*. For a descent route, they chose the steep *Gruberrinne*. "This descent was a lot more adventurous than I had imagined. Three times we had to rappel and the last time it took 3/4 hour hard work to retrieve the rope." Hurrying back to the Prielschutzhaus, they packed their gear, then ran down the trail to the valley for the last time.

Hans left Traun for Canada in late November. An old friend, Fritz Speer, recalled that Hans had no suitcases or trunks for his journey, so he gave him some strong boxes to use instead. Hans's family saw him off at the train station. For Hans, it was the last time he would see his mother. No doubt some of his climbing companions, such as Franz Dopf, were there. And likely Gretl Hackl, his girlfriend, was there, too, the first of many broken hearts he would leave along the way.

On November 28, Hans embarked for Canada at Genoa, Italy, on the *S.S. Saturnia*. A new world lay ahead of him.

PART TWO

A Mountain Guide in Canada

(1951–1957)

"Once I got here, things were fairly tough, and nobody was waiting for you to give you something. You had to make yourself useful. I was 19 years old. I realized you'd better look after yourself and if you wanted people to help you, you'd better do something for them in return."

Bleak Beginnings—Edmonton in Winter

After the war, many immigrants came to Canada from Europe. Some of them came from the Alpine countries, most notably Austria, Germany and Switzerland, and gravitated west to the mountains of Alberta and British Columbia. In 1951 alone, 3,500 young Austrians, many of them tradesmen, arrived in Canada. Among them was Hans, who disembarked in Halifax on December 7. He then boarded a train and began a week-long journey to Edmonton. Crossing the Atlantic provinces, the forests of northern Ontario and the windswept stubble fields of the Prairies, he must have been overwhelmed by the size of the country, and the bleakness. Arriving in Edmonton, he stepped from the station onto the cold, snowy street, sucked in his breath and hardened himself for the struggle that lay ahead.

Edmonton was harsh indeed. The visa officer had been mistaken and the city lay on the plains, 300 kilometres from the mountains, at the junction of rich southern farmland and endless boreal forest. Winters were bitterly cold, with temperatures as low as −40°C, and lasted for months. To Hans's eyes, it was a rough-hewn city of about 160,000 inhabitants, with little sign of the European culture that he was accustomed to. However, oil had been discovered nearby in 1947 and the economy was strong. There were jobs to be had and fortunes to be made.

Leo was already in Canada, having arrived on October 30. He had been working with a number of other immigrants at a sawmill at Spirit River, but the day before Hans arrived in Edmonton, he had had an argument with his boss and had quit. Coming back to Edmonton, he met Hans the day he arrived. Leo had $50 from his job at Spirit River, so he went into a pawnshop and bought a guitar for Hans. Luckily, there was a place where new immigrants could stay near the train station; they could get a bed and three meals a day for $1.50 on credit.

The next day, Hans and Leo found a job logging in the forest west of Edmonton near Whitecourt. On the train, Hans pulled out his guitar and Leo began to sing. Soon the other passengers had gathered round and requested they sing "Lili Marleen." Their spirits were high, they were in Canada and the adventure had begun. In Edson, they were picked up in a truck by the foreman and driven to a camp in the bush. This job didn't last long, either. While felling a tree the first day, they bent the crosscut saw and were sent packing. By now, both of them were broke, so they borrowed $20 from a Czech immigrant and made their way back to Edmonton.

It was about a week before Christmas and a cold wind cut through their clothes as they walked the cheerless streets. Hans recalled, "We were out on the street in a strange country, hardly knew the language and had no place to go." Remembering that Franz Dopf had an uncle living in Edmonton who worked in the taxi business, they asked a number of taxi drivers if they knew Louis

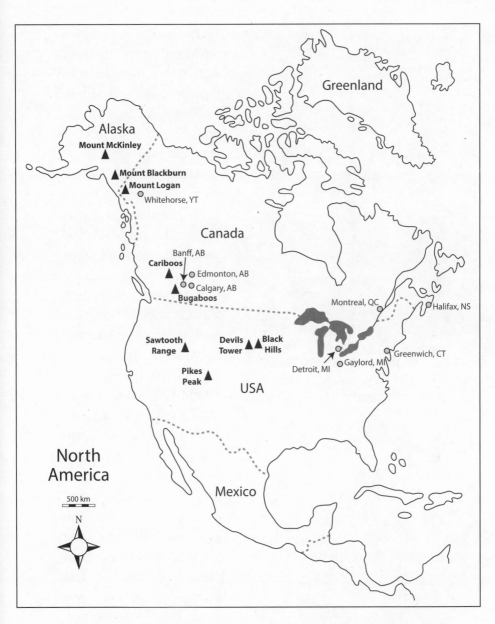

Dopf, but the reply was negative. Then they thought to look in the phone book, and, sure enough, there was his name. After writing down his address, they walked over to his house, where they were warmly welcomed and told they could stay for the holidays. It was surely a pleasant

Christmas for Hans and Leo, speaking their native tongue again and eating familiar food. Leo remembered, "It was wonderful. Louis was very nice to us."

After New Year's, Hans and Leo got jobs in Edmonton: Hans as an electrician, stringing power lines; and Leo as a plumber (Leo was a journeyman plumber). Things were looking up, and they even started to make a little money. With a small loan from Uncle Louis, they were able to buy two pairs of skis, boots and bindings, and on Saturday, February 2, they went to the local Whitemud Ravine ski hill. The sun was shining, the air was crisp and cold and they were at last skiing in Canada. "We were beside ourselves. We were so happy." Then Leo, showing off for three girls, wrapped himself around a tree and sustained a

Hans, on right, in coveralls, working as an electrician in Edmonton (above). Hans, the electrician, atop a power pole (below).

compound fracture to his right leg. Joy turned to despair. "That was the low point of our journey to Canada."

The break was serious, and at one point Leo even thought the leg was going to have to be amputated. The three girls visited him in the hospital, bringing flowers, and they became good friends, the girls later teaching the men English. Having no insurance, Hans and Leo were in a financial bind; Leo was in the hospital, and Hans earned just enough money to support both of them. For the next four and a half months, Leo would be in a cast, but luckily they had a safe and secure place to stay with Uncle Louis.

On the weekend of May 17–18, Hans and a new-found friend, Herbert Leinweber, hitchhiked from Edmonton to Banff, accompanied by Hans's new girlfriend Olive Mortimer. In Bowden, they visited Olive's parents, then continued to Calgary, where Olive decided to stay with friends while the two men hitchhiked west along what is now called the 1A Highway, through Cochrane (the present Trans-Canada Highway had not yet been built). From Calgary to Canmore the pair got a ride in a 1952 Super Buick. "In parts we went 100 miles per hour—it was terrific." As they approached the mountains across Morley Flats, Hans saw Yamnuska for the first time, rising sheer above the highway. He later wrote: "A silent and graceful silhouette. Massive and yet so elegant. I was fascinated. A beautiful rock face took shape. In one straight line it rose to the sky. My eyes were fastened upon it and as the mountain stood there solemn in this May evening, a silent promise was made."

That night, they arrived in Banff, Canada's premier mountain town, located in the heart of the Rocky Mountains. Under the stars, the men found a quiet spot in the trees beside the river and slid into their sleeping bags. Hans lay there warm and comfortable, listening to the wind sighing in the pine trees, and knew that he had come home.

Up at 6 a.m., they washed in the river, then "went in search of a suitable climbing mountain. For this 'thank God' there is no shortage, which gives us hope." Walking the streets of Banff, Hans had a serendipitous meeting: "Suddenly I saw two people out on a lawn and climbing skins hanging on the fence, their ski boots sitting on the lawn. So I immediately talked to them and it turned out to be Ken Jones and Lizzie Rummel. They had just skied out from Assiniboine." Both would soon become friends and mentors to Hans and would play a big role in his life.

Back in Edmonton, Hans made contact with the local section of The Alpine Club of Canada (ACC) and joined them on the Victoria Day weekend excursion to the Disaster Point hut near Jasper. Jim Walbridge picked Hans up at work and they drove west to the mountains. The next morning, the group set off early to climb Roche Miette, a modest peak nearby. "I could barely wait to get my hands on the rock.... I had a Hungarian Baroness and a Scottish doctor on my rope. Both were climbing for the first time. I looked for the most difficult route I could find." By 7 p.m. they were back at the hut, having reached the summit and "with a happy mountain experience filling our hearts." But the next afternoon, alone in the gloom of the immense expanse of the Athabasca valley, Hans was suddenly overwhelmed by homesickness. "It just came over me like a flood. I lay down and buried my face in the grass, I was so unhappy."

By the time he returned to Edmonton, however, he had changed his mind and wrote in his *Tourenbuch*: "On this trip I found something that I had been missing. The mountains are telling me something." And he had made contact with other mountain climbers such as Jo Kato, with whom he would be friends for a lifetime.

Rocky Mountain Paradise

The first week in June, Hans and Leo moved to Calgary, where they found room and board in the Mount Pleasant district at 714 23 Avenue NW, with Mr. and Mrs. Elmo Himmelreich. The two men shared a double bed and paid $60/month each. Hans found work with the Davies Electric Company as an electric motor expert. He managed to get Leo a job there as well, rewinding electric motors. For three weeks, Hans sat beside Leo and coached him on what to do, but eventually their employer caught on and fired Leo.

On their first weekend in Calgary, Hans and Leo went with their new landlords to the Saskatchewan River Crossing Lodge, along the Banff-Jasper Highway (now called the Icefields Parkway), where Elmo was installing a new oil heater. Hans helped by connecting the cable to the motor of the ventilator. In the evening, standing outside the lodge, they gazed west to the great peaks along the Continental Divide. "The mountains surrounding me had an unbelievable attraction and I felt an itch in my toes and fingertips."

Leo was still recovering from his broken leg, but Hans was fired up and ready to go. Making contact with climbers from the Calgary section of the ACC, he was soon out in the mountains every weekend. An ascent of Mount Edith "wasn't really a hard climb but it satisfied me." The rough, grey, limestone rock pleased him, for it was very similar to what he knew in the Totes Gebirge back home. Two weeks later, an attempt on Mount Verendrye was foiled by occasional rain showers, leaving Hans feeling none too pleased. "This was my first defeat in Canada and I don't adhere to the saying, 'One has to be able to turn around.'" Back home in Austria, he had often climbed in worse weather. The next weekend, the group returned to the mountain and climbed the southeast ridge. Hans wrote in

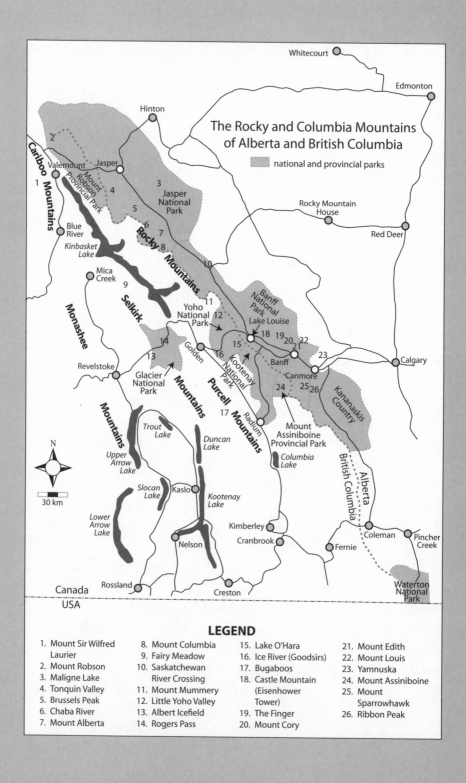

The Rocky and Columbia Mountains of Alberta and British Columbia

national and provincial parks

LEGEND

1. Mount Sir Wilfred Laurier
2. Mount Robson
3. Maligne Lake
4. Tonquin Valley
5. Brussels Peak
6. Chaba River
7. Mount Alberta
8. Mount Columbia
9. Fairy Meadow
10. Saskatchewan River Crossing
11. Mount Mummery
12. Little Yoho Valley
13. Albert Icefield
14. Rogers Pass
15. Lake O'Hara
16. Ice River (Goodsirs)
17. Bugaboos
18. Castle Mountain (Eisenhower Tower)
19. The Finger
20. Mount Cory
21. Mount Edith
22. Mount Louis
23. Yamnuska
24. Mount Assiniboine
25. Mount Sparrowhawk
26. Ribbon Peak

his *Tourenbuch*: "As we reached a peak, which we thought was the summit, a wonderful double pointed tower came into view. At the beginning it went quite easily, then we roped up and the climbing became more interesting. It turned wilder and wilder. Towards the southeast was a vertical drop of 700 m and in front of us a 30 m slab without any handholds. When Jim [Tarrant], who had led everything up to here, could not see any possibility of getting up,

Hans and Isabel Spreat on top of Mount Edith

he asked me. I didn't want to be asked twice and started to climb furiously. And to the amazement of the group I succeeded." Sitting on the summit, they had a terrific view and Jim pointed out, far to the southwest, the black towers of the Bugaboo Range. He said to Hans, "That is where the real climbing is."

Hans celebrated his 20th birthday on July 7, and Leo, in thanks for all of Hans's support, gave him a new nylon climbing rope. Together, they would use this rope on many historic climbs.

Hans went to the Alpine Club of Canada's summer camp in mid-July, held that year in the meadows below Mount Assiniboine. It was Hans' first visit to the mountain, one of the most spectacular in the Rockies. Shaped like the Matterhorn, it towers 2000 metres above verdant meadows, where thousands of alpine flowers carpet the ground. It is a mountain lover's paradise and one of the most beautiful places on the planet. For Hans, it would be love at first sight.

Getting there was not easy. After hitchhiking to Cochrane, he set out walking along the highway. "Late at night a good natured person took me to Canmore. I lay down beside the road and slept to a rainy morning." Then Hans continued hitchhiking, getting a number of rides along the Spray Lakes road. At last, he reached the Bryant Creek trailhead and hiked to Assiniboine Meadows, arriving there at 7 p.m. Not having enough money to pay $8/day for the ACC camp, he built a lean-to in the woods and rolled out his sleeping bag.

The next day, he joined an ACC group climbing Mount Sturdee: Hans led one rope, and Jim Tarrant, who was becoming a close friend, another. Later, he met Lizzie Rummel again and she invited him to her Sunburst Lake cabin, where he settled into the big tipi she kept for friends and penurious vagabonds. A few days later, he led Lizzie, her nephew Peter Lesher and Muriel Gratz to the summit of Wedgewood Peak. Afterwards, he wrote in his book: "I am very happy because my companions enjoyed it so much." The natural guiding instinct, where the guide derives his pleasure from his clients' pleasure, was coming out in Hans.

On leaving Mount Assiniboine, he wrote: "It was a hard goodbye. I went up to Wonder Pass and had to fight back tears.... They were days full of summit joy and mountain camaraderie, which lets one find sunshine during the grey everyday."

By this time Leo had found several different jobs. At Model Dairies, he worked for awhile making ice cream, but after several months he got fed up, quit and found work with Purity Flour Mills sewing flour bags. While Hans had been out climbing, he had been sitting at home, nursing his leg. Finally, at the end of August, he made his first excursion into the mountains. Hans was dying to show him the beauty of Mount Assiniboine, so they took the bus to Canmore, then walked all night along the road to the end of Spray Lake. After a short rest, they started walking up the Bryant Creek trail, Hans carrying his zither in his pack as he had often done back in Austria. For the rest of his life he would bring his beloved zither on most of his travels and mountain excursions. As they climbed the steep trail above Marvel Lake, it started to snow. "In a few minutes the snow was 2–3 inches deep. The higher we went towards Wonder Pass the worse it got ... On top of the pass there was a 1/2 foot of powder snow ... I barely could feel my feet. Leo was near the end of his strength and dragged himself along with iron willpower. [Leo was wearing running shoes.] I admired him. When I arrived at the cabin [Lizzie's Sunburst Lake cabin] I couldn't feel my feet at all. Leo rested at Strom's lodge and arrived 1 1/2 hours later. The end result; the front of both feet are half frozen."

Hans and Leo stayed with Lizzie in one of her wall tents and nursed their frozen feet. Barely able to walk, they spent a day chopping wood, then helped to shingle the roof of her cabin. In the evenings, at Erling Strom's Mount Assiniboine Lodge, they gave concerts of Austrian songs and music for the guests and staff; Hans played his zither and the pair yodelled. It must have started to feel a little more like the *gemütlich* evenings Hans and Leo remembered from their days in Austrian mountain huts.

Hans and Leo's mountain adventures continued all autumn. Leo, like Franz, was a perfect foil for Hans. The sixth of ten children, he had been raised in a musical home and his love of song ran deep. Although he was not as aggressive a climber as Hans, he was talented and had

Hans Gmoser playing his zither

climbed extensively in the eastern Alps: peaks such as the Grossglockner and the Dachstein, the main summits of the Totes Gebirge, and several routes in the Dolomites. Short of stature but powerfully built, Leo was charming and handsome. The girls liked him as much as they liked Hans. And Leo let Hans make the decisions. He would often remark that the only decision he ever made was to come to Canada and that after that Hans made all the decisions. Hard-working and loyal, he would become Hans's faithful lieutenant and right-hand man.

On the weekend of October 11–13, Hans and Leo visited Lake O'Hara for the first time, staying at the ACC's Elizabeth Parker hut. On the second day, with Milt Hicks, they attempted to climb the south ridge of spectacular Wiwaxy Peak. With frozen fingers, they worked their way up the steep quartzite rock, clearing powder snow from the small holds. But at about half height they turned back: "It is no pleasure to climb at one's limit in cold and snowy weather on an unknown face."[1] On the last day, they woke to five centimetres of fresh snow. "Hurray! Our legs itched and in our minds we could see ourselves gliding along on

Hans in front of the Elizabeth Parker hut at Lake O'Hara

our boards through the beautiful winter scenery. It won't be long now until we can."

A week later, they joined an ACC group hiking to the Stanley Mitchell hut, in the Little Yoho Valley. In knee-deep snow, Leo still in running shoes, they made their way through the autumn forest and up the steep Laughing Falls hill to the high valley. There they arrived at the rustic log cabin on the edge of a meadow surrounded by glaciated peaks with wonderful ski slopes, a veritable skier's paradise. Hans was just as passionate about skiing as he was about climbing and he wrote in his *Tourenbuch*: "The snow brought an irresistible magic for us. Every fibre in our legs itched and twitched and asked for the enchantment of the downhill ski run."

Hans tying into the rope below Yamnuska

The climbing season was, however, not quite over, and on November 23, Hans kept his silent promise with Yamnuska. As motorists approach the Rockies from Calgary, Yamnuska—or Mount Laurie (Îyâmnathka) as it is officially known—is the flat-faced monolith high above the Bow Valley on the right. The cliff rises 400 metres sheer from the scree, dominating the entrance to the mountains. It is a magical place where ravens ride the Chinook wind, and from its flanks one has an unimpeded view out onto the prairies.

Early in the morning, seven of the ACC group headed west from Calgary along the highway. Walt Sparling drove and the passengers on this momentous day were Hans and Leo, Isabel Spreat, John Manry, Jean Hewitt and one other identified only as Roy. Although it was late in the season, there had been no snow yet that year and Yamnuska was still bare.

Arriving at the base of the cliff, Leo was raring to go and soon was scrambling up the first rocks and scree-covered ledges. It had been a year since he had arrived in Canada and he had done no climbing yet. His leg was still weak, but, being a plumber, he had hands and wrists of steel. Stopping on a secure ledge, he decided he should tie in, so he hollered down to Hans to throw him up the end of a rope. Isabel tied in to the other end, and the pair began working their way up a line of cracks and corners that slants up the face just right of centre. To an experienced eye, it is the most obvious way to the top. Hans followed on a second rope with John and Jean, while Walt and Roy, on a third rope, brought up the rear. Before long, it became apparent that they were moving too slowly and that there was serious danger from falling stones, so Hans soloed on ahead to join Leo and Isabel, while the others began to descend.

At about two-thirds height, the trio arrived on a pedestal at the base of a ten-metre-high vertical wall. This tricky step offered small, square-cut holds overlooking tremendous exposure, but Leo made quick work of it, then scrambled up to the base of a large chimney. While belaying the others, he looked up and wondered if it would go; would the chimney lead to the top of the cliff, or would it pinch off into unclimbable overhangs? It was late in the day, and the thought of retreat was frightening. Also, the sky had turned grey and it was beginning to snow. The situation was becoming serious. Deep inside the chimney, Leo squeezed between the two walls, sometimes climbing with back and knees and sometimes with feet against opposite walls. After bringing the others up to a safe ledge, he explored a cave-like recess and was surprised to see light coming through a hole in the rock. Scrambling up, he poked his head out and pulled himself onto the windy crest of Yamnuska. They had made it!

With no pitons or carabiners, and with only the most rudimentary footwear, the trio had succeeded on a climb that in future years would frighten many well-equipped climbers. Isabel was wearing Vibram-soled climbing boots, but Hans wore leather ski boots and Leo only crepe-soled street shoes.

As the snow fell, they coiled their rope and prepared for the descent down the back side of Yam. By the time they reached the car, Leo's shoes were much the worse for wear, with holes worn through the soles from the rough rock. In honour of Leo's magnificent performance, the route would soon be called Grillmair Chimneys.

Although they did not realize it at the time, they had established the first modern rock climb in western Canada. They had climbed a steep rock face for the joy of hard climbing and not just to reach a summit. This ascent is now considered one of the most important events in Canadian climbing history, and Yamnuska itself has become one of the most popular mountains in North America. Summer and winter, thousands of climbers now challenge the face; and Leo and Hans's single line up the cliff has grown to over 100 routes. After being in Canada for less than a year, Hans and Leo had already made a significant contribution to Canadian mountain culture.

The next week, Franz Dopf arrived in Calgary. Hans had been sending letters, telling him of the many new

Leo atop a pinnacle near the base of Yamnuska

climbs to be done and the money to be made in Canada, and finally he could not resist. In their small room in the Mount Pleasant home, they set up a single bed where Hans slept, while Franz joined Leo in the double bed.

It was now ski season, and at Christmas, along with friends from the ACC, the trio made the arduous ski trek to the Little Yoho Valley. Starting out at 4 a.m., they broke trail through deep snow for 24 kilometres and reached the hut shortly after noon. In the evening, they lit candles on the freshly harvested Christmas tree and sang carols. Hans pulled out his zither, and the three Austrians sang songs of their homeland. With all the good food and drink

Franz, Leo and Hans in front of their Mount Pleasant home in Calgary

Franz, Hans and Leo high above the Little Yoho Valley
at Christmas, 1952

on the table and the fire crackling in the hearth, they must have thought they had gone to heaven.

For the first few days the weather was beautiful: –25°C with steel-blue skies. On December 26, Franz, Leo and Hans skied to Emerald Pass. "Splendid scenery opened up before us. One hundred metres below was a great ocean of fog, surrounded by majestic summits. We tore ourselves away from this splendour and in wonderful powder snow carved our tracks. Silently our boards slid over the white blanket. Turn followed turn as we descended. Then a short schuss and the last turn; it had been a great experience and an honestly earned descent."

The clear skies turned to grey, and two days later, when the trio left the cabin, they slid down the trail through new powder snow. It was heavenly, running through the silent, snow-frosted forest. The Little Yoho Valley had captured their hearts, and gradually thoughts of returning to Austria were fading. They were here to stay.

Hans was soon back at work in Calgary, but almost every weekend he went west to the mountains to ski at the fledgling resorts of Mount Norquay, Lake Louise and Sunshine Village. And on Sunday, February 15, at Mount Norquay, he broke his first ski in Canada. Meanwhile, Leo had headed north in January to make money to pay off the bills that still hounded him: $650 in medical fees, and also his passage to Canada. He would spend the next year at Cold Lake in northern Alberta, working on the construction of the new air force base.

March and April of 1953 were pivotal months that changed Hans's life. He worked for Lizzie Rummel at her cabin on the shores of Sunburst Lake, chopping wood, shovelling snow and leading guests on ski trips in this snowy paradise. Backcountry skiing in western Canada had begun here below Mount Assiniboine in March of 1928 when Norwegian ski adventurer Erling Strom and his partner, Italian nobleman the Marquis d'Albizzi, had led four American guests the 60 kilometres from Banff over two high passes to some rustic cabins that had been built earlier for summer tourists. Everyone had such a marvellous experience that Strom decided to build a lodge in the meadows and spend the rest of his life there. That summer, in partnership with the Canadian Pacific Railway, he built Mount Assiniboine Lodge. It thrived in the 1930s as western Canada's first ski lodge, but during the war it was shut down in winter. By the 1950s, however, it was back in operation again.

Lizzie's cabin was a smaller, more rustic affair, located about a kilometre away across the meadows from Strom's lodge. The owner and proprietor, Elizabeth von Rummel-Waldau, was, in fact, a German baroness and had grown up in cultured European society. In 1911, her mother had brought Lizzie and her two sisters to a ranch in southwest Alberta near Millarville. Lizzie's mother had actually won the ranch gambling, this being a favourite pastime of people of her standing. Marooned there three years later by the outbreak of the First World War, Lizzie had fallen in love with the rustic life of the Canadian West. In 1938, at the age of 41, she moved to Banff to make a new start in life. For ten years she managed Skoki Lodge near Lake Louise; then, in December 1950, she bought the Sunburst Lake cabin, where she realized a dream. Here she welcomed visitors from around the world and shared her love for Mount Assiniboine and for the Canadian Rocky Mountains in general.

Lizzie had been educated by private tutors, was well read and could speak French fluently. On the shelf in her little cabin were a number of books: a biography of Mozart; *Snow Structure and Ski Fields* by Seligman; and the works of Goethe, Schiller and other German masters. Hans read these books, and many nights the two sat up late talking. Often she would take down a book and show Hans a relevant passage. Hans was eager to learn. In another life he could, perhaps, have become a university professor or a doctor, but at the age of 15 he had been forced by circumstance to give up his education and apprentice at a trade. He still hungered for something more, and Lizzie could help. Years later, he recalled that the winter he spent with her had changed the course of his life.

Lizzie, who was 35 years older than Hans, had, in fact, become Hans's surrogate mother in Canada. She encouraged and supported his mountain career and offered him a window on a cultured world that he aspired to. For the rest of her life she would be one of his closest friends.

On Lizzie's bookshelf Hans also discovered *Where the Clouds Can Go*, the autobiography of Austrian mountain guide Conrad Kain, who had come to Canada in 1909.

Erling Strom and Lizzie Rummel soaking up the sun

Years later, Hans wrote the foreword to a new edition of this book: "Naturally the fact that he was a fellow Austrian and mountain guide had something to say, but here I read the words of a man who had been through the hard school of life. Yet he was never bitter: He was never afraid, even when, with torn shoes, infected feet, hungry and cold, he was tramping the roads of his native Austria, perhaps even unnoticed by other mortals. His straightforward philosophy of life, his respect for and tolerance of others no matter how they treated him, his gratitude for and loyalty to his friends all sank in deeply."

On March 2, Hans flew from Banff to Mount Assiniboine with Al Gaetz in his little Cessna 170 airplane. After landing on Lake Magog, they ferried loads up to Strom's lodge, where they spent the first night. Then they moved to

Sunburst Lake. For a week it stormed; the wind blew and the snow drifted around the little cabin. Hans shovelled, carried water up from the lake and occasionally ventured out on his skis for a few turns. Six days later, it cleared. "I just about shouted myself hoarse for joy—sun and blue sky. Heart, what more could you wish for!" Immediately, Hans and Lizzie were out on skis to the Little Nub and over to the Cerulean Hills. In the afternoon, they made the customary visit to Strom's lodge, and the next day they toured to Wonder Pass.

On March 10 and 14, Gaetz returned and Hans again ferried loads up from the runway on the lake to both Strom's and Lizzie's operations. Then the weather changed and it began to snow. On March 17, sitting around the radio, Hans and Lizzie heard the news that their pilot had been killed in a truck accident near Lake Louise. Al was their lifeline back to Banff and was to bring in guests for both lodges. Many guests cancelled, but some decided to come anyway, with Hans leading them the 30 kilometres from Sunshine Village ski resort to Mount Assiniboine. Hans had never travelled this route before and was used to the well-marked trails of Austria, so it would be a serious undertaking and a real challenge for one so young.

Hans was instructed to ski out to Sunshine Village with Al Johnston, who was working for Erling Strom. Al had never been on skis, so this was going to be an additional struggle to get him safely to the ski resort. Hans told the story years later:

> Lizzie primed me…. She tried to describe the route to me. I was pretty green, 21 years old. I'd never been in a place like that. Al and I left at 6:00 am and headed down to Og Lake and down the Valley of the Rocks and Golden Valley and I could see right away this guy is one helluva tough cookie

because he worked going uphill and he worked going down.

It was about 5:00 pm when we got to the top of Citadel Pass, out into the open between Fatigue Mountain and Citadel Peak. Al said to me "That's as far as I'm going today. We'll go down into the timber and spend the night." I said "No, tonight we'll sleep at Sunshine." I finally convinced him to keep going so we skied across and through the little neck and started to make our way to Quartz Ridge. By that time it was dark. I wasn't too worried because I knew Sunshine was on the other side of the ridge and it's got to be flat if not downhill from there. We got on top and looking over we saw a moving light. Al said to me "That's a car on the Banff-Lake Louise Highway." That didn't make sense to me. I had looked at the map enough to know that there was no way we could look down into the main valley. So I got out my flashlight and blinked it and sure enough the light blinked back.

What had happened was the snowmobile drivers at Sunshine knew that we were coming and when it got dark they took the Weasel [a type of large snowmobile] up to Brewster Rock to see if they could spot us. As soon as they saw my light they flashed back and then I could see the light moving down and coming across towards us. We skied down from Quartz Ridge and met them, jumped on board and spent the night at Sunshine.

In Banff, Hans went to Al Gaetz's funeral and did some shopping, then he returned from Sunshine to Mount Assiniboine with Al Johnston and two clients from Chicago. "It took us about 17 hours. It was a long trip and everybody got tired and I was tired.... We just got slower and slower and it was pitch dark when we came around Og

Lake." Here they came across a broken trail left by Lizzie, who had come to look for them. "When I hit that track it was like flying all of a sudden. I just went ahead and when I got to the other end of the meadow I looked around and there was no one in sight. They just couldn't keep up with me.... I actually lay down in the snow and had a little snooze. And then the three of them came and we went up the gully.... I still remember when we broke over the last rise and I could see the light in the kitchen and there was Lizzie sitting by the window, waiting for us."

That winter, Hans made two more trips out to Sunshine Village to collect supplies and lead clients back to Mount Assiniboine. On one of these trips, he led Elsa Wyatt, who would become a regular over the years. Hans was already making contacts and building up his clientele. While passing through Sunshine Village one day, he met another future friend, Philippe Delesalle, who was operating the little rope tow at the bottom of Strawberry Hill. Philippe "was intrigued by this 'wild man' hunched under a heavy pack, on his way into the no man's land that was in those days the flats of Citadel Pass in winter." Philippe was from France and, while on a trip around the world, had fallen in love with the Canadian Rockies. He was Gallic, emotional and exuberant. While he, too, submitted to Hans's leadership, and would play a key role in Hans's future success, this pair was not as well matched in temperament and occasionally argued.

On April 11, Hans left Mount Assiniboine for the last time that spring. The day before, he wrote in his *Tourenbuch*:

> I am really sad. I have spent six weeks here and I would count them as the most beautiful weeks of my life. I always felt at home and content. All the small trips between Strom's and here, the short trips to the Wedgewood Cirque, the trips I

did with Lizzie and various guests; they all cling to me unforgettably. But the most beautiful trips were those to Sunshine and back. Every time it was as if I left home and then came back again. Every time when I came over the first little hill and up to the clearing and saw my Wedgewood Face again, then I calmed down and was happy and I knew there was a small hut and somebody was waiting for me. There is my home. Now I am leaving for a long time; I will be happy when my trail leads back up to the little hut which has become my home on a strange continent.

Lizzie also wrote in Hans's *Tourenbuch*: "Hans was my faithful companion and I owe him a lot. He stood always helpful by my side and I hope we have happy moments again at our little lake and our darling Wedgewood Face. Many thanks, Hans. [Signed] Liesel Rummel"

Some time in 1953, Hans got a National Parks guide licence. It was ridiculously easy in those days. "All I had to do," said Gmoser, "was to go to the Administration Building [in Banff]. I think Herb Ashley was the Chief Warden, and he gave me this piece of paper. I stood at the counter and answered 20 questions and then I paid $2.00 and got this little badge that said National Parks Guide." It was not the sort of guides' exam that Hans had expected, but over the next few decades the qualification system would improve.

That summer was a productive one for Hans Gmoser the climber. Still working as an electrician in Calgary, he had only weekends and holidays to explore and climb, but he made exceptionally good use of his time. With Franz and Philippe and a new friend, Kurt Lukas from Austria, he climbed many of the Rockies classics such as Mount Victoria, Eisenhower Tower on Castle Mountain and the spectacular spire Mount Louis four times! He also made four very significant first ascents of difficult new rock climbs.

On May 10, Philippe was in the Banff Hospital, having burned himself at Sunshine Village when a coal stove back-flared in his face. Hans and Franz were keen on climbing a new route on the east face of Mount Edith, so they snuck into the hospital at 6 a.m. and whisked Philippe out the window to join them on the ascent. The climb went well, Philippe being careful not to disturb the large bandage that covered half of his face. They graded the route IV+ (about 5.5), Franz considering it not nearly as hard as what they had climbed in Austria. But the climb had taken a long time and it was evening before Philippe slipped quietly through the back door of the hospital and returned to his room. When the nurses discovered him, they were not amused.

The next weekend, Hans and Philippe made the first ascent of Wasootch Tower in the Kananaskis Valley, a climb that has become a local classic over the years. Philippe was not really a climber, but he was very strong and full of adventure and was ready to follow Hans anywhere. Leo was working in northern Alberta at this time, and Hans was often in need of a climbing partner.

On the weekend of June 13–14, there is an entry in Hans's *Tourenbuch* that is completely out of character: "Because of the tremendous drunkenness of Herbert and I, we were not able to go climbing!" A man who rarely drank to excess, Hans appears to have occasionally let down his guard and had a party.

For his holiday that year, Hans once again returned to Mount Assiniboine, this time with Franz and Philippe. Erling Strom warned them that there was too much snow and that the mountain was unclimbable. The trio ignored him, however, and on August 16 climbed Mount

Hans and Franz on the summit of Mount Assiniboine in 1953

*Hans (right) and Franz (centre) describe their ascent
of Mount Assiniboine to Lizzie Rummel
on the porch of her Sunburst Lake cabin.*

Assiniboine for their first time. According to Philippe, it was the first time the mountain had been climbed in seven years! Afterwards, seated on the steps of the Sunburst Lake cabin, Philippe captured his famous image of Hans and Franz relating the story of their ascent to Lizzie Rummel.

Hans, Franz and Philippe were not alone at Mount Assiniboine, having been accompanied by three girlfriends from Quebec who worked at the Banff Springs Hotel. Hans asked Philippe to walk out with the girls because they had to be back at work the next day, and as Philippe would say years later, "When Hans asked you to do something, you could not refuse." Unfortunately, Philippe would miss out on one of the best climbs of the summer: the first ascent of the northeast face of Sunburst Peak, a subsidiary summit of Wedgewood Peak directly across the lake from Lizzie's cabin. Hans and Franz graded this climb, which was steep and composed of excellent quartzite rock, V– (about 5.6).

Hans leading on the first ascent of the northeast face of Sunburst Peak

Afterwards, Hans met Edmund Petrig, one of the last of the Canadian Pacific Railway Swiss guides, who was guiding a client up Mount Assiniboine. They spent the evening together exchanging tales and developed a mutual friendship and respect for each other. He also met a young woman who would steal his heart away. On the evening of August 23, at Lizzie's cabin, "A lovely young lady came for a visit who I took home afterwards." Her name was Carter Meyer; she was 18 years old and was visiting Strom's lodge with her father, a prominent American banker. On the 26th she left Mount Assiniboine for Banff via the Allenby Pass trail, and Hans followed the next day. Arriving exhausted at 8 p.m., he found Carter at her hotel and spent the rest of the evening chatting with her. He was hooked.

On October 18, with Franz, Hans climbed a second new route on Yamnuska. Calgary Route, as they called it, followed a huge slanting gash just west of the summit. The crux came right at the end, a strenuous squeeze chimney that still proves difficult for climbers today. After the climb, Dopf and Gmoser crossed the summit and down-climbed Grillmair Chimneys, only a small slip away from eternity. On Calgary Route they had even placed a piton or two, likely the first pitons hammered into Yamnuska's grey and yellow rock. This one they graded V– (5.6).

Franz remembered years later, "You're 20 years old, you're invincible. That's how we felt." Hans, however, was more philosophical:

Everyone who climbs grapples with the question, "Why are you doing it?" I also feel everyone has a different way of explaining it or else you use a cliché. For me I came here with nothing as a young immigrant. At home you have your school friends, you have your family and your friends at work. You belong to a community. You come to a strange country like this and all of a sudden you are nobody. At home I had always been very happy in the mountains. I enjoyed the physical act of climbing, the physical surroundings, the rock features, the views and the camaraderie with people who did similar things.

Then Leo and I came here and we met a few people in the Alpine Club but their philosophy about climbing was quite different from ours. To climb a face like

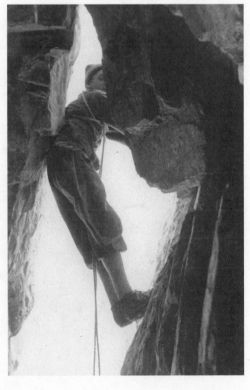

Hans leading the last pitch (the squeeze chimney) on the first ascent of Calgary Route

Yamnuska was almost a bit of a refuge in a way. To try to find that which you had left somewhere else. Trying to rediscover it. Trying to prove yourself.

It was basically trying to make yourself feel good. That was the only way I knew how to do it. Certainly when we were doing these climbs we felt very happy. Maybe because you thought you were doing something special or maybe there is really something up there that does make you feel good.

In what was becoming an annual event, Hans spent Christmas back in the Little Yoho with Leo, who had returned from Cold Lake, and Philippe, who was rapidly becoming the fourth member of the "Austrian group." Isabel Spreat and Rosemary Broady, their physiotherapist friends from Calgary, were there, as were Kurt Lukas and Hosi Weber, who was from Switzerland. On December 28, the group was crossing a bowl high on Mount Pollinger,

In front of the Stanley Mitchell hut at Christmas 1953.
Hans is at the extreme right.

Evacuating Leo to Field on a sled at Christmas 1953

Weber out in front, followed by Gmoser, Lukas, Grillmair and Delesalle. They were just coming to the end of a traverse when the slope started moving, very slowly at first but gradually picking up speed. The last three men were caught and carried over several cliffs. "It was like being in a concrete mixer," remembered Delesalle. When the snow stopped moving, everyone was on top, luckily, for they had no beacons, probes or shovels. Grillmair was hurt—a possible broken leg—and Lukas had lost his skis. The rest of their holiday was spent evacuating Leo on a sled back to Field. Lukas improvised a makeshift pair of skis from planks in the kitchen door and walked ahead of the others, packing a trail for the sled. It was all a false alarm, however, for Leo's leg was not broken after all.

In January 1954, Hans quit his job in Calgary and moved to Banff to live the life of the professional mountaineer and guide. There he found a cheap place to live in the garage of Muriel Gratz, a local schoolteacher and mountain lover. Hans would never have a nine-to-five job again in his life, and it would be decades before he had a regular paycheque. From then on he would live on his wits as a mountain guide and later as a lecturer. Franz, meanwhile, moved to Edmonton to work and live with Uncle Louis.

At that time, Banff was a small, quiet, mountain town and Canmore was a hard-working, coal-mining town. The village at Lake Louise was only a gas station, a general store, a one-room school and the small log Post Hotel. The Mount Norquay ski resort boasted a single chairlift and a couple of rope tows, Sunshine Village had a lone rope tow and a few log cabins and at Lake Louise there was only a Poma lift next to Temple Lodge. Summer tourists and winter skiers made their way along the Bow Valley on what is today the 1A Highway, or Bow Valley Parkway. The Banff Springs Hotel and the Chateau Lake Louise were closed in winter, and none of the many hotels that now line Banff Avenue existed. The original, wooden Mount Royal Hotel, filled with buffalo, elk, bear and moose heads, and the King Edward Hotel across the street were the only downtown Banff accommodation. Wardens still lived in backcountry outposts, and supplies for lodges such as Skoki and Mount Assiniboine went in, during the summer, on horseback. Local pilot Al Gaetz had been on the leading edge of mountain aviation.

When Hans returned that winter to Mount Assiniboine, he was hired to guide for Erling Strom at Mount Assiniboine Lodge. On March 2, he guided Fred Pessl from Detroit, Michigan, from Sunshine Village to Mount Assiniboine. It was a momentous meeting, the start of a long and rewarding friendship. For a number of years, Hans had been looking for the absent father figure in his life. Although Gmoser always spoke very kindly of Erasmus Hintringer, it is unlikely that his stepfather provided the strong role modelling that a young boy needs, and while the priest Dorfner had had a strong but brief influence on Hans as a father figure, it was Fred who would give him the leadership, support, love and inspiration that he craved. An immigrant from the same region of Austria as was Hans, Fred had made good in the New World; like Lizzie Rummel, he encouraged and supported Hans in his chosen career. Fred carried with him a 16mm movie camera and took footage of the action that spring at Mount Assiniboine. Little did Hans realize at the time that this was the start of his own career as a filmmaker and lecturer.

Hans carrying buckets of water from Magog Lake to Mount Assiniboine Lodge

For over two months, Hans called Mount Assiniboine Lodge home. He led guests on the usual ski tours to Terrapin Glacier, the Little Nub, the Towers and Og Pass, chopped wood and shovelled snow. And there was a lot of snow to shovel in 1954, for it was a record year. Stu Ames had taken over from the late Al Gaetz and was flying guests to Mount Assiniboine, but on occasion Hans made the trip out to Sunshine Village ski resort.

Franz came to visit, and on March 21 he and Hans attempted to climb Mount Assiniboine. Starting out in the dark, they climbed steep, avalanche-prone slopes, then snow-covered rocks to the plateau. It was a bitterly cold day, −30°C. The winter sun barely warmed them, and as they were wearing only single boots, their feet began to freeze. They made their way to the Red Band, 300 metres below the summit, then turned back, knowing that if they continued they would spend a night out. As it was, Hans froze the toes on his left foot.

Late in the season, Stu Ames crashed his plane. Hans was there and years later told the story:

> Stu landed and took off on the lake. At the lodge end there was a little hill. His tactic was to come in, make a turn at the head of the valley, touch down on the lake and taxi right up to the top of the hill and turn around. Then when he took off, he took off from the top of the hill, went down and usually got airborne shortly after he hit the lake. The tricky thing was that he was flying right towards the mountains, often with a severe downdraft. He had to make a turn at the most vulnerable moment. On this occasion we got him off, he had a good track, went down, got airborne, turned at the back of the lake and stalled. The wind coming down was so strong and he didn't have enough air speed. He just nosed in. Luckily he wasn't too high off the ground.
>
> We watched the whole thing and rushed across the lake. By the time we got there they had gotten out of the plane. They just left it there. Al [Johnston] and I often talked about getting it off the lake or getting the engine out but we never did anything.... When we went back in July there was still ice on the lake and the plane was still sitting there. But by that time it was too dangerous to go out. Within a week or so it all went. It's still at the bottom of the lake.

On April 18, Hans switched from writing his *Tourenbuch* in German to writing it in English. In midentry he made the change. He wrote: *"Mit Rael Charette nach Sunshine.*

Al Gaetz (right) and his Taylorcraft airplane in front of Mount Assiniboine Lodge. Gaetz would accelerate down the hill and across the lake, then after becoming airborne turn to the right before reaching the mountain wall.

Ski all day in Sunshine." He never went back, and all his future entries were in English.

Hans, Lizzie and Al Johnston packed up and headed for Sunshine on May 1, another biting-cold day. Hans wrote in his *Tourenbuch*: "This is the end of another season of spring skiing. We had great experiences and now we are on the lookout for new adventures."

Kurt Lukas (left) and Hans on their Chaba River adventure in 1954

Kurt Lukas (left) and Hans camped along the Chaba River

Hans didn't have to wait long and only three days later took the train to Glacier on the west side of Rogers Pass in the Selkirk Mountains: "We got out of the station and the snow banks must have been 10 feet high.... We skied up to Wheeler Hut. When you crossed under the telephone line you had to duck under the wire, the snow was that deep. It was fantastic and I was so impressed because here we were at the beginning of May, and man, there was snow!" Later in the day, he was joined by park warden Noel Gardner, his wife, Gladys, and Peter van Wagner, and for the next week Hans assisted Noel with his research. The Canadian government was considering routing the new Trans-Canada Highway through Rogers Pass, and Gardner was collecting information on avalanche hazard. On May 9, they skied across the pass to Stony Creek, taking photos of the avalanche paths, and two days later, with Jimmy Webb, an engineer with the national parks service, they skied in the other direction, towards Flat Creek, taking pictures. Then it began to rain and Hans decided to go home. On May 12, he skied alone to Mount Abbott. It was "[v]ery wet but terrific skiing. Too bad that this is the end."

A month later, Hans made his first foray into the wild and untracked wilderness of the Canadian Rockies. In mid-June he and Kurt Lukas set off with heavy packs and skis from Sunwapta Falls up the Athabasca River, in Jasper National Park. On the second day they were forced to strip naked and ford the Athabasca in water up to their waists. Continuing up the broad gravel flats of the Chaba River, they camped about three miles from Fortress Lake. Sitting around the smoky campfire, swatting mosquitoes, Hans realized that these mountains were completely different from the ones he had known in Austria: there were almost no huts, few trail signs and often no people, only tangled forest and wild rivers surrounded by a myriad of snow-capped summits. Maps at the time were still primitive and there was only one slim guidebook for the entire range. They attempted to reach the west Chaba Icefield below Apex Mountain, but it was just too far, so on June 25 they returned down the Chaba and Athabasca rivers on a raft they had built. "It was a great experience. We had a lot of fun in spite of a few narrow escapes."

In the summer of 1954, Hans returned to Mount Assiniboine, and so did Carter Meyer. Hans was guiding for Erling Strom and she was a cabin girl, doing almost everything except the cooking. They had an idyllic summer together, hiking, climbing and skiing (the heavy snowfall of the previous winter still persisted in the higher terrain). In fact, at the end of the summer, Hans felt guilty that he had perhaps neglected his duties as a guide. Carter would recall years later, "In the mountains I had absolute confidence in him. He was very good looking and had enormous charm. He played the zither and loved music and so did I."

Carter Meyer

This was the first summer that Hans worked as a climbing guide, and he kept a log with comments from his clients. One client wrote: "One of the best days of my life, and with the best guide I have ever had the pleasure of knowing." Another wrote: "My stay at Assiniboine was the most wonderful holiday I have ever had and Hans was largely responsible for that. Climbing with him was sheer joy thanks to his patience and agility." A young woman with whom he did a number of climbs that summer wrote: "Hans, it was so wonderful to go with such a good climber as you. Thank you so much for all you taught me. I love you." Most of the climbs that Hans led were not difficult, just scrambles really. Interspersed were ascents of Mount Assiniboine with a young friend from Banff, Jerry Johnston,[2] and the second ascent of the northeast face of Sunburst Peak, a

Hans on horseback in the summer of 1954

route that Hans had named the Elizabeth Route in honour of Lizzie. Hans befriended a group of students from the Varsity Outdoor Club at the University of British Columbia who were working at the Kananaskis Forest Experimental Station. On their frequent visits to Mount Assiniboine, Hans would teach them climbing technique during the day, and at night, sitting around the campfire, he would teach them to yodel. Pat Duffy remembered that one day Hans took four of them on a traverse of The Towers.

Carter returned to Banff on September 6, on her way back to school in the American Northeast, and Hans accompanied her. That night they had dinner together, talked and dreamed. The next day, they climbed the south ridge of Mount Edith and late in the day she left for home. It was a sad parting at the Banff train station, but Hans had plans to visit Carter in the United States. He returned to Mount Assiniboine for another month, then, on October 18, he, too, departed for Banff. That night, he wrote in his *Tourenbuch*: "This summer I was too much in love to be a good guide. When I look back, I am not satisfied with myself. <u>I will do better in the coming years.</u>"

In early November, Hans journeyed to the United States. He went first to Detroit, where he saw Fred Pessl, who presented him with 400 feet of edited 16mm film and suggested that he use it to promote his business. Hans then went to Greenwich, Connecticut, to visit Carter. This visit didn't go very well. Carter's father was chairman of the board of the J.P. Morgan Bank, one of the most prestigious banks in North America. He was not impressed with what he saw and for three days refused to speak to Hans. Hans was devastated. He was an immigrant, a tradesman with an accent. In those days, some would have called him a DP (displaced person). Hans left Greenwich and the Meyer family and made his way back to Banff. Later that winter, Carter's mother convinced her to end the relationship with Hans, but for years they continued to correspond, Hans relating to Carter all of his mountain adventures. Carter saved the letters, but the day she married she destroyed them. For Hans, the wound eventually healed and his iron resolve returned, but the scar would always be there.

That year of 1954, Austrian climber Hermann Buhl's biography, *Achttausend drüber and drunter* (Eight Thousand Over and Under), was published. It was (and still is) an inspirational tale of high adventure in the mountains, culminating in a solo ascent of Nanga Parbat, the ninth-highest mountain in the world. The original English title, *Nanga Parbat Pilgrimage*, tells it all. Hans bought a copy and devoured it from beginning to end. He even gave a copy as a present to Lizzie. A fellow countryman, Buhl was a mountain role model he could relate to. Hans decided he would devote all his energies to climbing and skiing adventures, and thoughts of serious romance and marriage would be set aside.

At Christmas that year, Hans and his friends returned to the Stanley Mitchell hut in the Little Yoho Valley. Somehow they lost the trail in the dark and found themselves working their way steeply up the creek bed. It was a painful ordeal, and one member of the group, Hans's new girlfriend, was not impressed. Thelma Maher, whom Hans had met the previous summer, had turned down a vacation in Hawaii to spend Christmas with him, and here she was, under the stars, cold and tired, floundering in deep snow. Arriving at the hut just before midnight, Kurt Lukas immediately went out and cut a Christmas tree. Franz and Philippe got the fire started, fetched water and took the shutters off the windows. Then, warmed by the crackling flames, they settled in.

Thelma, however, wasn't having much fun, so Hans accompanied her to Takakkaw Falls on December 27 and out to Field the next day, so ending their brief romance. Late in the afternoon, he returned to the warden's cabin at Takakkaw Falls, and in the morning, through 25 centimetres of new snow, he continued to the Stanley Mitchell hut. It snowed for several days and the skiing was excellent. On January 2, it cleared and the group ascended a small peak above the Glacier des Poilus. Thoughts of Thelma far from his mind, Hans wrote: "Terrific view and excellent skiing. I shall never forget this day. It was one of the best I had in the mountains."

The winter of 1955 was an incredibly active one for Hans, even by his standard. First, he and Jerry Johnston, staying at informal, rustic mountain huts or warden cabins, toured and explored in the area southwest of Banff. Shadow Lake, Egypt Lake, Sunshine Village, Police Meadows and Mount Assiniboine, and the connecting valleys and passes, were their kingdom, and a small log cabin with a wood stove

Hans teaching national park wardens
mountaineering techniques during the winter of 1955.
Left to right: Murray Dawson, Tom Ross and Hans.

was their castle at the end of the day. Without a care, young and free-spirited, Hans revelled in this good time.

Then came what Hans called "one of my biggest breaks in my career as alpine guide": helping Walter Perren teach a ski-mountaineering course to national park wardens. Perren was the last of the Swiss guides hired by the Canadian Pacific Railway. From 1950 until the autumn of 1954, he and Edmund Petrig, both from Zermatt, had led guests from Chateau Lake Louise to the surrounding summits. After their contract expired, Edmund had returned to Zermatt, but Walter stayed on in Canada. That summer of 1954, there had been a very high-profile climbing accident on Mount Victoria with four fatalities. The national parks service decided to develop a mountain rescue program and teach park wardens, most of whom were cowboys, the necessary skills, so they hired Walter to do the job. In February 1955, he ran a winter course from government cabins at Cuthead Creek in the front ranges of Banff National Park and hired Hans to be his assistant.

Despite temperatures that dipped to −38°C, they taught the wardens avalanche rescue skills, route finding in the mountains, and even ski technique, for most of the men were novices. Hans had a break in March and, with a warden only identified as Chris, went on a ten-day patrol in Banff National Park. Staying at warden cabins with romantic names such as Windy Cabin, Scotch Camp, Sand Hills Cabin and Little Pipestone Cabin, they covered almost 200 kilometres. For Hans, it was a wonderful opportunity to see new country. Later that month, Hans instructed another warden training school, based at the Columbia Icefield. After suffering temperatures reaching −44°C on March 24, Hans and the group of wardens went to Marmot Basin, a tiny ski resort near Jasper, to practise ski technique for three days. Then, on March 29, they were back at the Columbia Icefield, where they learned to blast overhanging cornices using explosives.

An Independent Guide

At Fred Pessl's urging, Hans organized his first independent ski camp in the spring of 1955. On April 28, he arrived by train at Glacier and skied up to the Wheeler hut. Two days later, Philippe, who would be his assistant, showed up, and on May 1 their first clients began arriving. Amongst them was Doreen Tynan from Calgary, who would soon become Hans's new flame. Pleasant, intelligent, outdoorsy and, of course, pretty, she was liked by everyone; the consensus was that she would be perfect for Hans. For two weeks, Hans led his guests on tours to the Illecillewaet Glacier, the Asulkan Glacier and Sapphire Col. Then, on May 12, disaster struck. Hans and Philippe had brought

Isabel Scott to the Glacier station for her return to Banff, and while waiting for the train, Hans broke his leg skiing on the snowbank behind the station. The leg was splinted and Hans was loaded on the train for Banff. Philippe took over for another week, and the camp wound up on May 20.

It was a quiet summer for Hans, and a difficult one. He had no money and no insurance and was without work. His friend Elsa Wyatt offered him a place to live at her house in Banff. Leo had a chance to repay the generosity that Hans had shown three years earlier and loaned him some money. Eventually, Hans found a job at the Bow Summit Fire Lookout, where, to strengthen his leg, he would ride a bicycle down the road and back up to the lookout. Meanwhile, Hans's friends from the Varsity Outdoor Club in Vancouver had not forgotten his kindness of the previous summer at Mount Assiniboine and they voted him an honourary member. Hans received the letter informing him of this honour on July 7, his 23rd birthday.

At the Bow Summit Fire Lookout in the summer of 1955.
Left to right: Leo Grillmair, Franz Dopf
and Hans Gmoser with broken leg.

Hans Gmoser leading the first ascent of the south ridge of Cascade Mountain in September 1955

He wrote in his *Tourenbuch*: "I am only too glad to accept this and will do everything to live up to expectations."

On July 20, Hans's mother, Rosa, died of cancer at the early age of 42 years. She had never been very supportive of Hans's climbing adventures and had not wanted him to go to Canada. No doubt Hans felt guilty that he had not returned to visit his ailing mother, particularly as Leo had gone back to Austria during the first four months of 1955 and had looked in on Rosa. She had asked Leo questions about the pair's adventures in Canada but had not criticized their decision to emigrate. Hans had tried to please her and show her that he had made a good choice. Now she would never see the amazing life he would live and the remarkable success he would make of it.

By the beginning of August, Hans was able to hike up small peaks again, and on September 18, with Franz Dopf, he was back on the rock. The pair climbed a difficult new route on the south ridge of Cascade Mountain, above the Banff airport, which Hans graded V (5.6–5.7).

In early October, Hans, Franz and Leo returned to Yamnuska. Inspired by the vertical lines on the great walls of the Italian Dolomites, they wanted to create a route that would rise directly to the summit from the scree. They climbed only two rope lengths that first day, and it was difficult climbing. A week later, the trio returned, joined by Kurt Lukas, and this time they made three rope lengths up the face. A bulging, rounded crack capped by an overhang was the crux. Hans had made wooden wedges and tied nylon loops through a hole drilled in the end. After driving these into the crack, he hung small rope ladders on the loops and climbed using direct aid. It was a new type of climbing that had rarely been seen in Canada before.

During the 1950s, rock climbing in the Canadian Rockies was a dangerous sport. Little information was available and the only guidebook that existed gave not much more than the latitude and longitude of the major peaks and the names of those who had made the first ascent. The hemp ropes that Hans would have used in Austria had now been replaced by hauser-laid nylon ropes, but he still tied in around the chest in the European fashion, there being no harnesses at the time. For protection, climbers carried a few soft iron pitons, heavy steel carabiners, and a few long slings. The piton hammer was simply stuffed in the back pocket. Many climbers wore full-shank mountain boots. There were no helmets, and a leader fall was to be avoided at all costs.

In the early winter, Harry Dempster, superintendent of Jasper National Park, hired Hans as an alpine specialist, but the job didn't last long. Hans wasn't happy in Jasper and "[t]here wasn't anything I could get my teeth into so I quit." According to Toni Klettl, an old-time Jasper park warden, Hans was fired. Clearly, Hans was not cut out for a government job.

It was another beautiful Christmas for Hans that year at the Stanley Mitchell hut, but it would be the last with his friends. He would return many times in the future, but it would now be as a guide with clients. Earlier, Fred had asked Hans to organize a spring ski tour for him and his son, and Hans had decided the hut would make a perfect base. For ten days in early February, Hans packed supplies up the Yoho Valley in preparation for this adventure. At the hut, he cut and stacked wood, which was hard and lonely work. Hans wrote in his *Tourenbuch*: "I wish I had somebody to ski with." On February 10, he finished the job and skied out to Field, where he wrote: "Boy am I ever tired now. It's good to relax once again." However, Hans's idea of relaxing over the next few weeks was to make more ski tours: to the Ptarmigan hut, near Lake Louise ski resort; up Redearth Creek to Egypt Lake; and from Sunshine Village to Mount Assiniboine.

On March 28, Fred arrived, and they spent two days warming up on the slopes above Temple Lodge.[3] Two days later, Hans, Fred and Aileen Harmon from Banff set off on skis up the Yoho Valley road, spending the first night in the warden's cabin at Takakkaw Falls before continuing up to the Stanley Mitchell hut. Late in the afternoon, Hans returned back down the trail to meet his assistant, Bob Price, who was leading Fred's 24-year-old son Skip. For some reason, Aileen returned to Banff on April 3, but Fred and Skip stayed and for the next two weeks explored the fabulous ski slopes of the Little Yoho Valley. There were tours to President Pass and even an ascent of The President on foot. Several days were spent skiing the northeast flank of The Vice President beyond President Pass. The slopes below Mount Kerr were another favourite location, as were the glaciers of Mount McArthur and Isolated Peak. Kiwetinok Pass, Whaleback Meadows, Emerald Pass: they skied them all. On their last day in the valley, they skied

*Fred Pessl (left) and Hans Gmoser on the way to
the Little Yoho Valley in early April 1956*

to the summit of Mount Pollinger, descended to Kiwetinok
Pass, climbed to the col between the two peaks of Mount
Kerr, then descended into the basin below Emerald Glacier.
To finish the day, they skinned up to Emerald Pass, where,
sitting in the golden light of sunset, they bade farewell
to the valley. It had been a superb two weeks, with good
weather and good snow. Fred had carried his movie
camera and filmed Hans, Bob and Skip in action. Some of
this footage would make its way into Hans's first film the
following year. In the hut logbook, Hans signed his name:
"Hans Gmoser, Guide, Banff, Alta." It was the first time he
had called himself a guide.

Hans had only a few days to prepare for the next camp,
and by the end of April he was at the Wheeler hut in Rogers

Pass. Several of his regular clients, such as Isabel Scott and Elsa Wyatt, were there, and for a month, ably assisted by Philippe, Hans led tours to many familiar destinations. On this camp, Hans discovered the Hermit hut and wrote in his *Tourenbuch*: "Certainly the spot I like best in the mountains of Canada. The cabin was all under snow and we had a hard time finding it."

Hans would guide spring ski camps at Rogers Pass for many years and eventually worked out a method of getting the best snow. Years later, he recalled, "We had a pretty strict schedule there. Everybody turned their clocks two hours ahead, so then we would get up at 4 in the morning, which was 2 in the morning, and leave the hut at 5, which was actually 3. We would be on top by 9:00.... Then, depending on how the conditions were, we would sit up on top for a while and enjoy the sun. It was actually very interesting skiing because you had to be right on with your timing. And when you were, you had really good skiing on top where it was flat, fast, then nice corn snow coming

Hans Gmoser at the Hermit hut, above Rogers Pass

down the steeper slopes, and you still had the track going down in the woods and out along the creek. So by 11 or 12 o'clock we were back at the Wheeler Hut."

Hans finished the ski season of 1956 with a brutally hard tour with Philippe. On May 28, they took the train from Glacier to Flat Creek, then shouldered their loads and set off on foot along the creek. Philippe had 56 kilograms on his back, and Hans 53 kilograms. Their goal was the Albert Icefield. After about one kilometre, they realized that the weight was just too much, so they began to pack their loads in relays. The alder bush was dreadful and they were forced to camp after only five kilometres. The next day, they were able to put their skis on and the travel became easier. At Camp Two, Hans wrote: "The waters are tumbling down from everywhere and we are excited to look at the country behind the skyline."

Putting on wet boots and clothing in the morning was hard, but over the coming week it became the norm. They became accustomed to the daily grind: crossing creeks barefoot and negotiating steep canyons while carrying immense loads. The weather turned miserable, but they kept going in rain and snow. At night, they sat around the campfire and tried to dry their socks and boots. Crawling into their sodden sleeping bags, they would shiver for hours before falling asleep. On June 3, they finally reached a glacier descending from the Albert Icefield and climbed a small peak that they called Arrival Peak. The next day, they ascended the glacier to a col, arriving in a lightning storm. In such conditions further travel was impossible, so they returned to their camp in pouring rain. Hans wrote in his *Tourenbuch*: "We are completely wet now and hope for some nice sun to dry our bones and clothes."

The sun didn't come, and instead they had "Snow, snow and more snow. We can hardly see 100 yards. We found a small cave and built a fire in it. It was pretty smoky and

Skiing high above Rogers Pass. The Trans-Canada Highway, under construction, can be seen in the bottom of the valley.

*Hans (left) and Philippe camped along Flat Creek
on their way to the Albert Icefield*

damp. We still kept our spirits up." On June 6, it was still snowing, so they decided to turn back. Quickly packing up, they jettisoned the extra food, then pushed rapidly down Flat Creek to the rail line, busting through the bush with brute force and walking in their soaking boots through the streams. "It was tough—perhaps the toughest yet but we made it by 7:15 pm."

That summer, with Franz and Leo, Hans returned to Yamnuska to push forward the line they had begun the previous season. "We progressed extremely well; mastered the big overhang and moved 6 more rope lengths up the wall, right underneath a 30 foot yellow roof. There we all were pretty tired and so we rappelled the 950 ft. back down." Only a day later, Hans was out with Ken Baker, making what they thought was the first ascent of a spectacular rock spire west of Banff called The Finger. Climbing the north ridge, they found it "a little tricky in places but spectacular and thrilling." On the summit, however, they discovered a small crumbling cairn, likely built by old-time Canmore climber and guide Lawrence Grassi many years earlier.

By this time, Hans was the only mountain guide operating full-time in Canada. The original Swiss guides such as Edward and Ernest Feuz had retired in the early 1950s. Edmund Petrig and Walter Perren, who had replaced them for five years, had now also moved on, and Bruno Engler was putting most of his energy into photography. Hans recalled, "When Walter Perren became the Alpine Specialist he called me in and said, 'I know you've got this license but I think for your sake I'm going to give you a four-day test and then you can legitimately say that you have actually passed a guides exam.'"

Early that summer, Walter gave Hans and Bruno an exam.[4] On Day One, the three of them went to Guide's Rock below Mount Cory for a test of rock-climbing and route-finding skills. On Day Two, they drove up the Cascade Fire Road to the Bonnet Glacier, where Perren examined them on ice-climbing technique, glacier travel and step cutting. On Day Three, they climbed Mount Victoria above Lake Louise, and on Day Four, Walter gave the

Hans Gmoser (left) and Philippe Delesalle after their Albert Icefield adventure

two aspirants written and oral tests. Both of them passed the exam, and Hans could now advertise himself as a certified mountain guide.

During the last two weeks in July, Hans guided for The Alpine Club of Canada at their 50th-anniversary camp at Rogers Pass. Here he had an opportunity to experience the old ACC traditions: the evening campfire and singsong, the Sunday-morning church service, followed by the club's annual general meeting, and the separation of the tents into men's, women's and married quarters. He also had a chance to meet many Canadian mountain icons: outfitter Bill Harrison, who, with his team of horses and cowboys, set up and managed the camps each year; ACC old-timers Rex Gibson, Don and Phyllis Munday and Eric and Emmie Brooks; and Swiss mountain guide Ed Feuz Jr. He made connections with Dolores Lachapelle and Sarka Spinkova, who would both share future adventures with him, and with club members Roger Neave, Bruce Fraser and Dave Fisher, with whom he would work on future camps. And, of course, his old friend Jo Kato was there, with whom he had shared his first climbing trip to Roche Miette in May 1952. Hans had come a long way in just five years.

Hans had one other big guiding engagement that summer. From August 15 to 30, he guided at the Iowa Mountaineers' summer camp, leading Mount Assiniboine on three occasions. He shared the guiding duties with Ken Jones, Canada's first Canadian-born mountain guide, whom he had met that first morning in Banff in 1952. He also met Clair Brown and Wally Adams, with whom he would share a great adventure on Mount Robson the following year.

Perhaps his most notable meeting occurred in October, at a Thanksgiving gathering at the Stanley Mitchell hut, when he was introduced to a 22-year-old British climber newly arrived in Canada. Of medium build, with sandy brown hair and a sharp intellect, Brian Greenwood came from a working-class Yorkshire background. Averse to work himself, he would later devote himself entirely to rock climbing. The vanguard of an invasion of British climbers to the Canadian Rockies, he would establish dozens of very difficult climbs over the next two decades and become Hans's great rival in the climbing community.

In early December 1956, Hans drove east to Quebec, where he was certified at Sainte-Marguerite as an assistant ski instructor. Then he crossed the border into the United States at Detroit, Michigan. For the next three months, on Fred Pessl's recommendation, he worked as a ski instructor at the Otsego Ski Club, in Gaylord, Michigan. Fred lived in Detroit, where he worked as a mechanical engineer for General Motors; on the winter weekends, like many others from Detroit, he made the five-hour drive to Otsego, located in the state's lower peninsula. Otsego did not have much of a hill, only about 130 metres vertical. There were several rope tows, a rather elegant clubhouse with a lounge and restaurant and a number of individual resident cabins. It was a private ski club whose members, many of them well-to-do, came from the greater Detroit and Chicago areas. One of the members, Pete Parish, remembered, "Hans not only taught

Hans (right) entertaining at the Otsego Ski Club in Michigan during the winter of 1957

us, he also skied with us and our children when he was not instructing. In fact, he would often take the children on his back and race down the slope, much to their glee." Of course, Hans entertained club members and their families in the evenings, playing his zither or guitar and singing Austrian songs. And he interested some of the more intrepid members in a ski adventure to the Stanley Mitchell hut in the Little Yoho Valley. About eight signed up, despite the fact that they had never ski toured before. They trusted that Hans would take good care of them.

Canada's Leading Mountaineer and Guide

Hans returned to Canada on March 9 and with Leo's help began preparations for the forthcoming ski camp in the Little Yoho. Over a period of two weeks, the pair relayed almost 600 kilograms of food from Field to the hut. The cooks were Renate Hick and Sigrid Wirte,[5] two adventurous young women from Germany. They had met Hans the previous autumn at Lake O'Hara and again in December in Montreal, where he asked them to help at the camp. Although they had no cooking experience and had skied very little, they accepted. They arrived at the hut on March 24 and set to work.

Guests started arriving in Field on March 30 and Hans and Leo led them to the Little Yoho. Hans remembered, "None of them had ever ski toured. I would pick them up off the train at two o'clock in the afternoon in Field, ski to Takakkaw Falls, cook them supper and get them all bedded down in the back of the warden's cabin. Then I would mount Trima skins[6] until about one o'clock in the morning. I had a little hand drill. The next morning we

*Hans negotiating a cluster of brassieres and panties
to light the stove in the women's room at the Stanley Mitchell hut*

skied up to Angel Falls and that's where we put on skins and went up over the first little hill. For most of them that was the first time they ever experienced that."

At the Little Yoho, the day would begin early with Hans lighting the stoves in the hut at about 5 a.m. The women all slept in the side room off the main dining room, and they would often tease Hans by hanging their brassieres and panties near the stove for him to negotiate in the morning. Renate and Sigi made a breakfast of bacon and eggs, pancakes and coffee, then everyone would go off skiing. The two cooks took turns, one going skiing each day. By noon, some of the group were back in the hut, where they would enjoy soup, salami, cheese and bread for lunch. Most days they would go out again after lunch (or would stay out all day), then come home late in the afternoon and lie in the sun drinking tea and eating fresh-baked cakes

Fred Pessl (left) and Hans enjoy a quiet moment in the Stanley Mitchell hut

and cookies. Dinners were simple, with lots of beef and some vegetables. In the evening, Hans played the zither, Leo sang and Sigi joined in, as she had a good voice. By 9 p.m., it was off to bed. Renate remembered that she and Sigi were paid $50/ week, which they split between them. About Hans she said, "He could so easily fly into a rage; little things could upset him. But most of the time he was nice."

They made the regular ski excursions to The President, Mount Kerr

Renate Hick and Fred Pessl
in front of the Stanley Mitchell hut

and Emerald Pass, and Fred again carried his 16mm movie camera and filmed the tours. On leaving, Fred wrote in Hans's *Tourenbuch*: "Another [camp] has passed and with it one of my most treasured 3 weeks. Your friendship and true understanding of the spirit of your mountains is something that will always call me back as long as my old legs will permit me to do it. Let's keep our friendship alive by enjoying these wonderful skiing trips together."

At the end of the camp, Hans wrote in the hut logbook:

We have been here for five weeks now and we enjoyed our stay thoroughly. Many, many trips were made in bad and good weather. We visited most of the peaks around here and the most popular one was undoubtably Mount Kerr. The President thrilled us with an unforgettable view and of course everyone liked the smooth expanse of its glacier. As the climax we can call Mount des Poilus, which we visited on the last day we had. The tremendous view and its steep slopes will be remembered by all of us. The steep slopes of Mount Pollinger were another favourite playground. A beautiful evening on Emerald Pass still lingers in my mind as well as a traverse of Mount McArthur one recent afternoon. Tomorrow we will be on our way to Field. We are sad yet content. We are rich—full of the adventure we have lived in this little valley home.

The camp was deemed a great success, and for the first time Hans may have made a little money for all his hard work.

The ski season was not over yet for Hans, and for three weeks in early May he led another ski camp, from the Wheeler hut in Rogers Pass. Hans led all the standard tours that he was beginning to know so well, and one day he led a spectacular new tour right to the top of Rogers Peak on skis! It was certainly a steep and exciting run back down the mountain.

In early July, Hans and Leo found themselves at a party on the shores of Ghost Lake, in the foothills west of Calgary. The setting was the summer home of the parents of Doreen Tynan, Hans's girlfriend at the time. Leo arrived with his girlfriend, a young Québécoise. Also, there was Doreen's new roommate, a 25-year-old Austrian girl by the name of Elfriede Steiner. Adventurous and smart, Elfi,[7] as she was called, fascinated Hans, and he spent much of the evening in conversation with her. Hans, Leo and Elfi sang Austrian folk songs and reminisced about their homeland. At the end of the evening, Leo drove his date home first, then returned to drive Elfi home—something that has always perplexed Elfi. In less than a year, on May 3, 1958, the pair would be married. Leo was, however, not the first to tie the knot: Franz had married a Calgary girl, Garnet Mellon, in July of 1957.

Hans was still single, with no thoughts of marriage, and itching to climb. In later years, he would consider the summer of 1957 his best season as a climber and guide. On June 4, with two naval officers—Lieutenant Fred Crickard, RCN,[8] and Lieutenant Commander Bob Higgens, RN—Hans led the first ascent of Ribbon Peak via the south face. Two days later, from a camp in Galatea Creek, they made the first ascent of a peak they called The Tower, later known as The Fortress. Cloud obscured the summit, but they set out anyway. The crux was low down, climbing a 30-metre vertical slab to a col on the northwest side of the mountain. Fred Crickard wrote:

> With a "here-goes-nothing" attitude Hans led the way. The first 40 feet were steep and the holds small but good for a change. Hans soon reached a point halfway up where he deliberated for a while. Finally he decided, and drove in a piton. This was the first hardware used in a week of climbing and it immediately told Bob and myself sitting on our airy platform that there was fun ahead. Hans is not a man to use pitons unless absolutely necessary. In this case it certainly was. The pitch from the midway point was a smooth 80-degree convex slab providing nothing but the smallest protuberances for holds. The only thing to be said for it was that

the rock was sound. Hans led magnificently. It was a joy to see him moving slowly and methodically over this steep and exposed Grade 5+ slab.

Visibility improved and the trio reached the summit without further difficulty.

In late July, while guiding for The Alpine Club of Canada at their camp in the Tonquin Valley, near Jasper, Hans met Austrian Frank Stark. Three years older than Hans and from the South Tyrol, Stark had also been certified a mountain guide by Walter Perren. Hans asked Frank to join him on what would be his boldest guiding objective yet, an ascent of Mount Robson, the highest and most difficult peak in the Canadian Rockies. At 3954 metres, Robson towers more than three kilometres above the Yellowhead Highway and is often enveloped in cloud. In 1957, the mountain had not been climbed for years and the peak had not been guided since 1939. It was an enticing but daunting undertaking. Hans had met all his clients before and knew them well. Sarka Spinkova was a gymnastics teacher from Toronto, Wally Adams and Clair Brown were members of the Iowa Mountaineers and Neil Brown was a bacteriologist from Calgary and a very committed mountaineer.

The weather that summer had been poor in the area, so it was a pessimistic group that peered through binoculars up at Mount Robson. The peak was deep in snow, and one could easily detect the long snow feathers that had built up on the ridges into giant mushrooms. Late in the morning of August 6, the group set off up the trail for Kinney Lake. Stark was still taking down the ACC camp and would join them later that evening.

That night, they camped in the rain at Kinney Lake. Stark arrived in the dark and, unable to locate the camp, was forced to spend an uncomfortable night huddled under a tree. At midmorning, the reunited team started

Setting off to climb Mount Robson. Left to right: Neil Brown, Sarka Spinkova, Clair Brown, Hans Gmoser and Wally Adams.

bushwhacking up to the south face of Robson. The angle was steep and the going difficult, so at 6:30 p.m., still two hours from where they planned to place their high camp, they set up their tents in a small depression. The next morning, in pouring rain, they negotiated a steep rock pitch and reached high camp in a notch below Little Robson.

On August 9, Hans looked out of the tent at 3 a.m., but the weather was so uninspiring he decided to wait another day for improvement. Later in the morning, however, the skies cleared, and the group climbed to the summit of Little Robson, where they had spectacular views of their objective.

The following day, the group rose early and by 4:20 a.m. were on their way. One after the other they passed below threatening ice walls out onto the glacier, following the Hourglass Route. The snow was firm and the trail breaking, shared by Hans and Frank, was easy. Although clouds lay deep in the valleys, the peaks were bathed in golden sunshine. Spirits and expectations were high. As the day progressed, the clouds rose, enveloping the climbers in a mist so thick they could barely see each other, but they pushed on in silence, gradually gaining altitude. At last, the terrain flattened and the clouds were swept away by the wind to reveal the final ridge: a truly Himalayan sight.

Hans advanced across the windswept plateau, then up the ridge. In the *Canadian Alpine Journal*, Sarka Spinkova described the final climb:

> Suddenly Hans left the ridge and advanced to his left onto the face. Huge featherlike snowy curtains obstructed the going on the ridge. If you touched these beautiful creations of nature, powdery snow showered on your head and swirled in front of your face. The going was now slow and difficult, and Hans proceeded alone. A milky mist was steadily descending and visibility became very poor. I proceeded after him slowly, following the rope which was my only guide. Going was very precarious as the snow was so powdery that one had no feeling of stability. Finally, I spotted Hans perched on a narrow ledge around the corner, with white masses hanging over his head. His smile was encouraging even though slightly worried. I made a stand for myself by tramping the snow into a more solid base and signaled the next man.
>
> Meanwhile Hans started on his way again; as far as I could see, his movements were rather those of a swimmer trying desperately to make his way through a waterfall. Snow swirled around him and slowly he disappeared into the mist. I had to concentrate on the approach of the third man who, because of his weight, had more difficulties than I

in the soft snow. As soon as he reached me, I started on. Now I understood those swimming motions of Hans; it was a sort of snowy chimney we had to go through. Everywhere you put a hand or foot, hoping for a firm hold, the snow powdered away and one had to use knees and elbows and snake one's way upward. This tricky spot was the huge mushroom we had seen from the valley and dreaded.

Once we were through this, the going did not present any more difficulties. We still climbed one after another, belaying each other, for the slope above the mushroom was very steep and the snow very unsettled and light. Soon I heard Hans' joyous shout: "Sarka, come fast, there is nothing above me!"

I found Hans crouching on a little platform still surrounded by the heavy mist, with apparently nothing above him but the sky. In a short while Clair joined us, and at this moment a sudden gust of strong wind lifted the heavy curtain of mist and there, in the distance, the real summit of Robson gazed down upon us. As though hypnotized, we started on, Hans first, I following him and Clair remaining behind, unroped, to shoot the movie. Within 20 minutes, at about 12:30, we stood on the top of this giant of the Rockies and gazed out amazed at the marvelous view it offered us. Mercifully, all the clouds drifted away. There, 10,000 feet straight below us, the greenish mirror of Kinney Lake shone—this was a sight truly unforgettable.

The clear weather did not last long, and it was soon apparent that a storm was approaching. Rushing down from the summit, they met Frank, Neil and Wally on their way up. At the snow mushroom, Hans prepared a rappel anchor, driving three axes deep into the snow. After Clair

Hans and Sarka Spinkova on the summit of Mount Robson

and Sarka were safely down, he descended, bringing the axes with him. Below the col, "the leaden skies began to pour on us tons of hail which bounced off our heads and shoulders and with a sizzling sound rushed down the steep slopes of the ice-falls, forming numerous streams. The streams were so deep that they almost reached our knees and so powerful that it took all the strength we could muster in order not to be swept away. Thunder roared around us, doubled by its echo; blueish and greenish lightning gave us the eerie look of ghosts dancing madly under the open sky. Nevertheless, slowly, and taking all possible precautions, we proceeded step by step."

By 5 p.m., in bright sunshine, they were back at their tents. "Looking up at the beautiful mountain, everything seemed like a dream."

In late August, Hans served again as a guide at the Iowa Mountaineers' camp. Located at the south end of Maligne Lake in Jasper National Park, it was an opportunity for Hans to get to know another rarely visited area of the Canadian Rockies. Here he met fellow Austrian Willy Pfisterer, who was also guiding at the camp and would later join Hans on one of his great expeditions.

On September 14, Hans returned to Yamnuska for a fourth attempt on the direct line to the summit. Leo was with him, as was a young German immigrant by the name of Heinz Kahl, who had come to Canada just the year before and would soon be a mountain guide, certified by Walter Perren. Happy and carefree and passionate about climbing, Heinz would play an important role in Hans's adventurous life.

The trio parked their car not far from the highway and wandered through aspen poplar forest turning gold with the autumn frosts. In the open places, daisies and Indian paintbrush, the last of the summer flowers, bravely waited for winter. The trail then turned steeply upward and they climbed pungent slopes of creeping juniper and kinnikinnick, reaching the base of the cliff after about 90 minutes. Dropping their packs, they looked upward, examining the face. It was a sunny day and the rock looked inviting. Could they find a way this time? They talked little, quickly sorting the gear, then tied into the rope.

In the *Canadian Alpine Journal,* Hans would later tell the story of his relationship with Yamnuska:

> We came again and again, and each time this mountain became dearer to us and each time our ties grew more intimate. So far we had picked the

Heinz Kahl

easiest routes. But every time when we came our eyes would wander across the smooth rock, trying to find another route, an ideal route—direttissima—a route following the line which a water drop would take falling from the summit. Was it possible? Here the rock was smooth and near the top a big roof hung far out over the face. We made a few meager attempts. Franz would be out of sight and every now and then the rope would move a little. Then we would hear him drive a piton. Silence—another few feet—another piton. An hour would pass then another one and then he would announce his retreat. He would be very exhausted and discouraged. My turn; the same performance.

What were we trying to do? Were we trying to show off? Were we trying to kill ourselves?—No! We wanted to inhale and breathe life again. We were rebelling against an existence which human kind has forced upon itself. We were rebelling against an existence full of distorted values, against an existence where a man is judged by the size of his living room, by the amount of chromium on his car. But here we were ourselves again; simple and pure. Friends in the mountains. Removed from the noise of our cities, removed from the meaningless and unimportant complications of our everyday life, we were close to the land we live on and what's more, we were close to each other. We could appreciate the friendly sunlight, we could appreciate a little ledge to sit on, we could appreciate the encouraging handshake of a friend and we were ready to trust each other, help each other and give to each other our everything.

This mountain to us is not a sports arena. To us it is a symbol of truth and a symbol of life as it should be. This mountain teaches us that we should endure hardships and that we should encounter the difficulties and not drift along the easy way, which always leads down.

On the previous attempts, Hans, Leo, Franz and Kurt had managed to climb about 270 metres to the base of a large yellow overhang. Now they were going to try to find a way around it. After tying in at the bottom of the climb, Leo led off, climbing up and left to a small pedestal. Continuing up the overhanging crack, he traversed out right to a good ledge. Here Heinz went ahead, weaving his way up corners and chimneys and through small overhangs. Early in the morning, the grey limestone rock was still cold to the touch, and as the void below them grew larger and larger, it took willpower not to find an excuse to go down. Hans took over and traversed right, climbing a difficult slab to a good ledge. Stepping boldly around a corner to the right, he led up to the big yellow roof, their previous high point. This time, Hans cracked it, climbing up and left over a steep wall to the base of a long chimney. Heinz took over and led up the chimney, surmounting small overhangs to a deep recess at the base of the final overhang. Then, legs spread wide apart against opposing walls, he bridged his way up. Beneath him was a 400-metre drop straight to the scree. Reaching over the overhang, he found a solid hold and pulled himself up. A few more metres of easy climbing and he was on top. Rapidly, the others followed.

Heinz Kahl (left) and Hans Gmoser below the big overhang on the first successful ascent of Direttissima, September 14, 1957

Hans wrote: "Our joy was indescribable. Heinz lifted me right off my feet when I came to the top and threw me over his shoulder in an outburst of joy. We were really lost for words and simply laughed and shook our heads. It had been so difficult and at times so frightening that now the feeling of relief and joy was simply overwhelming. Silhouetted against the evening sky stood Leo, coiling up the

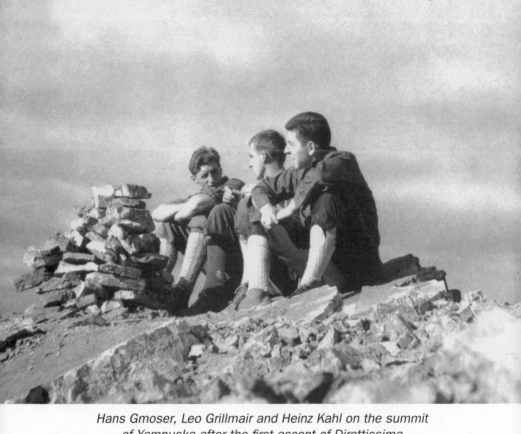

*Hans Gmoser, Leo Grillmair and Heinz Kahl on the summit
of Yamnuska after the first ascent of Direttissima*

rope which had tied us on many a fine climb. Then he threw
it over his shoulder and slowly we walked away."

They named the new route Direttissima because it
climbs the highest part of the wall, directly to the summit.
Sixth-grade climbing, as originated by the great European
masters of the 1920s and 1930s, had come to Canada.

PART THREE

The Great Communicator

1957–1965

"A man should have wings to carry him where his dreams go but sometimes a pair of skis makes a good substitute."
—Hans Gmoser, *Canadian Alpine Journal* 44 (1961): 1

With Skis and Rope

In the autumn and winter of 1957, Hans began a new phase in his life—that of filmmaker and expedition leader. His first film, titled *With Skis and Rope*, was a marvellous, poetic evocation of the mountains. At every venue, Hans gave a personal narration in his lilting Austrian accent that was both lyrical and humorous, his style capturing the hearts of audiences across North America. He began his first film with the words:

> The pictures I am showing here tonight are taken in surroundings and describe activities known to only a few people. Skiing is of course a very popular sport today. However, one finds the majority of skiers in places where the crowds gather. They stand in long lift lines, come down the many marked trails and slopes, which are very often hard and packed with moguls, and then, of course, one indulges in a great variety of social activities. As you will see in this film, the kind of skiing I portray is quite different. First of all we have no lift lines. There are simply no lifts to line up to. We have no moguls on the slopes. The terrain we ski on is so immense

and varied, and by the time we get around to ski a slope for the second time, new snow has covered our tracks again. And to come back to the social life, it is of a very quiet nature. After a day of such skiing, you are perfectly content to sit around the fireplace after supper, have a little drink, sing a little, crack a few jokes and then get a good night's rest, because you certainly need that.

Part One of the film was largely Fred Pessl's footage shot at Mount Assiniboine in 1954, at Rogers Pass in 1955 and at Little Yoho in 1956 and 1957. The film opens with a figure slowly ascending a slope on skis. Then the spectacular scenery of the Little Yoho unfolds and soon the audience is swooping with Hans down the Emerald Glacier. For a few minutes there is footage from several locations all mixed up—Assiniboine, Skoki and the Little Yoho—but few would notice, captivated by Hans's magical narration. There is sunshine and storm, and shots of camp life: chopping wood and carrying buckets of water up to the cabin. There are close-ups of Renate, Sigrid, Fred, and Pete and Sue Parish, all wearing corduroy knickers and snowflake-patterned socks. Then Hans leads the group to the summit of The President. After ascending the glacier, they traverse in a howling wind out to President Pass. On foot and tied together with a rope, they climb carefully through deep snow and over rocks to the summit. The panorama from the top is spectacular, particularly the view south to the Goodsir peaks towering on the horizon. After climbing carefully back down to the col, the group straps on skis and, with Hans in the lead, glides and turns down the glacier to the valley. The ski part of the film ends with an ascent of Rogers Peak at Rogers Pass. Starting out at dawn from the Hermit hut, they cross the glacier, then, putting their skis on their shoulders, kick steps to the summit.

After taking off skins and tightening boots, the group then sets off down the 40-degree corn-snow slope.

After an intermission Hans was back with the climbing part of his film. First, he presents a sequence of his adventures the previous summer with the sailors Fred Crickard and Bob Higgens—likely his first effort at filming. Some footage of climbing

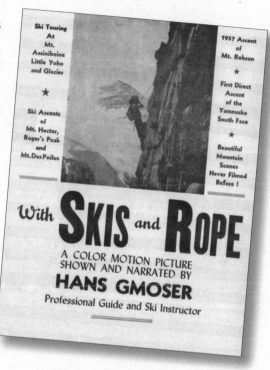

The poster for Hans's first film

Mount Assiniboine follows, but the highlight is the ascent of Mount Robson shot by Clair Brown, the farmer from Solon, Iowa. Considering the rigorous nature of the climb, the film is amazingly good and shake-free. The shot of Hans and Sarka Spinkova reaching the summit in mist and wind is the highlight. Their summit kiss and Hans's friendly pat on her back are charming.

The film ends with a short sequence shot by Hans on the first ascent of Direttissima. There are good scenes of Heinz Kahl and Leo hiking up to the base of Yamnuska, then of Heinz leading out on difficult rock. Hans must have given the camera to one of the others, as there are some images of him leading the leftward traverse out under the overhang that cracked the climb. The film ends with a magical shot of Leo coiling the rope on the summit by the light of the setting sun.

It was a completely new type of entertainment, never witnessed before in North America. Karl Ricker, soon to be an expedition companion of Hans, commented, "The show was the antithesis of the John Jay and Warren Miller ski movies that came to Vancouver every year." It was simple yet professionally made and presented, and showed that Hans had lost none of the romantic love of nature that he had acquired in Europe.

His Catholic faith hadn't fared so well in the Atlantic crossing, however, and after arriving in Canada he rarely made reference to God. According to Leo, Hans went to church once in Edmonton, then never returned. Another friend remembers Hans saying that he was offended when they passed the collection plate around.

Mount Blackburn (5037 m)

In March and April, Hans once again led a ski camp in the Little Yoho, with the assistance of Adolf Bitterlich, from Port Alberni, BC. Adolf had come to Canada in 1954 from Germany, where he had already done a lot of hard climbing, and he was full of drive and ambition. It was likely through his recommendation that Hans became involved in the 1958 Mount Blackburn expedition. This undertaking was conceived and organized by Leon Blumer, an Australian-born climber living on the West Coast who had attempted the mountain in 1955. Rounding out the team were Adolf and two experienced Alaskan climbers: Bruce Gilbert from Yakima, Washington; and Dick Wahlstrom of Seattle. This would be the only undertaking in Hans's life where he was not the leader.

On May 17, the five climbers assembled in the ghost town of Chitina, Alaska. Blumer wrote in the *American Alpine Journal*: "That we all met on the appointed date was a masterpiece of personal organization, considering that two of the five drove up the Alaska Highway and another hitchhiked the same route carrying all climbing gear and a pair of skis."

It was Hans who had hitchhiked to Alaska, and at the US border he had run into difficulty. To enter the country, he needed $200 cash, but he didn't have this much money, so he wired his bank in Banff and they sent the money along. With the $200 in his pocket, he was free to pass back and forth cross the border as he pleased. When Bitterlich and Gilbert arrived, Hans was ready and waiting for them on the Canadian side. Adolf also had little money, so Hans slipped him the $200, enabling him to enter the United States. By this time the border guards knew Hans and let him cross without showing his cash.

On May 18, the clouds cleared and Hans saw the Wrangell Mountains of Alaska for the first time. He wrote in his expedition journal: "Later on it cleared and we were able to get a few glimpses of the big mountains. What giants! It is hard to believe that anything so big can exist. After all the mountains I have seen, this was such an overwhelming sight. I feel now so little and am both excited and afraid. What will it be like? Are we fit for this?"

The next day, a light rain fell and Hans lazed in his tent. Impatient to get going, he wrote: "There is a sad loneliness in this inactivity which isn't a deserved rest at all. The goals you strive for seem so inaccessible, time seems to stand still and you seem to get nowhere. It is depressing. But there is nothing you can do about it. Relax and wait until conditions are right. The sun came out. There was the smell of spring. Flowers on the meadows, new leaves on the trees—a beautiful little valley beneath gigantic mountains."

The bush pilot they had initially engaged to fly them to the glacier below the mountain had not been able to fit skis to his plane, so they had found a replacement in the legendary Don Sheldon, who flew 320 kilometres from Talkeetna to help them out. At 37 years of age, Sheldon, who had flown over Europe in B17 bombers during the war, had already acquired a considerable reputation in Alaska as a pioneer of mountain flying and glacier landings. Sheldon arrived on the evening of the 19th and the next morning began ferrying one person at a time to 2135 metres on a side glacier northeast of Blackburn. Blumer went first, then Gmoser. "What country—it was far beyond anything I had ever seen. Tremendous glaciers came way down below timberline and pushed enormous moraines ahead of them. We flew along jagged ridges, crossed over cols, cruised underneath threatening icefalls and at last arrived over the big neve [icefield] which covers a great part of the Wrangell Range. Here we turned sharply south and soon came in for a landing. It was somehow strange to see one lonely tent on this vast expanse of snow and beside it one man."

Sheldon made another trip and deposited Bitterlich just as the weather was changing. On the fourth flight, the clouds were heavy and it had begun to snow. The trio heard Sheldon circling, looking for a hole, but finally he left.

Over the next two days, Hans, Adolf and Leon pushed supplies higher up the glacier, depositing a cache at 3050 metres. Hans wrote: "We really worked hard and changed leads constantly. As we came higher we encountered a strong downdraft and it made the going even harder. At times it was a fight for every step and we moved very, very slowly. The wind grew stronger all the time and the drifting snow covered our tracks immediately." Meanwhile, Sheldon arrived at base camp with Gilbert late in the afternoon on the 22nd, then he made a short trip to pick up Dick Wahlstrom, who had been deposited two days earlier, eight kilometres lower down the glacier.

Wahlstrom had been left with no tent or stove and for two days had been frantically trying to find the others.

From base camp they could see their route, and it looked like quite a challenge. At 4250 metres, their glacier joined the east ridge, which then dropped 300 metres to a kilometre-long, knife-edge crest. Further along, two steep bumps would have to be crossed to reach the summit of the lower east peak, after which a long plateau led to the true summit.

On May 23, while Dick and Bruce rested, the others established a high camp at 3350 metres. By the time they had pitched their tents, a full-scale blizzard was in progress. Blumer wrote: "We had dug a large platform, but the driving snow gradually piled up on the side of the tent and sifted in through every small opening. Then my tent cord broke; so I had to crawl outside and try to re-erect the tent in the fury of the storm. My fingers froze within minutes, which compelled me to leave everything and squeeze in

Leon Blumer at camp below Mount Blackburn

with Adolf and Hans, bringing snow into their tent in the process. It was a hellish night, cold and damp, with no chance to cook a good meal. Every three hours we had to crawl outside and dig away the drifts."

The next morning, it cleared. Hans wrote: "I don't think I have ever enjoyed the sun so much! At 6 am it was already warm and there was hardly a breeze except for the high ridges. It is impossible to capture the greatness of this country in words." They dug out their camp and dried their sleeping bags in the sun, then Adolf and Hans dug a giant snow cave. In the afternoon, it stormed again, but Adolf and Hans descended to 2750 metres to collect more supplies. As the storm intensified, they climbed back up to the high camp. "The storm was now pretty bad and was

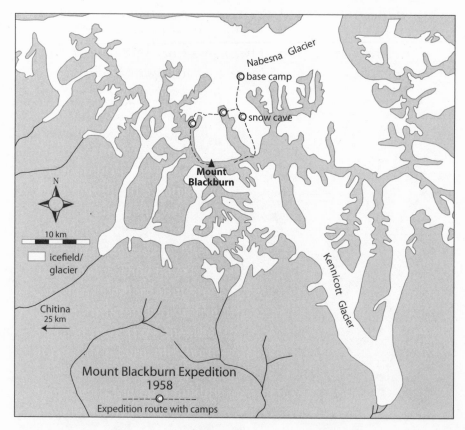

Adolf Bitterlich at camp below Mount Blackburn

increasing all the time. Soon the wind almost knocked us over and our progress became slower and slower. At times we couldn't even see each other. We were getting cold and slightly worried." At last, they reached the snow cave. "The hole was completely drifted over and I feared that Leon had already suffocated. We dug frantically and found him happily cooking our supper."

It stormed all night, and in the morning they had a terrible time pushing their way out the entrance. Leon wrote: "We had put skis and poles across it, which acted as prison bars. It gave us a horrible trapped feeling." In the afternoon, Gilbert and Wahlstrom arrived, and for three days, while the wind blew and the snow fell, all five of them remained in the snow cave, passing the long hours as best they could.

By noon, on May 27, it had cleared, and Gilbert dropped down to get more food from the cache while the others reconnoitred the ridge above. Skiing to 4250 metres, they

On the summit ridge of Mount Blackburn

looked along the crest. Blumer wrote: "It was obvious that with doubtful weather and heavy packs the knife edge section, exciting enough under milder conditions, would be a difficult proposition indeed. We would have to rappel onto it, fix ropes, and also place another camp or snow cave before the long climb to the main summit over the slightly lower east peak." In Hans's opinion, "the ridge ahead was out of the question. So we returned to camp. We had good skiing down. It was a beautiful evening, but I was a little disappointed, because our Alaska mountaineers were nowhere as good as I thought they should be." The east ridge of Mount Blackburn they named "Blumer's Folly."

On the 28th, they descended with huge packs and camped in a little col at about 2300 metres. From here, Hans and Adolf could see the north face and wanted to attack the north spur directly to the summit. Gmoser wrote: "There is an easy and direct route to the summit from here but those guys know so little about mountains that they are afraid to try it." Blumer's authority as leader prevailed and the team directed their efforts to the northwest ridge, even though he had failed on this route in 1955, stopped by "an enormous ice tower fronted by a crevasse." Blumer wrote: "Morale had dropped a bit at this point, and we were becoming a little impatient." However, the weather had cleared and would remain good through the rest of the expedition.

Camp in a snow cave was established on the northwest ridge, and the next morning, Friday, May 30, they set out at 3 a.m. for the top. Hans described the ascent in his journal:

> Why does one get out of a warm sleeping bag at one in the morning and start cooking breakfast in a snow cave? I can't explain it. I am sure that I have no idea why I do it. I only know that there is a desire or will within me which pushes me along. Actually not only along, but up—and up. Always seeking the difficult and at the same time I am looking forward to a well deserved rest, once the difficulty is overcome. There was this giant mountain rising 5000 feet above us and we wanted to reach its summit. If one has never seen such a big thing one cannot imagine its dimensions. For us it is even difficult to get the proper scale. There is an ice tower. It looms small but when you are underneath it, it becomes a monster. To me this was a new world full of new wonders. Yet I feel at home and relaxed. More so than my friends. It was a mountain and my life is in the mountains. There was the first ice tower and I took great joy in climbing it. This was the beginning and it was a good one. It was just like shaking hands with an opponent before a set of tennis. Our grip was firm, warm and friendly. It was to be a fair game. He

was the big mountain, we five little human beings. He was to give us unforgettable moments while climbing and traversing the steep slopes and the joy of a towering summit. A higher summit than any of us had ever reached. We were to fight hard, defeat our weaknesses and fears and bring forth in us a determined, strong and pure man. What a great way of life, what a great land to live in. All those moments and sights. Above us silhouetted against the morning sun, Leon and Bruce climbing on the steep ridge—ahead a steep buttress of ice—a fine climb around it—a long traverse underneath the seracs—and a long, long slope to the crest of the ridge. We all moved silent and steady, ever scanning the mountain and the sky. The weather was getting better all the time and soon we knew it would be up to us to make it. Adolf in the lead we went up on the long ridge. With every step we got higher and our horizon grew bigger. Mountains, mountains, mountains—clouds and sky. Below the rugged peaks and glaciers stretching into the green valleys. Soon we were higher than anything around us. The broad ridge stretching to the summit like a giant dome. Our steps grew shorter and we began to breathe harder. High up we stopped— Adolf in the lead—and we had a leak. "This is an honorable moment," Adolf said. "The highest piss we ever had." If this shocks you, then you are a phony! This is one side of our life and our life is so strong in its elementary lines that we can accept it and appreciate all aspects of it. We walked for a long time, slow and breathing hard—and then we could see down all around us. We shook hands. There was Dick, dead tired but so happy. It was his third mountain. And Adolf, the mountaineer, the conqueror. He cried. What a fine true man! We were soon all together. What should I say about the summit? How could I ever describe it? Could you tell me how it is in heaven? It is too much for us, we can't really conceive the whole of it. Surely I can tell you that we saw tremendous cloud banks, mountains in all directions and even part of the sea to the west. But how they impressed us, how we saw them, I cannot put into words. We climbed down through the clouds, our faces burning, our throats dry and our heads aching. The wind was blowing hard and we were glad to have the shelter of our cave and to sleep.[1]

Back at base camp, they waited five days until Sheldon returned to fly them to Chitina. It was a boring time, and at one point Hans just lay in his sleeping bag for 27 hours straight, at times philosophizing in his journal: "You think about many episodes in your life but you cannot decide whether or not you did the right thing. Your own life seems like such a shambles at times. All the foolish things you did, all the good chances you turned away, all the fine girls you left behind."

On June 5, they finally flew out, one by one: "We landed right next to the river, I piled out and was left in a cloud of dust as the plane took off again. As the dust settled I found myself in a beautiful, green valley. A cool breeze came down from the mountains; the air was rich with the smell of grass and fresh leaves. What a fine evening, what a pleasant change after three weeks among the snows of Mount Blackburn. I took my pack and walked up to the village. The adventure was over."

Back in the Rockies that summer, Hans returned to guiding clients on mountains he was becoming very familiar with: Mount Edith, Eisenhower Tower on Castle Mountain and Mount Assiniboine. Then he made his way to the Alpine Club of Canada's summer camp, held that year at the head of the Blaeberry River, below the Mummery Group of mountains. From July 21 to August 1, Hans led climbs, including two traverses of Mount Mummery. At the annual general meeting, Adolf Bitterlich, who was also serving as a guide, "set off an explosion." Hans later wrote an article called "The Young Ones and the Old Ones," in which he put forward his own point of view:

> One could sense a rise of feelings against him [Bitterlich] as he spoke and one could sense that many people took the things he said personally and were really hurt. What hurt them was not so much what he said, but the manner in which he said it. At the time he asked the club to help in opening up new areas even if it meant losing money and he also asked that the club should help the YOUNG ONES so that they can make expeditions into some of the more inaccessible regions and of course he meant that the OLD ONES should foot the bill. As far as I know he might have spoken strictly for himself. Yet whether he knew it or not he made himself spokesman for a new element, a new force within the club. He called them THE YOUNG ONES. That in itself created a lot of bad feelings. Unfortunately whenever we make a sharp definition such as Adolf did, we are apt to hurt some people's feelings. This however, is largely due to lack of understanding on their part. It was really disheartening to have heard the flood of narrow minded, opposing comments, for this wasn't just a question of a few eccentric characters asking for money or for that matter for a job. The issue is far more important and to realize what there is to it all, we must first understand what this new force, this new element, the YOUNG ONES really are.

Today we find a large number of what people call "bums" in the mountains. I cover about as much mountain territory in a summer as anyone, and I am astonished at the ever increasing number of people in the mountains. Those people don't stay at the CHATEAU or the JASPER PARK LODGE, some of them don't even have a tent. Well what is the matter with them? Why don't they work and save their money so that they can afford to do all those things in proper style? It has always been said that the friends you make in the mountains are the best friends, and we always feel that the people we meet in the mountains are fine people. How come there are all of a sudden so many "bums"? Or are they "bums"? Let's look at the situation a little more carefully and let's see if we can understand the true reasons behind it. What would a bum be doing in the mountains anyway? Under a bum we mostly understand a person who is too lazy to work and to look out for himself. But does that apply to the people we find in the mountains? I should say not! The fact that they are there alone proves that they are not lazy. Perhaps they are too lazy to work at a conventional job and rather spend their energy in the mountains? Or is there even more to it than that? Yes, I believe there is.

Let's take a youth full of ideals and full of the feeling that the world lies before him, full of the urge to do great things, willing to learn, willing to observe, full of respect for the great people in our time, full of admiration and envy for his elders, and what happens to him? Every time he turns around, every time he looks at something, every time he listens to something his ideals are being shattered. Instead of the wonderful world he has imagined he finds a world full of artificialities, falseness, corruption, and a world in a hopeless shambles of political and social affairs. He finds wherever he goes he is not wanted as the person, as the man he is, but rather as the guy who hauls so many loads of gravel a day, or the guy who sells so many insurance policies a week or for that matter as the executive who saves the company so much money a year. Today those things hit us with so much more impact than they might have 50 or even 30 years ago. Every time we read a paper, listen to a radio or just walk down a city street this material world stares and blares at us. There is no room and no need for such a youth to develop his human potentialities. He is only a piece of machinery, a tool.

Is it any wonder now if these young ones try to escape from such a world. Even if it is just for a little time. Even if it is just long enough to regain faith in themselves and in their ideals again, to regain enough strength to face this world again. And is it any wonder if this escape leads them to the mountains. However inexperienced, however poorly clad, however poorly equipped, they are not "bums". Here we have human beings fighting for the realization of their ideals, whether they are aware of it or not. Wandering through this unspoiled garden, they can see that there are still places on our earth where man can rejoice in watching things take their natural course. Living in this garden brings them close to the land again. They learn to see again, they learn to hear again, they learn to notice all the many living wonders which surround them and which have almost vanished from our cold cities and parts of the land we inhabit. They seek truth, pride, hope, satisfaction and strength in the mountains. Here while enduring the hardships of a difficult climb, they grow close to each other again. Here the true friendship is born, the kind of friendship which knows no limits.

Here where the feeling prevails that one stands for the other, they feel again deep admiration and great respect for their fellow men. Here they experience some of the greatest moments in their lives. Without many words great things are done. And the great things are not to climb a difficult overhang or to surmount an absolutely smooth slab. No! A great thing is done when your friend tells you, "If you want to get up there you better get going." This is friendship so strong! When you both realize that this could be fatal and you both have been sitting there for the longest time not saying a word, and struggling with yourself, and then comes this remark from him. This remark so simple and said so calmly expresses everything you could ever expect from a friend, everything a friend could ever be. It shows this great confidence in you and if it had to be, even his willingness to die with you. But we don't want our friends to die, and here we surpass ourselves. Here we do the impossible. Here is where we find truth. Here is where we find strength. Here is where we find pride, pride in ourselves, pride in our friends, pride in people, yes, pride in humanity. If we, if our friends, if people are still able to do great things then there is still hope, then the world can't be so bad; it must be good, because people are good if inspired to be good. With their ideals strengthened those young people can believe in our modern world again and who knows perhaps shape it according to their ideals. This I think we have to take into consideration to appreciate the young ones.

Yes the ALPINE CLUB OF CANADA as such has a great obligation to all people of Canada, especially to those young ones, and must realize its responsibility. We have to fight to establish ourselves as a national institution for the benefit of all people interested in mountains, be it that they pick flowers, scale the north face of Mt. Temple, ski on the slopes of Mt. Norquay, or traverse the Columbia Icefield on skis. The mountains represent a great source of spiritual strength and wealth. This strength and wealth must be made accessible to as many people as possible. For one thing we must make people realize that this source of strength and wealth is existing and we must make it possible for them to get their share of it. We must give them the means and the opportunities, and we must teach them how to enjoy our mountain heritage. If the ALPINE CLUB OF CANADA fails to recognize this we will very shortly have a number of small clubs (which is partly the case today) all essentially striving for the same goal but yet all competing with each other and thereby accomplishing very little. One strong club can definitely accomplish much more than many small organizations. I realize what the club has done and is doing in that direction, but we are doing it too informally and on too small a scale. Certainly it is nice to belong to a club where you have the feeling that everyone feels the same way you do and where you know almost every member personally, but today it is important for us to cover all people concerned with mountains. The social and informal functions will be taken up by smaller groups within the club. With the present interest in mountaineering we could be 10 or perhaps 20 times as strong as we are now and this would give the club enough financial and even political strength to carry out such a program.

This article was never published, and Hans's fears came to pass. The leadership in the Canadian climbing world passed for several decades to smaller clubs such as the Calgary Mountain Club, while The Alpine Club of Canada gradually lost its energy and initiative. Hans continued his close relationship with the ACC for many years, but Adolf never again had much to do with the club.

In 1958, Hans plucked another feather for his cap when he guided two of his most capable clients, Sarka Spinkova and Neil Brown, up Mount Alberta, north of the Columbia Icefield, in Jasper National Park. Such was the difficulty of the mountain that it had been climbed only twice before: in 1925 by a group of six Japanese led by three Swiss guides, who had come halfway around the world just to climb this mountain; and again in 1948 by two exceptional American mountaineers. A remote monolith of steep, loose rock, Mount Alberta was regarded as one of the most difficult climbs in the Canadian Rockies.

On August 16, Hans, Leo, Heinz, Sarka and Neil stripped off their clothes and in hip-deep, ice-cold water forded the Sunwapta River. After following a large creek for a while, then bushwhacking through heavy forest to avoid a canyon, they struggled up 800 metres of steep scree to reach what is called Woolley Shoulder. The view of Mount Alberta, standing alone and aloof, was impressive, and Sarka was inspired to write: "There, still two large glacier-filled valleys away, stood our mountain—a huge, long, massive wall, strong, dominating, inspiring awe rather than admiration in its beauty." It was luckily a dry season and the rock was completely bare of snow, which would make for easier climbing. Battling strong winds, they continued on, eventually finding a rocky peninsula in the sea of ice. Setting up camp, they examined the mountain and discussed their route in more detail. It began at the lower left-hand corner and worked its way right up broken ledges and gradually steepening black cliffs to a narrow, serrated ridge that would be followed for several hundred metres to the top.

Two days later, they set out in the dark and by daybreak were at the foot of the face. From afar, the wall had looked impregnable, but closer up they could see the possibilities for a route. As they began scrambling up the loose, scree-covered ledges, "some of the party lost their early enthusiasm. Everything had to be tested, and several times after a thorough testing a seemingly firm hand or foot-hold would give way. If one could adjust his mind to this fact, one found the climbing excellent; not easy and yet not difficult, quite exposed and yet not frightening."

Two hours of scrambling brought them to the black band. "The pitches became steeper and thinner and required great care. Our nerves were quite tense and we could only relax momentarily to look at the ever changing scenery." After 500 metres of climbing on friable rock, they reached the summit ridge. Only two or three feet wide in places, with immense drops on either side, it proved a delicate balancing act. After nine hours on the move, they reached the summit "exalted and joyous." Almost 2000 metres below was the golden thread of the Athabasca River, and around them were other great peaks, such as Mount Columbia and The Twins. "Only a sharp eye could distinguish the green and yellow dots of our tents against the greyish background of our small rock-island."

The descent gave them no end of trouble. As they were making 200-foot rappels, the rope often became tangled or stuck and knocked down showers of rocks. Finally, they stopped for the night on a ledge four or five feet wide. "Close to us the sudden fall of loose rock in the stillness of the night, the shining stars above our heads and the distant lightning behind Mount Columbia seemed to add something almost fairylike to our adventure." In the

On the summit of Mount Alberta with the North and South Twins
and Mount Columbia in the background.
In back: Neil Brown, Sarka Spinkova and Hans Gmoser.
Heinz Kahl in front.

morning they reached their tents, exhausted but happy, and after a short rest, broke camp and "bade farewell to this lonely mountain, remote but incredibly beautiful".

There were two other important events in 1958: on August 28, Hans became a Canadian citizen, and that autumn he returned for the first time to Austria. Little is known of that trip except that he met Renate Hick in Germany and asked her to be his cook again in the Little Yoho. The pair flew from Frankfurt to Montreal, where Philippe, who was studying architecture at McGill University, picked them up at the airport. Then they drove to Detroit to see Fred Pessl and continued across to Calgary, where they began preparations for the spring ski camp in the Yoho. For six weeks, from March 10 to April 25, Hans once more welcomed ski guests to the little cabin in the Canadian wilderness. Then he turned his attention to his next expedition.

Mount Logan East Peak (5900 m)

While hitchhiking with Adolf back from Mount Blackburn the previous summer, Hans had admired the peaks of the St. Elias Mountains in Canada's Yukon Territory. These mountains are some of the wildest in the world—wilder perhaps than the Himalaya, where there are trails and villages in many valleys. In the St. Elias, there is no such habitation; it is one of the largest glaciated areas outside the polar regions, with glaciers as wide as 20 kilometres across and over 100 kilometres long. Climbing in these mountains in the late 1950s was a serious undertaking: climbers were on their own, and there was little chance of rescue in the event of problems.

As Hans had sat on the edge of the road, admiring the peaks to the west, he had known that somewhere beyond the horizon was Mount Logan, Canada's highest mountain, massive and covered in snow and ice. A seed was sown, and when he returned to Banff he immediately began planning an expedition to the mountain with himself as leader. By 1959, Mount Logan had only been climbed a few times. The first ascent, in 1925 by a joint Alpine Club of Canada/American Alpine Club expedition, had been a horrendously difficult undertaking involving three separate expeditions: one to explore a feasible route to the mountain, another to place a cache of food and supplies at the base of the mountain and then a third to actually climb the mountain. Lost in a blizzard on the summit plateau after reaching the top, six men had wandered for several days in −30°C temperatures, sleeping only for brief spells in holes scooped in the snow. At last they had found their tents and had made their way back down the mountain with badly frostbitten fingers and toes. The struggle was not over yet, however, and they still had to walk 240 kilometres back to the road. It was a daunting tale and enough to frighten any mountaineer. Understandably, the mountain was not climbed again until 1950.

Hans's objective was the east ridge, climbed only once before by a five-man American expedition in July of 1957. Almost 4000 metres from bottom to top, the route followed a long, knife-edge crest, then climbed steep, windswept slopes to the summit. The Americans had spent 22 days climbing the mountain and had established nine camps.

Hans's team was composed of five men, all Canadians: his friend Philippe (29); Willy Pfisterer (33), with whom he had guided at the Iowa Mountaineers' camp in 1957; Ron "Alpine" Smylie (26), who ran a mountain equipment store in Calgary; and two young men from Vancouver who were both members of the Varsity Outdoor Club, Karl Ricker (23) and Don Lyon (22). Gmoser himself was only 26 years old. Although young and inexperienced in expedition

Hans hitchhiking along the Alaska Highway to Mount Logan in 1959

climbing, they were enthusiastic and full of the spirit of adventure.

All winter long, Hans prepared for the expedition. Money was a real issue, but Hans was lucky enough to enlist the sponsorship of *Weekend Magazine*, which donated $1,500. The team members all dug deep into their own pockets for an additional $1,200, and Head Ski Company donated six pairs of their new metal skis.

On May 18, the team gathered at Ron's Calgary store, where for two feverish days and nights the last food and equipment was checked and packed. Ron and Willy then set off with all the supplies in Willy's overloaded station wagon for the 2400-kilometre drive to Whitehorse. The next day, the remaining four drove in Hans's Nash to Whitecourt; then, as Hans was unwilling to take his overloaded vehicle on the rough gravel of the Alaska Highway, they began hitchhiking north.

Assembled in Whitehorse on May 24, the six men moved into an abandoned house, where Hans wrote in his journal: "Being the leader of such an expedition is quite different from being just a member of the party. Even though our friends are very independent and everyone does his share of the work without having to be urged to do it—I feel that all the responsibility rests on me and in the end I will have to be the driving force in the party."

Hans had originally intended that they would fly to the base of the mountain as they had for Mount Blackburn, but in Whitehorse there was no one with retractable skis and wheels on their aircraft. In fact, there was no pilot who

The Mount Logan team at the abandoned house in Whitehorse. Left to right: Don Lyon (behind), Karl Ricker, Ron Smylie, Philippe Delesalle (behind), Willy Pfisterer, Hans Gmoser.

was familiar with the St. Elias Mountains at all, and Hans had great difficulty finding anyone who would even fly over the mountains and place an airdrop. Eventually, he was able to locate a pilot by the name of Jim, who agreed to help them.

Leaving Hans in Whitehorse to deal with the airdrop, the other five drove to Kluane Lake and set up camp in an abandoned sod-roofed cabin. The plan was that they would all walk the Slims River valley, then follow the Kaskawulsh Glacier to the base of Mount Logan. On May 27, four of them set off, and that same day Hans managed

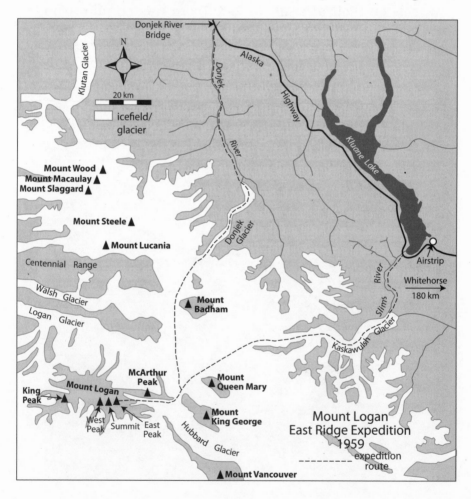

to make the airdrop. From the air, he had an opportunity to see the route that they would be taking: "It is quite frightening. Just like an immense river the glacier winds itself right down into the forests. It is impossible to describe those great mountains ahead of us—they are just so big— much, much bigger than anything I have ever seen. I must confess they are frightening. I wonder if I, if my friends are strong enough to climb such a monster."

At the base of the east ridge, above the Hubbard Glacier, Hans made the first airdrop. The pilot was afraid to fly very low and the gunny sacks containing their food dropped a long way before hitting the snow. Turning north, they flew over the route Hans intended to walk out and Hans dropped three life rafts at the toe of the Donjek Glacier. Returning to Kluane Lake, they loaded up again with more sacks for the base of the east ridge. After dropping these sacks, the pilot let Hans out at the airstrip at Kluane Lake, and with Karl, who had waited for him, Hans set out along the dusty gravel flats of the Slims River. By nightfall, all six men were reunited just short of the Kaskawulsh Glacier.

Carrying 40 kilograms on their backs, they made their way the next morning over a jumble of moraine and ice blocks to the glacier. When they reached the snow line a day later, they put on their skis, which made travel easier. On their feet they wore foam-padded Kodiak duck-hunting boots in which they had filed a heel groove for the cable binding. Moving slowly on the smooth expanse of the glacier was boring: "We counted our strides in an effort to keep our minds occupied." The next day, they set out at noon in fog. The snow texture changed constantly and they were forced to wax their skis a number of times.

On June 1, the fog cleared and they got their first view of Mount Logan, one of the most impressive sights in the world. Almost 40 kilometres from end to end, Mount Logan is the largest mountain mass in the world and one

Reaching the Kaskawulsh Glacier

of the most heavily glaciated. Great glaciers hang from
the walls and ridges of the peak, and the summit plateau,
which is 15 kilometres long and all above 5000 metres, is
itself a vast icefield from which several summits protrude.
As they descended out onto the Hubbard Glacier, the east
ridge came into view, a beautiful, aesthetic line rising
directly to the East Peak.

Clouds loomed on the horizon and it looked as though
a storm was approaching, so Hans and Willy pushed on
quickly to locate the airdrop, still 25 kilometres away. At
about 2 a.m. on June 2, they spotted the first parcels in the
snow; then, after rounding them up, the men collapsed
exhausted into their tent. Late in the afternoon, the rest of
the team arrived and they were all safely reunited at the
base of their route. They had travelled about 135 kilometres
in only six days, so to celebrate they ate a dinner of salami

sausage, soup and condensed milk. The group was in good spirits, and expectations were high.

At 3 a.m. on June 6, they skied to the base of the ridge, then climbed steeply to gain the crest. Karl Ricker recalled, "Gradual dissension and lack of teamwork hit the expedition thereafter ... when Hans rejected the track set by Willy and Philippe on the steep upper slopes. With the feeling that their hard work had gone for naught they were most unhappy." Hans saw things differently and wrote in his journal: "Willy and Phil went ahead with light packs, to fix up a trail for us. There was a 600 foot snow slope, which led up to the ridge. To me the obvious thing to do was to gain the ridge as quick as possible. Willy somehow kept working on the rocks and when I finally asked him what he intended to do he got quite mad and went back to base camp." Hans, Ron, Don and Karl reached the ridge, dumped their loads, then returned to base camp. Hans continued in his journal: "Willy, Phil and I had a good talk after I came back and now that we have settled our differences we are in the best of spirits, full of great hopes and we know we are good friends!"

On June 7, they were up at 2 a.m. and on their way. Leaving their skis behind, they climbed in two hours to their food cache on the ridge, then continued along the crest to 3290 metres, where they established Camp I. While Ron and Phil dug platforms and put up tents, the others dropped down and picked up the food cache. The next day, Karl and Ron went ahead with light packs to break trail, while Hans managed to film spectacular footage of the others climbing along the knife-edge ridge. Leaving their loads at 3990 metres, they returned to Camp I; then, on June 9, they pushed the route higher, establishing Camp II at 4345 metres. Hans wrote: "Today there is quite some fog around us and it was quite eerie as we traversed on a steep snow slope, thousands of feet above the glacier. To break trail at this altitude with a big load is unbelievably hard. I was always looking ahead for some level spot but the slope rose up and up into the fog. Finally I just had it. Willy took over." Then Hans and Willy dropped down to retrieve the loads they had left the previous day at 3990 metres.

Karl had a different view of the events and wrote: "Two days later the teamwork fell apart on the first knife-edge, with Hans storming across it, unroped, saying that we more cautious ones were too slow, and he repeated the performance on the second knife-edge in the afternoon. After dumping the loads and setting up camp, his sense of urgency sent he and Willy back down the knife-edges to retrieve more loads. However, Don and I said no, we needed rest and would do our second load tomorrow. Surprisingly Hans agreed."

On the 10th, while Don and Karl rested late in their sleeping bags, the others pushed on to the summit plateau at 5075 metres, where they dropped their loads and then returned to Camp II. The following day, they all struggled up the steep slopes and established Camp III at 5075 metres. The weather was bitterly cold and a sharp wind stung their faces. Hans wrote in his journal: "Willy and I certainly have to take the most unthankful job on this trip. Both Philippe and Ron don't seem to realize that one has to accept a lot of physical punishment in climbing such a mountain. They always want to stop and thereby slow down our progress. On an expedition such as this each member really must hold up his end of the deal and simply force himself to do better.... Karl and Don on the other hand felt very good today and wanted to go further. It is quite difficult to please everybody and at times I just feel like telling everyone to go to hell and climb this peak with Willy." In Philippe's defense, it must be said that he had spent the previous eight months at university in Montreal and was not as fit as Hans and Willy, who had been skiing and guiding all winter. Hans's lack of sympathy for a man who was one of his best friends seems terribly insensitive.

Suffering from altitude, they all slept poorly on the night of June 11. According to Karl, "The 292's we took at breakfast had little effect and although the day was very clear I didn't seem to be interested in our objective. It seems to have taken four times as long as usual to wrestle our boots and mukluks on." But by 7 a.m. they were on their way to the summit. Hans described the day in his journal:

Those are the great days of our life. We experience greatest triumph and we can feel how little and inadequate we are against such a big mountain. It is silly to think that we can stand against such a giant. I think it is much more that such a mountain lets us be with him. In spite of all our fears and anxieties we feel somehow safe and secure. Once I set foot on him I feel so much part of him. Everything I do seems natural and almost instinctively I know where to put my foot and which way to take. We just must trust in him. People are often scared to walk on a sharp ridge or to traverse on an icy slope, but those places are really safe. Your footing, however small, is very solid. I don't think we should always regard the mountains as challenging, they are just as much of a retreat for us. Here we have truth, strength and soundness of the highest quality and this is something every man yearns for. And with this approach we feel good on the mountain. Of course we must realize that there are many dangers along the way and those we have to look for. But there is nothing sneaky about the mountain and we must keep alert to recognize the signs soon enough. These were my thoughts as I slowly broke trail from Camp III towards the summit of Mount Logan. We couldn't have asked for a better day. The sky above us was perfectly clear, only far to the north there were some cumulus clouds in the low valleys and there wasn't a breath of wind. I was very happy and felt like I did as a little child on Christmas Eve before we got our presents. 3000 feet above us rose the East Peak, a beautiful snow pyramid. We walked very slowly but the progress was noticeable. At first we headed towards the north ridge and then we made a long traverse across the East Face towards the East Ridge. Up to that point we were all pretty close together, but shortly before we got onto the ridge I became very exhausted and Don was even more so. We had a long rest, the altimeter showing 18,500 feet [5640 m]. But this was the turning point. Some of my friends just folded up, vomit—stagger on and fall down again. It was a real struggle for the summit now. We all had terrible headaches and only Karl and I had any push left. Karl was breaking trail now and Don on his rope fought to his utmost to reach the summit. It was a proud and happy moment.[2] At a time like this a man is opening a book. There are the ones to whom it is just a record—something accomplished. There are those who are too tired and who are afraid of the remoteness and then there are the men I admire, the men who cry and go out onto the point of the ridge and sit there moved to tears by the greatness of this moment. This is the time and the place where you see the man as he is. In spite of all our many layers of clothing we are naked to each other. We see into the inner depth of each other. "A flicker of light in our walk through darkness."

The walk down—our heads throbbing like mad. Our legs heavy as lead. Down, down—staggering always further down. Far below, lost in the immense expanse of ice, two little specks—our camp. How

The only surviving photo of the team on the East Peak of Mount Logan

far—how many miles—how many thousand feet? Go, keep going—don't think! Step after step—just keep moving. Forget your aching head—don't think about those dead legs—Ah hell I am too tired. Lie down in the snow, sleep, breathe deeply! Ah how good it feels—Oh what a relief. We must go—go on—go down to those little specks far away. Put one leg ahead of the other, you must go—go, you cannot stop, not here. How far? A mile? Half a mile? Maybe less? Another half hour. Don't think—just walk, walk—Ah, those are the tracks I made this morning when I took a picture of camp. Step. Step. Step. Only 30 feet. Soon you are there—Drop in the snow—Close your eyes—Breathe—Breathe long and deep. An ordeal!

The next morning, they began their descent to base camp. Ricker wrote:

> The descent of the east ridge was not quite an epic. Reaching the top of the knife-edge on the following day, everyone agreed that the snow was too soft for a descent in the afternoon sun (and no wind). But Hans was on a mission to go down the entire ridge that night. The knife-edges were still dicey when we set off (too early), and all were very tired after moving through the lower one. But onwards the leader pushed, reaching the point to get off the ridge in twilight. In semi darkness our ascent route was found to be "schrunded"—a rappel was set up to move over it—no complaints there, but several

Descending the east ridge of Mount Logan

thereafter of having to ski from the base of the ridge back to base camp—dead tired, with heavy packs, and little ability to control the descent on crusting snow![3] One by one the members sketched into camp, luckily without injury. The teamwork had at best been shaky through the descent.

The team rested at base camp for two days, lying in the sun and eating a meal every three hours. Hans wrote in his journal: "At this point I must confess that often I feel quite foolish and think that with all my fears I have no business being here. Often it is a constant inner battle to keep strong and to keep moving ahead. In such a dead world man is simply nothing and once you realize this it takes a lot of spiritual strength to retain optimismus and confidence."

At 10:30 on the night of June 15, they left base camp and began the journey back to civilization. Ron's skis were used to make a sled that the other five pulled while Ron steered and walked. The sled didn't work very well, and soon there was disagreement. Ricker wrote:

> Reaching the Hubbard Glacier Willy rebelled, saying it was time to dismantle the sled, eject the gear not vital to our way out, and why can't the team go out the way they came in? (A question he asked about 12–16 hours earlier.) Surprisingly Hans agreed, the sled was not working as planned, but he held firm on going out via the Donjek. The exit became an individualist mantra, each designed their own personal sled to haul the vital gear and supplies, and each walked their own pace to the head of the Hubbard-Donjek divide. Several kilometres separated the first and the last in the long procession. Individualism reigned on the descent of the Donjek Glacier with lack of concern

or help at the many crevasse crossings, although Hans did lead the way off the budding chaos of ice to the left lateral moraine.

Reaching the outwash apron at the snout of the glacier after a full day of slogging, the anxiety in Hans' rush became apparent. The air-dropped rafts were on the other side of the Donjek River and he cursed himself soundly for making such a mistake. The pressure was on, would the river be crossable in the early hours of the following A.M. Willy was asked to join him in the attempt. Bravely they set off with air mattresses to act as life savers should the swift, deep and cold current knock them off their feet. It was a nail biter watching them attempt each of the many channels at several spots on each, but slowly they succeeded after several close calls, and then they were gone for the rest of the day, searching for the rafts. Finally at dinner hour they reappeared, each in a raft, bobbing like corks on the swells and troughs in the rapidly moving current.

Unfortunately, one of the rafts had landed in a tree and had been impaled by branches. With 96 holes, it was unrepairable. They now had only two rafts—not enough for six men and all the gear. Philippe and Ron volunteered to walk, and they set out that evening while the others built two equipment rafts from air mattresses. In the morning, they launched themselves on the river. Ricker wrote in the *CAJ*:

> By picking the deepest channels we usually stayed out of trouble, but sometimes the projected route was missed. There was cause for alarm when we bounced along a bluff and more alarm when the rafts were filled with water in a whirlpool. After 15 miles of travel in just one hour the foot traveller's

Loading the rafts used to descend the Donjek River

camp was sighted on our left, four to five channels away. By putting more air mattresses under the equipment rafts, we managed to add the remaining two prospective passengers to our cargo.

Once again the rafts raced at a terrific clip with the current; as they were at the stream's mercy we bobbled like corks over four-foot waves in mid-channel. Unexpectedly Ron in the last raft yelled that he was sinking due to slow leaks. All of a sudden Hans' life raft blew a hole in one of the two air compartments and in the swift deep channel the paddles churned with fury to the shallow water. In a thigh-deep shallow all leapt overboard to pull our sinking rafts to a gravel bar.

It was decided that Ron and Willy would continue downstream in the one remaining airtight raft with the heavy gear and packs on the air mattress, while the other four would walk the 45 kilometres to the Alaska Highway. Departing the driftwood fire, they set off across the gravel flats, crossing many side streams before reaching the road, where Hans knocked on the door of a gas station at 1 a.m. The proprietors, Mr. and Mrs. Conway Bradley, took them in and gave them food and shelter. "With gnashing appetites the food was wolfed down as fast as she could take it from the shelf."

The next day, they drove to the Donjek River Bridge, five kilometres away. "Ron and Willy had been there since 11:30 pm the night before and by the look on their faces something was wrong. The story came forth—the river had been a nightmare of floating trees, and in order to save themselves from shipwreck they were forced to cut their entangled equipment raft loose. Only one and a half miles upstream the raft hit a snag and gradually the equipment sank from view."

Mr. Bradley helped Hans locate a boat, and they made a salvage attempt, but all they recovered were three tents and a rope. "In the silt-loaded waters of the Donjek lay $1500 worth of equipment and more important, almost all of Willy's, Phil's and Don's pictures lay in the murky depths—never to be recovered. Lady luck had finally run out on the Canadian Mt. Logan Expedition."

Over 1,300 slides were lost. Hans's movie film almost shared the same fate, but just before the raft and the hikers split up for the last stage to the highway, Hans realized that his pack was too light and that he could carry more, so he opened the large sack that he had lashed to the raft and reached inside. Right on top was his exposed film. He pulled it out and added it to his load. In later years, he would joke about how easily it could have been a bag of dirty laundry that he had saved.

Karl Ricker concluded: "The shock of the wild trip ending finally wore off on reaching Whitehorse. Hans had done a remarkable job of pulling us back together after such a tense trip that lacked cohesive effort when the

The Logan team safely back in Whitehorse.
Left to right: Hans Gmoser, Philippe Delesalle, Don Lyon,
Willy Pfisterer, Karl Ricker and Ron Smylie.

climb actually began and stayed that way until the rescue boat was pulled out of the Donjek River."

Back in Calgary, there was a party for the returning climbers at the home of Ethan Compton. Philippe remembered, "The next morning when I woke, Hans was sitting at the typewriter, bare-chested as usual, his pack with his crampons ready and he was writing a business letter. He was going climbing with a client…. This man was so focused."

That summer, Hans had two important guiding engagements: the Alpine Club of Canada's summer camp from July 19 to August 1, and the Iowa Mountaineers' camp from August 11 to 23. Both these camps were located in the Bugaboos of southeastern British Columbia. It was the first time Hans had visited the range and he was impressed by the spectacular spires, cascading glaciers and lush green forests, and by the granite rock, which was excellent for climbing. At the two camps he led ascents of the major summits, including Bugaboo Spire, Marmolata, Pigeon Spire and Snowpatch Spire.

During the autumn, with Frank Stark and Heinz Kahl as partners, Hans incorporated his first company, Rocky Mountain Guides Limited. Although the company had been operating since 1957, it was not incorporated until November 26, 1959. In addition, he prepared his second film, one he called *Vagabonds of the Mountains*. The film was edited at home on simple equipment and accompanied by classical music chosen by Jim Tarrant, Hans's friend from his early ACC days. Hans recalled, "We spent countless nights at his house. He had this terrific record collection. We would look at a piece of film and he would pick a record." For example, while Leo chops down a large tree, we hear the thump, thump, thump of Stravinsky's *The Rite of Spring*; while skiers waltz effortlessly down powder slopes, we hear exhilarating strings and woodwinds; and while Hans's friends sit on the porch of the Wheeler hut, singing and drinking, we hear delightful Austrian accordion music and yodelling.

The film opens with Hans's friends, the "vagabonds" of the title, walking down a muddy road near Rogers Pass, carrying their skis. "Let's face it—our vagabonds are a little crazy. They have to be. If they were too practical they wouldn't be here. But since it doesn't matter to them that their hair is messed up from the wind—that their faces are burned from the sun—that their clothes are wrinkled and torn a little here and there—that their pack is heavy—and that their skis are digging into their shoulders—they can enjoy walking on a muddy road beneath great mountains on a fine spring day."

Soon the audience sees a lone skier, breaking trail through knee-deep snow. "It's hard to imagine that one's desire could be to plod through the deep snow. But let's be frank. In spite of all the arguments against it, don't we all have the desire to prove our physical prowess—to overcome our own weakness—to make ourselves do something which is difficult and thereby lift ourselves above the dull everyday."

It is remarkable how quickly Hans had learned English. At the start of the decade, he could barely speak the language, and here he was lecturing to audiences around North America, occasional small grammatical errors only adding to the charm. And Hans was often very funny. In *Vagabonds of the Mountains,* he shows Leo repairing a ski boot with a hammer and file: "He told me he always wanted to be a dentist." Above all, Hans was poetic when he spoke of the beauty of the mountains. "On such a morning everything seems fresh and new. You feel as though all this had just been created last night. All the mountains in the distance, which you have seen so often, all of a sudden, seem to have grown out of a grey snowy curtain into a dark blue sky. It is like an awakening of nature. The sun lights up the snowy faces of the peaks and draws sharp shadows across the smooth glaciers. The air is crisp and still, all is silent except for the rhythmical hiss of our skis."

Part Two, the ascent of the east ridge of Mount Logan, shows all aspects of the trip from beginning to end. Action shots are interwoven with scenics and little bits of camp life. The scenes of climbers inching their way along the knife-edge ridge, the great peaks of the Hubbard Glacier in the distance, are alone worth the price of admission. And the integration of script and music with the visuals is uncanny, the music swelling or diminishing just at the appropriate time. Hans carries his camera, a Eumig

C-16, right to the summit of the East Peak; then, after capturing his teammates shaking hands, he pans across the surrounding horizon, showing Mount St. Elias, Mount Augusta, the Malaspina Glacier, the Pacific Ocean and Mount Cook.

Hans describes the summit day:

> It turned out to be the greatest day we had on the entire trip. Just like a gift from Heaven. There wasn't a cloud in the sky, not a breath of air. The temperature was 12 below as we started on our final stretch to the East Peak of Mount Logan, still 3000 feet above us. We had actually come up here much too fast and now we had to pay for it. We weren't at all acclimatized. We could hardly breathe. Each one had a splitting headache and every time we ate something we threw it up immediately.
>
> Even a man like Willy Pfisterer, of whom we all agreed that he was just like a horse on two legs, even he was just staggering along, hardly knowing where he was going and what he was doing. Alpine Smylie, whom Willy called Alpine Slowly, was really living up to his nickname.
>
> Quite a ways ahead of us were Karl and Don, already very close to the summit. Then at last all of us were on top and my first reaction was, well thanks God we don't have to climb any more. After a few minutes we all recuperated enough to really appreciate that we were at last on the summit and we had reached our goal. To say the least we were quite proud and happy. It was interesting to watch the different reactions in everyone and I knew then that each one of us came up here for a different reason.

As the team exits via the Donjek Glacier and the Donjek River, Hans keeps the camera rolling. There is footage of the rafts bobbing in the waves on the rushing Donjek, and even shots of the final march over the gravel flats to the highway. The last scenes in the film are of the rescue boat making its way upstream to search for the lost equipment. Hans's dedication to his filming task was amazing.

After showing the film across North America, Hans was back leading ski-touring camps. By this time, he had developed a regular program: a week at Mount Assiniboine in February, five or six weeks in the Little Yoho in March and April, then two or three weeks at Rogers Pass in May. As might be expected, by springtime of 1960, Hans was ready for another adventure.

The Canadian Icefields Expedition

Along the Continental Divide of the Rocky Mountains, between Lake Louise and Jasper, lie eight major icefields— the Waputik, Wapta, Freshfield, Mons, Lyell, Columbia, Chaba and Hooker[4]—the biggest in area being the Columbia at over 300 square kilometres. The idea of a traverse over the icefields had been an object of discussion since 1932, when J.M. Thorington wrote an article in the *American Alpine Journal* entitled "A High Level Route from Jasper to Lake Louise." It was obvious that this could be a 300-kilometre-long wilderness version of the celebrated Haute Route in the European Alps. The first serious attempt was made on skis in April 1954 by a group from eastern Canada. Heavy on sponsorship but light on experience and know-how, the group captured a lot of media attention but progressed only a short distance. No doubt Hans had watched them with great interest.

During the winter of 1960, Hans decided to make his own attempt on the traverse. His team would be much stronger and more experienced than the 1954 group: old friends

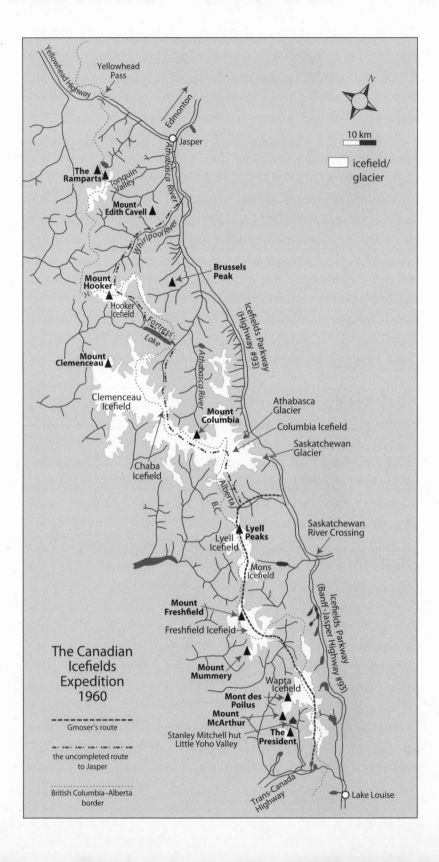

The Canadian
Icefields
Expedition
1960

- - - - - -
Gmoser's route

- - - -
the uncompleted route
to Jasper

· · · · · ·
British Columbia–Alberta
border

N

10 km

icefield/
glacier

Yellowhead Highway

Yellowhead
Pass

Edmonton

Jasper

The Ramparts

Tonquin Valley

Mount
Edith Cavell

Athabasca River

Whirlpool River

Brussels
Peak

Mount
Hooker

Hooker
Icefield

Fortress Lake

Icefields Parkway
(Highway #93)

Mount
Clemenceau

Athabasca River

Clemenceau
Icefield

Mount
Columbia

Athabasca
Glacier

Columbia Icefield

Saskatchewan
Glacier

Chaba
Icefield

Alberta

B.C.

Saskatchewan
River Crossing

Lyell
Peaks

Lyell
Icefield

Mons
Icefield

Mount
Freshfield

Freshfield Icefield

Icefields Parkway
(Banff–Jasper Highway #93)

Mount
Mummery

Wapta
Icefield

Mont des
Poilus

Mount
McArthur

Stanley Mitchell hut
Little Yoho Valley

The
President

Trans-Canada
Highway

Lake Louise

Kurt Lukas, Neil Brown and Philippe Delesalle; and two easterners who worked for the Canadian Broadcasting Corporation, Pat Boswell and Pierre Garneau. Boswell had been a member of the 1954 team and was familiar with the problems.

Sponsored by the *Calgary Herald* newspaper, the expedition attracted a great deal of publicity. Hans was successful in rounding up contributions from boot, ski and dehydrated-food manufacturers and had lots of support in the community, with many people helping out in ways large and small. Laura Gardner—the wife of J.S. "Smitty" Gardner, Hans's doctor—spent weeks baking dozens of loaves of what was called Logan bread, a heavy, nourishing bread suitable for an easy breakfast meal. She did this for all his expeditions. Meanwhile, her husband provided medical services to Hans free of charge. In return, he asked Hans to occasionally take his son Don mountain climbing.

One of the problems on the 1954 attempt had been the placing of food caches along the route, so Gmoser enlisted the help of a young pilot from Banff by the name of Jim Davies. Jim was 22 years old and had grown up in Banff, where his dad was a park warden. After a winter ski-racing in Europe, he had enrolled in art college but had soon quit and had launched himself on the career of pilot. By the winter of 1959–1960, when he helped Hans place the food caches, he had only 78 hours' flying time under his belt. In February, Jim flew Hans over the route in his Piper Super Cub aircraft. It took five hours and the temperature was −30°C. Bundled up in heavy clothes and with sleeping bags over their laps, they had a cold trip, and Hans could barely walk when they landed back in Banff.

Hans wanted to drop his food caches from the air, so he and Jim practised the technique. "Jim got this bomb rack which he fitted to his undercarriage. Then we got these ammunition boxes from the army. I knew we couldn't just drop them in the snow; we had to mark them. So we put two 12-foot poles alongside these boxes with a little flag at the end of each pole. And then we experimented on Lake Minnewanka, at what altitude he would have to release the thing so that it would actually hit the ground perpendicular.[5] At 500 feet it worked perfect. The thing would just go in an arc and hit the snow. And in the soft snow that thing went in about five feet."

Over several occasions in March, the pair flew the route and dropped seven caches, each containing four days' food and fuel. On one trip they landed on Fortress Lake, but when it came time to take off, the plane was too heavy with Hans on board. "[So Jim said,] 'You go and push on the strut and when I nod my head you jump in.' That's what we did. I remember running down the lake watching his head and at the right moment I jumped in and away we went."

On April 2, the group set off from the Trans-Canada Highway at Kicking Horse Pass up the trail to Sherbrooke Lake. Hans wrote in his journal:

> The confusion before such a trip is unbelievable. After a most hectic day, which lasted until 2 in the morning, we spent the better part of the day assembling and packing our gear. The Calgary Herald had 3 people present; CBC was represented by Bruno Engler with 3 other fellows and then of course there were John and Gertie [Hartefeld] at whose house all this took place. Finally we could drive up to Lake Wapta where the Gardners were waiting to bid us goodbye and at 3:30 we took off accompanied by Bruno and his gang. It was quite a shambles, as we couldn't see the trail at first. There was actually a very good trail to Sherbrooke Lake at the end of which we set up our camp in a heavy snowfall. We have quite an elaborate tent

Hans Gmoser and Jim Davies in 1960

and it will take time before we can set it up fast. We spent the evening with Bruno exploding flash bulbs and drinking some wine. It will still take a few days before we are all close to each other. But there seems to be a fine spirit among us.

The next day, carrying 30-kilogram loads that towered over their heads, they progressed up the valley in a wet and heavy snowfall to the Niles-Daly col, at the edge of the Waputik Icefield. On April 4, the weather cleared, revealing magnificent mountains surrounding them. Hans wrote: "It is unbelievable how long it takes us to get going in the morning. We were finally off by 10 am. I must say the views were unbelievably beautiful but our packs were still too much of a burden to let us really enjoy this trip." In a

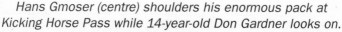

Hans Gmoser (centre) shoulders his enormous pack at Kicking Horse Pass while 14-year-old Don Gardner looks on.

The Icefields Expedition team:
(left to right) Hans Gmoser, Pierre Garneau, Philippe Delesalle,
Kurt Lukas, Neil Brown and Pat Boswell

violent wind they crossed Balfour High Col and descended to Balfour Pass, where they placed a camp near Mount Olive. During the night it stormed and in the morning it was still socked in, so they didn't get underway until noon. By the time they crossed the Olive–St. Nicholas col onto the Wapta Icefield, it had cleared, but the wind tore at their clothes. That night they found their first cache, near their camp at the head of the Peyto Glacier.

On April 6, they skied to a high col east of Mount Baker. The view was incredible. "Even though you can almost imagine the impressive panorama that awaits you on the other side, it always takes your breath away when mountain range upon mountain range unfolds before you— hundreds of peaks, many of them old friends, many of them strange, new, mysterious and tempting." Then the six men set off down the Baker Glacier to Wildcat Creek, where they had lunch in the sun. From there the descent to the Blaeberry River became tricky as they negotiated cliffs, bush and soft snow.

On April 7, they travelled a short way up the Blaeberry River, then rested in the sun, drying and repairing clothes and equipment. On the 9th they made their way through the maze of the Cairnes Glacier icefall, hoping to reach the Freshfield Icefield. "Back and forth we switched through crevasses and seracs, across some narrow ridges, and then there was just a large ice wall ahead of us. It started to snow hard and a strong wind drove the snow-like needles into our faces. We tried to find a way but there was always either a vertical ice cliff or a huge crevasse which stopped our progress. Finally we dropped down into a crevasse, went along it on a snow bridge, took off our skis and climbed up for 60 feet—we were on top of the Cairnes Icefall."

Reaching the Low-Barlow col, they coasted out onto the Freshfield Icefield and set up camp. Later that night, Hans wrote in his journal:

> One cannot imagine how hard we have to work here—people tell you to "have a good time" and the like—"have fun", etc. They are idiots and haven't any idea what they are talking about. Surely we enjoy such a trip, but in a very special way. It couldn't possibly be fun. We have to fight constantly for our survival. Everything we need to live has to be carried on our backs. If the weather closes in for a long period we won't find our next cache and have to starve. People die up here, if they take life too easy. The enjoyment comes largely from realizing that one can survive in such a place and that one can find his way in the snowstorm. The actual doing of it sometimes demands the ultimate from the man—so it was today.

For the next few days the weather was good, and after finding their second food cache they made rapid progress, crossing Niverville Col and descending to Bush Pass and on down Forbes Creek. Then they ascended steep forest towards a pass between Golden Eagle Peak and Cambrai Mountain. Near the top, Hans cut steps up a short ice chimney, then climbed snow slopes, exiting up and over a cornice onto the Mons Icefield. As Lukas climbed over the cornice, it broke and he tumbled 20 metres, by some miracle stopping just above a rock cliff.

So far the weather had been good, but that was all about to change. As they pushed across the west slopes of Division Mountain, between the Mons Icefield and the Lyell Icefield, it began to snow. By the time they had pitched camp, the storm had moved in, the snow building up so rapidly that it was crushing their tents. For two days it snowed and they simply waited it out, slowly running out of food. On the night of the 14th, Hans wrote in his journal: "We are now cooking our last supper and tomorrow we still have one breakfast."

Hans cooking supper at camp on the Lyell Icefield

The weather cleared the next morning, enabling them to search for a cache that they knew was located only a kilometre away, but it had snowed so much during the last few days that they were unable to find it. They were planning to ski out to the highway

On the Freshfield Icefield.
Pierre Garneau on left and Hans Gmoser standing at right.

for more food, when Jim Davies flew over. After they communicated their predicament to Davies, he flew back to Banff and returned four hours later, dropping the much-needed food and fuel. Once again optimism was high, and they continued a short distance up the icefield to a camp just below the Lyell peaks.

The following morning, in fog and wind, they crossed the highest point on the route, the glaciated 3380-metre pass between Lyell No. 2 (Edward Peak) and No. 3 (Ernest Peak), and began the descent of the 1800-metre-high Alexandra icefall, one of the most serious portions of the traverse. Gmoser wrote in the *CAJ*:

> The fog was so thick that it was difficult for us to tell between up and down. After checking the map once more, we traversed in a westerly direction, under Lyell Peak No. 3. The object was to reach a steep, narrow ridge which led to the Lyell/Farbus Col. We kept very close together. All of a sudden there was a break in the clouds, and after hastily sizing up the situation, we began to ski toward what we thought was the col. The fog closed in again, and as though warned by an inner voice, I stopped abruptly. Only a few feet below me, there was a 2,000-foot sheer drop. We were too far east of the col and had almost skied over this enormous precipice.

After climbing back up, they carefully worked their way west, then down into the col, below the thick clouds. Here they were forced onto the left side of the steep glacier below the slopes of Farbus Mountain. "All of a sudden, we heard the noise of a huge avalanche and saw it coming right at us. Luckily there had been several slides before and the ground was so broken up that the avalanche stopped when it hit the glacier. Cautiously, we threaded our way through the labyrinth of crevasses. It was impossible to find a straightforward route, because we could not see where we were going. We constantly had to detour and retrace our steps. On one such occasion, the snow gave way under me and I felt myself falling for a long time. When I finally landed on my head and back, I was far down in a crevasse. Some light came through a small hole about 70 feet above me." Luckily, Hans was unhurt, and after his companions threw him a rope, he was able to climb out of the crevasse. "That evening as we camped in the valley among the trees, the campfire was a real symbol of life."

At this point, Neil Brown decided that he had had enough and chose to ski out the Castleguard River valley to the Icefields Parkway. The others pushed on towards some cabins reputed to be located near Watchman Lake on the east side of Mount Bryce, where they felt there would be food. Hans wrote: "When we finally arrived at Watchman Lake and realized that there was no cabin, I was near collapse, as were most of the others.... Once more we dug deep into our small food bag." The next day, the group skied out to the highway, where they "were welcomed at a national park road maintenance camp and in short time devoured five pounds of roast beef, 22 eggs, two cakes and drank two gallons of milk." At this point, Pierre Garneau also called it quits.

The reduced team of four was not finished yet, and after a day and a half of rest, they skied up to the ACC hut at the toe of the Saskatchewan Glacier. Philippe remembered years later: "That night the tension among the remaining four was high. Hans, bare-chested in the overheated hut, decided to wax our skis, a favourite activity of his—never really trusting our casual approach to this important factor of performance. Without a doubt, a trivial remark of ours ignited the explosive atmosphere in the hut! Hurtful words flew ... difficult to digest by loyal friends." The next morning, Philippe put on his skis and headed back to the highway. The remaining three—Gmoser, Boswell and Lukas—continued a short distance up the glacier, but after 12 days of bad weather and with the wind sweeping deep drifts of snow across their path, progress was very difficult. Exhausted and dispirited, they, too, returned to the highway. The trip was over.

Hans had made no entries in his journal since April 15. On May 1, he wrote again. "There is no real reason for finishing this diary now; the trip has long been over. It was a failure and what I have to say now is no one else's business but mine." Respecting Hans's wish that the diary entry remain private, I will not reproduce it in its entirety. Suffice to say that Hans was severely depressed. This was the absolute nadir of his life. He wrote that if it weren't for all the people who depended on him, he would just run away. There was nothing for him to do but wait and suffer until gradually the memory faded.

It seems strange, perhaps, and even a little melodramatic, that Hans took his failure so hard. After all, he and his team had given the traverse a good try and had succeeded in covering half the route. But failure was not for Hans, particularly in front of the national news media. And the acrimonious way the trip ended must also have deeply troubled him. Although the friendships survived, the bitter memories would always remain.

During the summer, Hans returned to his guiding work and on July 8 led Jack MacKenzie up the prominent crack that splits the west face of Mount Cory, near Banff. MacKenzie wrote in Hans's *Tourenbuch*: "Hans Gmoser is an excellent leader for an inexpert climber, for he is careful, alert and considerate, but nevertheless an expert rock climber who can inspire and instruct you to do your best.

A new route, unhesitatingly and unerringly led." It was the beginning of a long friendship that would later grow into a successful business partnership.

That year, the ACC's summer camp was held at Fryatt Creek in Jasper National Park. At the end of the camp, Hans and Heinz made what was likely the third ascent of Brussels Peak. After acquiring a reputation for being unassailable, this rock tower had finally been climbed in 1948. The first ascentionists, two young Americans, had even drilled holes in the rock and driven in expansion bolts to aid their progress, a technique that had provoked outrage in the conservative Canadian climbing community. Hans and Heinz did not find the climb anywhere near as difficult as they expected, and climbed the mountain in impeccable style:

Hans climbing what would later be called the Gmoser Crack on Mount Cory

I admit Heinz Kahl and I were scared before we took off to try Brussels Peak. We both tossed and rolled in our sleeping bags and were glad to be at last on our way from Fryatt Creek to the Christie-Brussels Col. We went fast and didn't speak much. Shortly after the col we roped up and Heinz went ahead. We found the climb most interesting and the rock very good. The climb is actually quite short. There are only four rope lengths which we took alternately. The formidable Lewis Crack which had been surmounted with bolts and the "flesh crawl technique" before, was this time climbed with one piton below it and by simply utilizing the two sides of the outer crack. Apart from being the hardest part of the climb it was also the most enjoyable. There was certainly no need to kick the air with your feet.... To sum it up, Brussels Peak is a wonderful climb. It is not easy but neither does it take superhuman beings to climb it. I go as far as saying that if one wants to make a point it can be climbed without pitons.

Later that summer, Hans guided for the Iowa Mountaineers at their summer camp in the Sawtooth Range of Idaho, a group of jagged granite spires located at the head of the Salmon River. It was his first guiding engagement outside Canada. He led ropes up Mount Heyburn, Chockstone Peak and the Grand Aiguille. In addition, he made a number of first ascents: Quartzite Point, Black Aiguille, Eagle Perch and Flatrock Needle. Many of these ascents he climbed with his friend Clair Brown.

In the autumn, Hans sat down and prepared another film for the coming winter. *Of Skiers and Mountains* is not one of his best. Perhaps he was still suffering from the depression of the previous spring. The commentary, however, gets off to a good start: "Many people wouldn't think in terms of skiing unless they had a lift to carry them to the top of the slope. To be bound to one slope, even to one mountain, by a lift, may be convenient but it robs us of the greatest pleasure that skiing can give, that is, to travel through the wide, wintry country, to follow the lure of the peaks which tempt on the horizon and to get away from all the noises of our technological age into some clean, mysterious surroundings."

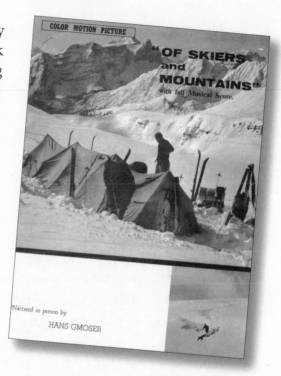

The poster for Hans's 1960–1961 film

The first half of the film is about a ski holiday at the Wheeler hut, at Rogers Pass. Despite the best efforts of Jim McConkey, who is the star of the film, the skiing on spring corn snow is not dramatic and the storyline seems forced and contrived. Choppy editing and music that often does not fit the action also detract from the film.

Part Two of the film is the Canadian Icefields Expedition story. Once again, there is the spectacular scenery, but the commentary is matter-of-fact and muted and the usual magic seems to be missing from the show. There is no mention of the interpersonal drama, and Hans concludes his presentation with the words, "In spite of not completing the trip, we were quite happy about it. We had some wonderful experiences, saw some terrific country and hope that in years to come it will be possible for many people to ski those great mountains which few people have ever seen."

Expedition Interlude

For the next two years, Hans undertook no major expeditions and concentrated on his guiding. By the spring of 1961, the business end of things was getting too much for him and he asked Elfi Grillmair to be his business manager. Back in Austria, she had spent two years studying at business college, and she was familiar with accounting and could type. In Canada, she had enrolled in 1956 at the University of Alberta, graduating three years later with a B.Sc. in Geology. She agreed to Hans's request and for the next six years would run the office of Rocky Mountain Guides Limited from her Calgary home at 83 Armstrong Crescent SE. She was a busy woman indeed: raising three children; working part-time identifying microfossils for an oil company; and dealing with the comings and goings of clients as they passed through Calgary—feeding them and doing their laundry. Hans had a key to the house and came and went as he pleased. Leo and Elfi's daughter, Elizabeth, recalled recently, "When I was little I thought that Hans lived with us."

Actually, Hans still lived in Banff in an assortment of basement suites and small apartments. At times he stayed with John and Gertie Hartefeld in their house on Muskrat Street. Originally from Germany, John was a big, strong man, the shop teacher at the Banff High School. He and Gertie took good care of Hans and became another set of parents in his life. During this time, Hans's girlfriend was Peggy Telfer. Originally from Rossland, BC, she worked in the oil patch in Calgary and was a ski instructor on weekends at Mount Norquay. As an old friend commented, "Women were very much attracted to Hans." Although Peggy would have likely made a good wife for Hans, he was not ready yet to settle down, or perhaps he had not yet met his soulmate.

In July of 1961, Hans guided again for the ACC at their Ice River camp below the Goodsirs. Reverend A.F.T. Thompson wrote in the *Canadian Alpine Journal*: "Hans Gmoser was our most capable guide. One of the nice things about Hans, from the point of view of a newcomer to the mountains, was his propensity for murmuring a dulcet phrase or two from *The Magic Flute* with an awesome chasm gaping at his feet." Returning to the United States in August, Hans led members of the Iowa Mountaineers on climbs in the Needles in the Black Hills of North Dakota and also on

The Iowa Mountaineers gathered at a summer camp.
Hans is in the back row, right centre, wearing his trademark white cap.

A group of Iowa Mountaineers on top of Devils Tower, Wyoming.
Left to right: Earl Carter, Hans Gmoser, Bill ?, unidentified,
Annie Carter, Celia Ekie, Sue Prince and Harvey Carter.

an ascent of Devils Tower in nearby Wyoming. At the end of the month, Hans led his last cutting-edge rock climb: a new route on the southeast face of Mount Louis near Banff, which is now known as the Gmoser Route. With his friend from Mount Robson, Clair Brown, and two other clients, Jeff Pope and Christian von Allmen, he established a line that is still graded 5.8 and remains one of his best.

After repeatedly viewing the spring ski sequences in the previous year's film, Hans must have realized that powder-snow skiing was much more photogenic and exciting for his viewers. Consequently, his creation for the autumn of 1961 was titled *Deep Powder and Steep Rock*. The commentary begins, "Powder snow is no doubt the ultimate of snows and the very mention of it suggests a host of impressions. Mostly it brings to mind a sunny day, a wide open, untracked snowfield and big plumes of powder behind the skiers who carve their turns into this fluffy white." On the screen, Jim McConkey and Ted Johnston are seen racing effortlessly through deep snow down the steep slopes of the ski resort at Alta, Utah. At Mount Norquay and the growing ski resort at Lake Louise, the stars are locals such as John Wackerle and Bob Meggs.

Back in form again, Hans is poetic and philosophical about ski touring:

> While you climb up mainly for the run, you encounter so many other thrills, beautiful sights and unforgettable experiences that this alone makes the climb worthwhile. This then reduces the run itself practically to the role of a bonus. Mind you, at that a bonus which I wouldn't want to miss for anything. Furthermore, only while you are climbing can you experience the many moods of the mountain, and if done properly, climbing is such a pure, rhythmical motion. Especially if you lay a track which snakes up the mountain, as if you were a part of it. And when this track leads you to the top of some steep, untouched slope on some early morning just as the first suggestion of sunlight rests on the peaks, then you have added another priceless pearl to your collection of memories.

And Hans has his sense of humour back as well. "One morning my good friend Ethan Compton and I were sitting out there [on the newly constructed outhouse] and Ethan turned to me and said, 'You know, Gmoser, you have a lot in common with Tchaikovsky.' I said, 'What do you mean?' 'Well,' said he, 'Tchaikovsky composed the Nutcracker Suite, but you built it.'"

The brochure for Hans's 1961–1962 film presentation

Hans again presents an ascent of The President from President Pass, followed by some remarkable footage of Jim McConkey skiing the steep west face to the Emerald Glacier. Then he finishes with a ski tour from Sunshine Village to Mount Assiniboine. "With all its thrills and excitement, this life is very relaxing and goes on at a rather slow pace, a pleasant change from our usual life. Everything is very quiet and the mountains seem to guard the privacy of those places themselves."

Unfortunately, neither the commentary nor the film of Part Two has survived, so it is uncertain what it contained. Likely, it showed some very dramatic footage of Hans's recent climb on Mount Louis.

Hans set a terrific pace for himself that winter as he toured the film around North America, giving 50 presentations. Travelling in his little Volkswagon Beetle, he often curled up in his sleeping bag in the back to save money on hotels. In October, he began in Denver, CO, then drove to Revelstoke, Rossland and Nelson in British Columbia, then continued to Lethbridge, Calgary and Edmonton in Alberta. In November, he did 17 shows: Boston, MA, Concord, MA, Oneonta, NY, Chicago, IL, Cheyenne, WY, Bozeman, MT, Missoula, MT, Idaho Falls, ID, Spokane, WA, Seattle, WA, Portland, OR, Vancouver, BC, Los Angeles, CA, San Francisco, CA, Salt Lake City, UT, and two shows in Berkeley, CA. In December, he was in Fort Wayne, IN, Northfield, VT, Lewiston, ME, New London, NH, and Grosse Point, MI, then up to Banff, AB, Vernon, BC, and Penticton, BC. At Christmas, Hans would come home to rest with friends. Flush with money from his lectures, he would pay Elfi, who had been keeping track of her hours for months. The pace continued in January with Espanola, Sudbury, Collingwood, Toronto and London in Ontario, Montreal, QC, Mount Snow, VT, Waterville, ME, Hanover, NH, Fresno, CA, Sugarbowl, CA, and Richland, WA. Then, in February, it was Salt Lake City, UT, Alta, UT, Aspen, CO, Tonasket, WA, Dawson Creek, BC, and Windermere, BC.

It was quite a schedule, and Hans needed a lot of help to make it work. In almost every town he had friends who would help organize the shows. According to one friend, "Hans used a lot of people over the years, but they liked it and wanted to help him make his way in the mountain world." A young friend, Don Gardner, remembered that Hans would drop by the Gardner house for dinner when he was in Calgary. With his rigorous guiding schedule, film presentations and active social life, Hans was often exhausted and would literally fall asleep at the dinner table.

In February, while skiing at Alta, in Utah, Hans broke his leg. He still had several engagements left on his schedule, so Leo came south and drove him from venue to venue. By early May, Hans's leg had recovered sufficiently to allow him to lead a ski excursion to the heavily glaciated Cariboo Mountains of British Columbia. This trip was different in two ways: Hans had hired Jim Davies to fly his group in his Cessna 180 aircraft high into the mountains and land them on the glacier; and, for the first time, the tour was set up exclusively as a film shoot. As stars of the film, Hans had brought with him his old pal Jim McConkey and three members of Canada's national women's ski team: Nancy Greene, her sister Elizabeth and Nancy Holland. While waiting in the valley for good weather, Hans wrote in his journal:

> What a way to spend time? While most people are busy pursuing their goals, we sit here lazily, practically within reach of our goal and yet unable to reach it. A ray of sun hits the paper through the rain sprinkled windshield, warming me, while all around us the clouds hang low on the mountains. A mood to make you sad; melancholy and yet full of peace. What is peace? Is it the orderly falling into place of everything? I somehow don't think so because if I view the situation I can only see chaos. Chaos of emotions. Actually a very morbid state of mind and yet it doesn't feel too sad. Mind you there is a slight hurt and you could easily feel sorry for yourself. But then when you are in such a mood you feel so self righteous and see so many faults with your companions. A mood which gets me thoroughly pissed off with myself and which makes me glad that I feel pain. There is nothing worse than to feel sorry for yourself. It is all in your own hands and you have to be able to shape your own life the way you want it. If you can't cope with

it any more then it is time to change the course and if you have hopelessly gone astray then it is time to stop it before you make a bigger mess out of it.

While I am not entirely in accord with ending your life I think it unwise to continue a life which yields no pleasure and cannot surmount the barriers it has come up against.

What a grey world! Yet you know there is also a sun. You can almost see it, feel it—can it ever make its way through those clouds? At a time like this it seems impossible. But I have also seen times when you thought it impossible that there would ever be a cloud to cover the sun. A world of extremes, and no matter how determined we are, at times you can't escape the feeling that we are being tossed around like a little ball, from one side to another.

What in hell can we do against it? I want so badly to take things into my own hands and many times I feel like I do, but then at times like this I feel utterly helpless—helpless. It would be easy to resign and hope—hope for what? Can we hope? It is such a passive, stupid way of life. It is the life of a slave. Unable to think and do for yourself. Just "hoping" for handouts. God I want to bust those chains, get the things I want myself.

Patience and equanimity were not Hans's virtues, and he was clearly growing irritated by the slow pace of his commercial success. Leo, Franz and Philippe were all working at steady jobs, married and raising families in their own homes. Hans, however, was going his own very individual way and was paying a price for it.

Eventually, the weather cleared and Jim flew the group to 2850 metres at the head of the Canoe Glacier, below Mount Sir Wilfred Laurier. In the sunshine, and surrounded by glorious mountains, Hans's mood improved and he somehow managed to film the action with his cast leg in a mukluk fitted with a short ski. To provide some excitement for the camera, McConkey performed a remarkable stunt: he built a kicker from snow and jumped over the parked plane. Davies remembered that it took five tries for McConkey to get it right. He kept rebuilding and adjusting the takeoff and had four spectacular crashes before he succeeded. Jim, who had starred in Hans's movies several times before, was one of Canada's first daredevils on skis. Six years older than Hans, he was originally from Barrie, Ontario. After a brief stint as a ski instructor at Gray Rocks in Quebec, he migrated west, first to Banff in the late 1940s, and then south to Alta, Utah, where he met Hans.[6]

After his leg had healed, Hans was busy guiding all summer, but in September he was seriously at work producing another film, this one called *To the Forbidden Snowfields*. No commentary of this film has survived, but the

The brochure for Hans's 1962–1963 film presentation

film itself is spectacular. The Cariboo Mountains, draped in snow and ice, are an incredible backdrop for Jim Davies's flying and Jim McConkey's ski stunts, and the shots of Nancy Greene racing flawlessly past gaping crevasses are breathtaking. In just a few years, Nancy would win both the 1967 and 1968 women's World Cup championships, and silver and gold medals at the Grenoble Winter Olympics. Hans introduces his audiences to a new star, Mike Wiegele, a fellow Austrian six years his junior and a champion ski racer, who is featured skiing on the Athabasca Glacier, near the Columbia Icefield. Climbing sequences starring Mike, Hans and Peter Fuhrmann, a German-born, Canadian-certified mountain guide, on Castle Mountain add variety and were likely shot by Clair Brown.

By this time, Hans's presentation had become the social high point of the season for many North American mountain lovers. Dressed in their best Norwegian ski sweaters and sealskin après-ski boots, they would gather at the local auditorium or school gymnasium. At intermission, Hans would mix in the foyer, greeting old friends and clients. With his winning smile and personality, he had become the mountain idol of the early 1960s.

In February 1963, Hans tried helicopter skiing for the first time. Calgary geologist Art Patterson, who worked summers in the Canadian North, travelled much of the time by helicopter. In the winter, these helicopters sat idle in the hangar, costing their owners money; so Patterson, who was an avid skier, got the idea that they could be used for skiing. "The original proposal that I had was to go from the top of the Standish lift up to Twin Cairns and at Lake Louise from the top of the Larch lift up to Purple Bowl.... But I got shot down thoroughly by Parks." Unfazed, Patterson "still felt that helicopter skiing would be a great sport. I knew lots about helicopters and I knew lots about mountains, but I knew absolutely nothing about snow, so I had to get hold of a competent mountain guide. I went to Ethan Compton, who in those days ran Premier Cycle and Sports in Calgary, and I told him my idea, and I said I need to know a good mountain guide to get this going, and he said, 'Obviously you've got to get hold of Gmoser.'"

Patterson phoned Gmoser, who "sounded a little stunned" but agreed to help with the idea. They met one Saturday late in the month at a restaurant at Dead Man's Flats, about ten kilometres east of Canmore. Associated Helicopters of Calgary was having a training day nearby, so there was a machine available. With pilot Murray McKenzie, Gmoser and Patterson flew all over the Kananaskis region, scouting for suitable spots for skiing. Gmoser remembered, "We landed on the Sparrowhawk shoulder and skied down. We actually ended up skiing down Cautley at Assiniboine, too. We flew all around trying to find places to ski. We decided that for the next day Sparrowhawk would be one possibility, and from Sparrowhawk across the lake, from a subsidiary peak of Mount Nestor, there is a little glaciated valley that ends up at a campsite on Spray Lake. So we used these two runs but the conditions were terrible. The wind was blowing."

On Sunday, Patterson and Gmoser met about 20 clients who had paid a nominal fee for a day of heli-skiing. It was a slow process getting everyone to the top of the mountain in the piston-driven helicopter of the era. Gmoser recalled, "I'd fly up and wait for a few, and then we'd just start skiing down. Everybody else would just follow the tracks down."

In early May, Hans tried helicopter skiing again, this time in the Cariboos. By now, Jim Davies was flying helicopters; assisted by pilot Russ Timrick, he deposited high on the Canoe Glacier a group that included Jim McConkey; Bob Smith (later a designer of ski goggles); US national team ski racer Starr Walton; photographer Fred Lindholm, on assignment from *SKI Magazine*; Canadian national team ski racer Linda Crutchfield; and Hans's friend Mike Wiegele. Once again, this adventure was designed primarily as a film shoot, and it is clear that Hans was enlisting talented people who could help him in his aspirations. Building a snow cave, they weathered a two-day storm; when it cleared, Davies returned, picked them up and landed the machine right on top of Mount Sir Wilfred Laurier (3516 m). From here, they had an outstanding run of 1200 metres down to the campsite. Afterwards, Lindholm and McConkey opted to fly back to Valemount, but the remainder of the group skied the Sand Glacier to Tête Creek, then bushwhacked for 15 kilometres to a logging road. It was a brutal trip, with dense bush and creek crossings that took them almost two days.

During the spring of 1963, the Association of Canadian Mountain Guides (ACMG) was formed. Since that first exam back in 1956, Walter Perren had been certifying Canadian guides, often on the strength of a letter of recommendation written by Hans. Eventually, Perren suggested that they get together and form their own association. Nine men met at Heinz Kahl's cabin at Lac des Arcs, east of Canmore: Austrian-born Gmoser, Grillmair and Willy Pfisterer; German-born Peter Fuhrmann and Heinz Kahl; Swiss-born Hans Schwarz; and three English-born guides, Brian Greenwood, Eric Lomas and Dick Lofthouse.[7] Gmoser brought his girlfriend, Peggy, to take minutes of the meeting. Fuhrmann was elected president, Greenwood was voted secretary and Gmoser became standards committee chairman. His first job would be to write a guides' manual and to formalize examination procedures. On May 23, 1963, the Association of Canadian Mountain Guides was registered under the Alberta Societies Act.

Mount McKinley, Wickersham Wall

At the end of May, Hans set off on his biggest expedition ever. His goal was to make the first ascent of the north face, or Wickersham Wall, of Mount McKinley. Almost 4000 metres high and set at an angle of about 40 degrees, it is potentially a huge avalanche slope; should it snow heavily, climbers are exposed to great risk. This would be the most demanding climb of Hans's career and prove the truth of the statement, "On an expedition with Hans, suffering was mandatory, pleasure was optional."

At 6193 metres, Mount McKinley, also known by the Native name Denali, is the highest mountain in North America. It had first been climbed to the lower North Peak in 1910 by a group of Alaskan sourdoughs (local miners and prospectors), but the highest point, the South Peak, was not reached until 1913 by an expedition led by Hudson Stuck, Episcopal archdeacon of the Yukon. Like Mount Logan, this mountain is a daunting undertaking; it was not climbed again until 1932, by none other than Erling Strom, Hans's boss at Mount Assiniboine Lodge, who made the ascent on skis. By 1963, the mountain was gaining in popularity, most climbers opting to ascend the West Buttress route, pioneered in 1951 by Bradford Washburn. Air access to the Kahiltna Glacier, on the west side of the mountain, made the ascent considerably easier, but even so, it was still a cold and fearsome experience.

In the early 1960s, climbers were looking for new challenges in the Alaskan mountains. The major summits had all been climbed and young alpinists were interested in either smaller, unclimbed peaks of a difficult nature or in new routes on the biggest peaks. The Wickersham Wall was one of the plums waiting to be climbed and Hans wanted to get it.

After driving over 3000 kilometres along the Alaska Highway, the team gathered on May 27 at the Mount McKinley National Park ranger station on the east side of the mountain. In addition to Gmoser, there were seven other climbers: his close friend Leo Grillmair; Pat Boswell, a teammate from the Canadian Icefields Expedition; mountain guide Hans Schwarz; Calgarians Gunti Prinz and Dieter Raubach; and two Americans, Tom Spencer and Hank Kaufmann. Ahead of them was a daunting task: to walk 50 kilometres to the base of the mountain, climb the wall carrying their food, supplies and skis, then traverse the mountain and descend the Kahiltna Glacier on the west side. It was to be an epic expedition and come within a hair's breadth of tragedy.

They drove to the Eielson Visitor Center, parked their cars and set off under enormous loads along the McKinley park road towards Wonder Lake. Hans wrote in the *Canadian Alpine Journal*:

> Without pause sweat beads formed on my forehead, gathered into little driblets, ran down the corner of my eyes where they lingered for a little while before running across my cheeks and then dropping into the dusty road in front of my feet. I watched this play, just to keep my mind off the murderously heavy load on my shoulders and the seemingly endless way we had to go. When I lifted my head I saw another huge pack ahead of me and the two legs beneath it seemed able to move only with the greatest pain and effort. Beyond that stretched the tundra, and in the distance, towered a giant white mountain. It seemed so far away and our progress so slow, that I couldn't possibly bring myself to recognize this mountain as our goal. All I wanted just then was to take off this bloody pack

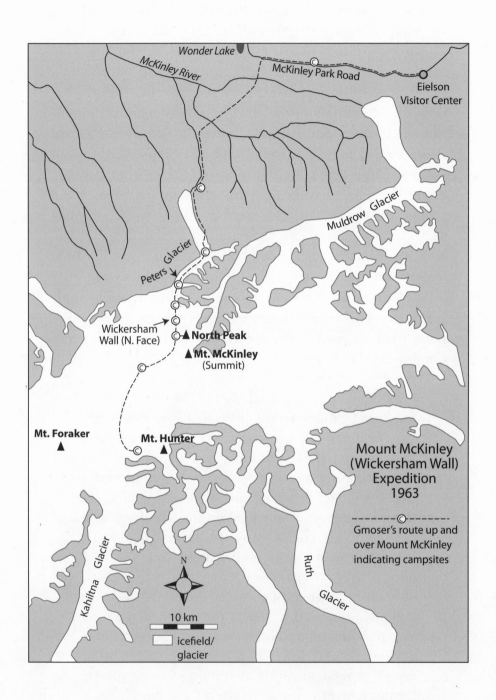

Wonder Lake

McKinley River

McKinley Park Road

Eielson
Visitor Center

Muldrow Glacier

Peters Glacier

Wickersham
Wall (N. Face)

▲ North Peak

▲ Mt. McKinley
(Summit)

Mt. Foraker
▲

Mt. Hunter
▲

Mount McKinley
(Wickersham Wall)
Expedition
1963

————————©————————

Gmoser's route up and
over Mount McKinley
indicating campsites

Kahiltna Glacier

Ruth Glacier

N

10 km

icefield/
glacier

and lie down. Anything beyond that didn't interest me in the least.

On the second day out, while crossing the tundra, they had a bear encounter. "Then there was another big grizzly! At first not particularly interested in us. So we got out of his way and lost sight of him, but not for long. And he began to intercept our path. This time we would have been going away from him so we decided to stop and let it come to a show down. The bear kept coming closer so we got our ice axes out and began to bang on the pots. The bear still kept coming and then only 150 feet from us he wheeled around and galloped over the hill. We breathed a sigh of relief and continued our trip."

They reached the Peters Glacier on May 30 and ascended to the base of the mountain the next day, setting up camp on the Jeffery Glacier at 2150 metres. While waiting for Don Sheldon to drop the bulk of their food and supplies, Gmoser, Schwarz, Spencer and Grillmair reconnoitred to 2900 metres, where they were stopped by a gaping crevasse. Clouds hung low on the mountain the morning of June 2, but late in the day it cleared and throughout the following day the sun shone brightly. Meanwhile, the men waited expectantly for Sheldon, but he did not come. Then it began to snow.

To their amazement, Sheldon roared out of the mist at 10 p.m. on June 4. Gmoser wrote: "I stuck my head out just in time to see a gas can land 30 feet from our tent. For the next half hour or so we were literally bombarded as Sheldon dropped our 25 parcels, some of them so close that we were afraid for our tents. This airdrop was one of the best spectacles I have ever seen. Like a ghost the plane would soar out of the driving snow, drop a parcel and vanish into the mist again with the red tail light flickering."

Late the following day, the sun came out, "[a]nd then the Wickersham Wall came alive. Everywhere avalanches cascaded down the steep ice and snow slopes."

Camp II was established at 2750 metres on June 6, and the following day they reached the crevasse that had stopped them. The problem was solved by Gmoser, who crawled gingerly across a fragile snow bridge, then walked along the upper lip to where it overhung the lower lip, and anchored a rope ladder. Above this impasse, they put on their skis and continued to 3050 metres, where a protected spot was found for Camp III. Everyone's spirits were high and they were optimistic about the outcome of their climb. Hans wrote in his journal: "Now that the weather seems to be with us we have lots of enthusiasm and are quite eager to do our work."

From this point, the wall rose in a long, exposed sweep for 2000 metres. Because it offered only one campsite along the way that was reasonably safe from avalanches, the group decided to push on as rapidly as possible. Gmoser noted: "In retrospect that was a mistake because it meant we went up too fast."

Just three days later, the entire party was installed in Camp V at 5060 metres. Hans wrote in his journal:

> We are on top of the Wickersham Wall! But at what a price! From 13,000 feet [3960 m] we moved our whole camp to 16,600 feet [5060 m] and this was about all some of the fellows could do. It was almost pathetic to see us set up our camp; tempers would flare up at the slightest provocation, all we could think of was to get the tents up, get something warm into our bellies and then go to sleep. That is, if we can sleep. Up here it is quite difficult to get a good nights rest, because of the thin air. We have come up here in four days from 9000 feet [2740 m]

Hans Gmoser leads his team
up the Wickersham Wall

and it is surely telling on us! But through all our tiredness we felt the impact of what we have just accomplished. We have for the first time made a trail through the Wickersham Wall—apparently the world's longest ice and snow face, and while we congratulated each other, I came close to crying and for a while all our troubles and differences had disappeared.

The following day, most of the team descended to Camp IV to fetch more supplies. Climbing back up, Raubach was so tired that he fell asleep in the snow 150 metres below camp. Prinz went down with water and some "pep" pills, revived Raubach and got him safely up to the tents. Meanwhile, Gmoser and Schwarz carried loads even higher up the mountain to Camp VI at 5500 metres. Even Hans's "legs felt like jelly and I was frantically gasping for air. But we moved on and on. One step; another step and another step. Oh I am so bloody tired. I am working so hard and don't seem to get anywhere."

Hans had promised his team that June 12 would be a rest day, but as it was sunny with hardly a breath of wind, he decided to move up to Camp VI. He knew he was tempting fate, but still he pushed on. On the morning of the 13th, thin streaks of cloud stretching across the sky foretold of a storm. "Morale in camp had reached an all-time low. Tom was moaning and unable to keep any food down. He just lay there in his bag with a blank stare, unable to move. During the night Hank felt very sick. Everyone else complained of severe headache and it seemed to take forever to even lace up your shoes."

At 11 a.m., six of them set out for North Peak (5934 m). Schwarz and Gmoser pulled ahead and after two hours reached the summit. As they waited for the others to arrive, it began to snow. Chilled after 20 minutes, they could wait no longer and began to descend. A short distance below the summit they met Gunti Prinz, who was still pushing upward, so they waited while he climbed to the top; then the three of them descended back to Camp VI. Hans wrote in his journal that night: "Everyone seems to be sick now and unable to eat. It is snowing quite hard now and I just hope that it will stop during the night. This kind of weather is not very much appreciated in such a place."

Their epic descent of the mountain was well described by Gmoser in the *Canadian Alpine Journal*:

> All night long the wind tore at our tents and I looked out often to see if everything was intact. By morning there was still no let-up in the storm, but Hank and Tom were so sick that I felt we simply had to take them down and set up our camp at 16,600 feet [5060 m]....
>
> However, I completely underestimated the ferocity of the storm. Visibility was nil and at times the wind literally took your breath away. We broke camp, nevertheless, and started to go down the ridge—it was impossible. After we had moved 200 yards we gave up our attempt and pitched the tents again. To do this we had to dig out platforms in the lee of the ridge. At the moment this seemed pretty good; at least we were somewhat sheltered from the wind. But the drifting snow piled higher and higher between the tents and the ridge.... I was quite worried; would the tents stand up under this tremendous load or would they collapse? But we were too tired to do anything about it.
>
> Those marvelous tents stood up all night even though 7 feet of snow had piled on them. But there was hardly any room left inside. I began to dig a snow cave. Just then it looked as though it might clear up a bit and we decided to move down to

16,600 feet [5060 m]. The plan was for Hans Schwarz to take Tom and for me to take Hank. The rest of the group were to dig the tents out and bring them as soon as possible. Hans and Tom started right away. Half an hour later I took off with Hank. The wind was still very strong and bitter cold, but visibility was good. All of a sudden Hank slipped and I found myself hurtling through the air, flying right over him and landing below him in a pile of soft snow.... Hank was delirious and didn't seem to care what went on; he was almost sleepwalking. As we continued I was very careful, but felt quite insecure with Hank on the rope and a heavy pack on my shoulders. By the time we came to the rocks the storm had regained full force, blowing snow in our mouths, noses and under our goggles. For a while I thought I would suffocate. Hank just wouldn't move because he couldn't see and it seemed a long time before we got down the few rocks. Once on the snow again, our progress was faster, except that the visibility now was zero. Since the wind blew straight from the north I kept at right angles to it and so hoped to find our cache which was marked by two large boulders in the saddle at 16,600 feet [5060 m]. I worried now

Hank Kaufmann leans exhausted on his pack during the storm

about the rest of the party, wondering if they had been able to move at all…. If they didn't come, what could we do? They had all the tents. Would there be suitable snow to build a snow cave?

Suddenly like a ghost the two rocks loomed in front of us. What a relief to see them! Hans and Tom had already been there. They had left their rope and taken the snow shovel. I bedded Hank down in the lee of the rock and then went to look for Hans. This was rather hopeless and I gave it up. All our skis were at the cache so I began to build some sort of shelter for Hank and myself. Suddenly Hans came out of the snow and said he had found a somewhat sheltered spot and that he had built a snow cave there, but needed the skis to finish it…. It was just big enough for Tom and Hank to lie in. To me it looked like a big coffin. Then we dug a hole for ourselves and tried to get some sleep….

Early in the morning I got up and walked over to the cache to see if our friends had come. There was no sign of them. I began to work on a big snow cave, one which would hold all four of us. After he had cooked breakfast, Hans helped me and by noon we could move into our new quarters. Things looked much better now and Hank seemed to regain a little strength. In the evening we talked over our radio and asked Sheldon to fly in if at all possible and look for our friends. This uncertainty hung over us like a big dark cloud.

Again I walked over to the cache in the morning and was glad to see that the storm had died down. However, there was still no trace of our friends. They would have to show up soon or it would mean trouble. Then at 10 a.m. two figures appeared on the ridge. We waited in vain for the other two, but they never came. What does it mean?

After a couple of hours, the two men, Gunti and Pat, arrived in camp.... Their story was grim: After also digging a snow cave in the storm, Leo had passed out and temporarily lost his eyesight. He had been very ill ever since, and Dieter had stayed to look after him.

Hans and I left immediately to bring Leo down. By now we were well acclimatized and in an hour and a half we reached the upper camp. Dieter was busy drying out things and Leo was propped up in a corner of the cave looking terribly ill. I heated some water to dissolve a fudge bar and then gave him two dexodron and two 292 tablets. The way he looked, I felt he needed some drastic action. Fifteen minutes later I had him tied to the end of my rope and slowly we started down. Hans and Dieter packed up the remains of the camp and followed us. In a couple of hours we were down and already Leo had visibly improved. When Hans and Dieter staggered in, they looked beat under their heavy loads. While we set up the tents, Dieter all of a sudden came around and motioned that he had lost his speech and was paralyzed on one side. I thought we had reached the last straw. Hank and Tom still fairly sick, Leo completely exhausted, Dieter half lame—what next? There was one more tense moment when Hank, a normally very amiable fellow, almost went berserk. By now it took only the slightest disagreement and he would start screaming at the top of his lungs. At last we were bedded down for the night and everyone's condition had improved considerably.

On June 18, the weather cleared and the entire team managed to traverse around the mountain to the West Buttress route. To do this, it was necessary to descend 450 metres, cross a bowl, then climb another 300 metres up to a pass. Most of the group was struggling, but Gmoser was strong, breaking trail upward through the deep snow. On reaching the pass, they had a well-marked route to follow, made by parties climbing the mountain from this side. After descending fixed ropes for 500 metres, they put on their skis and continued to Windy Corner. There they were forced to wait for Kaufmann, who was still feeling the effects of the ordeal. Eventually, Gmoser and Schwarz started back up to look for him. In his journal, Hans wrote: "By now we were both mad. Because lately we had done nothing but nurse sick people down the mountain and now that we are on easy terrain, we still have to do the same."

It began to snow again, and Gmoser led his group through the mist:

> We quickly lost our way and soon I found myself out on a steep, huge slope. The snow was so deep that I expected the whole thing to avalanche any minute. There was no turning back! There was the lower lip of a giant crevasse, which was the only flat place on this giant slope. I let myself drop on it and felt immediately that I had gone into a trap! How can I get out of it? I took off skis and pack and literally dug my way up the hill in the chest deep snow. In the meantime the fellows above, especially Gunti Prinz, let a rope down to me. Once tied into it I felt somewhat more secure and thought that my friends could hold me in case of an avalanche. I made about three trips up and down to retrieve all my gear. I couldn't believe that I was still alive when it was all over.

That night, everyone made it down to below Kahiltna Pass at 3050 metres, where they camped next to a group led by Dick McGowan. The next day, Sheldon arrived and dropped some supplies to the men; then, after they had packed a landing strip for him, he touched down in the snow. Soon he took off again with McGowan on board and roared into the mist.

All day on the 20th it continued to snow and they waited and waited, but Sheldon did not return. On the 21st he was back. Hans wrote: "We didn't think he would land, especially since the runway wasn't packed either and there was a foot or so of wind packed snow. But in he came and I must say it was one of the most frightful landings to

Hans relaxes in the tent on the descent from Mount McKinley

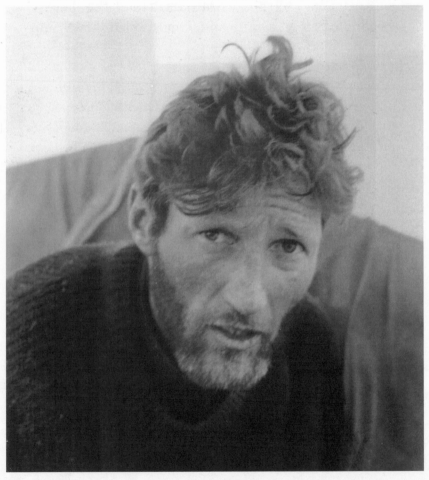

watch. He came in sideways and then bounced over the wind ripples till he finally got stuck in one of them. We now pushed the plane to the end of the runway, turned it around, loaded Jim Laithrop aboard [he had a frostbitten foot] and then Sheldon tried to take off. But with the deep snow and wind he never made it."

The mist came back, it began to snow again and for two days Sheldon and his aircraft were stuck on the glacier. Everyone lay in their tents and waited. Hans wrote: "What a great relaxing feeling—to have absolutely nothing to do! Our tents are pretty well buried under the snow, but now the winds are quiet again and while breakfast is prepared I dig out our tent and then lay back to read and enjoy this lazy day. It is not too often that I get such a rest. Nobody comes to see you; you don't have to go anywhere; no telephone rings. Everything is peaceful and time seems to stand still. Yet there is still enough to do to keep yourself from getting bored—mainly resting. To me this is a perfect holiday."

At last, on June 23, Sheldon managed to get airborne and the climbers broke camp, shouldered their packs and continued down the mountain to the regular landing spot at 2150 metres. It was another two days before Sheldon was able to fly them all out. On the last night, Hans made a final entry in his journal:

> Once again it is all over, like many another trip and yet this is different. While always on such trips there is a certain element of danger present, it was much more so on this trip! God, at times while on the wall I would wake up at night and a loose thought would size up our situation and would almost drive me out of my mind for fear. You quickly have to forget, think of something else and get yourself under control again. Our situation could have been deadly, had the weather turned on us while we were

on the wall. We were very lucky and that's why we are still alive today—and that's why it was such a different trip—and after all we made the first ascent of the Wickersham Wall—probably the highest snow and ice wall in the world!

Birth of an Idea

Back home in the Rockies, Hans was soon busy guiding. He initiated what he called Canadian Mountain Seminars, a trial one-week course at Lake O'Hara that offered instruction in climbing technique to young people. Perhaps he had taken Adolf Bitterlich's comments about reaching out to young climbers to heart and was attempting to do something about it.

In late August, I met Hans Gmoser for the first time. I had discovered the mountains the year before, and my mind was full of dreams of adventure. I read books of the great European climbers in the evenings, and every weekend—summer and winter—was spent in the hills. A mutual friend, Don Gardner, who often assisted Hans at ski camps, asked me if I would help Hans and Leo carry a cookstove to the Stanley Mitchell hut.

Early in the morning, we met at Takakkaw Falls. I was, of course, awed by Hans, who had a tremendous reputation by then, and I said little. Sitting on the tailgate of a truck was a blue-black cookstove and I could hardly believe what was going to happen. After first removing the door, the plates and anything else that was loose, Hans and Leo strapped the frame of the stove, weighing at least 70 kilograms, onto a Kelty pack frame. Hans then slipped his arms through the straps, slowly took the weight on his shoulders and set off for the ten-kilometre walk to the hut. After struggling for 30 minutes along the trail, he rested

Leo and Hans setting off on another adventure

the stove on a log and Leo took his place. All day long the men took turns with the immense load. The 500-metre climb up the Laughing Falls hill into the higher valley was particularly hard, but they struggled on, cursing under their breaths. Gardner and I, along with another friend, Gerry Walsh, struggled under our 30-kilogram packs, which were full of miscellaneous bits of stove. By late afternoon, we reached the hut, and Hans and Leo installed the stove that would be used at their ski camps the next spring.

Following dinner, I stood outside and admired the alpenglow on the surrounding peaks. The rush of the stream, the hoot of the evening owl and the smell of woodsmoke were magic, like some fairy tale that I had only read of. As the stars came out, I returned to the warm hut and climbed the ladder to the sleeping loft. Tired after a hard day's work, I lay there in my sleeping bag and listened to Hans play his zither in the main room below while Leo sang. I was enchanted, and life would never be the same. I became another of the thousands whose lives had been changed by their association with Hans.

In September, Hans was busy with his little editing apparatus. This year, the title of his film was *Skis Over McKinley*, and it was truly spectacular. The opening shots of Mount McKinley towering high above the tundra are beautiful and the river crossings are obviously very dangerous. The footage of Sheldon zooming out of the mist with his red lights flashing, dropping a parcel, then disappearing into the mist, are dramatic. Once again, Hans carried his camera, a Bolex H-16 Rex, right to the summit. It must have been incredibly difficult for him to keep shooting film in the bad weather and after a hard day's work, but he managed it right to the end of the expedition. He knew that he must have a complete story to tell.

The brochure for Hans's film presentation in 1963–1964

In October, Hans presented his film at the Jubilee Auditorium in Calgary. I was there in the audience, along with two thousand other mountain lovers. Hans was in good form, telling his story to the hometown fans, and at intermission we all migrated as usual to the large foyer for a drink and to socialize. Hans joined us and worked the crowd, speaking with old friends and new. As he neared me, my heart beat more quickly; then he smiled and said "Hi, Chic. I hope you are enjoying the show." He had remembered my name! The master charmer knew that the nicest thing you can do for anyone is to remember his or her name.

After the intermission, Hans presented some footage showing helicopter skiing on Mount Sir Wilfred Laurier the previous spring. When he showed the film at MIT (Massachusetts Institute of Technology) in Boston, Brooks Dodge, the legendary US Olympic ski champion, came up to him after the show and said he was interested in bringing a small group to western Canada for some ski touring, and enquired "about having a helicopter for one or two days." Back in Canada, Hans worked on the idea. Initially, he thought the ideal location would be Rogers Pass, as there was great snow, great skiing and a helicopter stationed nearby in Revelstoke, but he was unable to get permission from the national park authorities. In the end, the trip with Dodge did not materialize.

However, Hans's ski-touring program for the late winter and early spring of 1964 went ahead, but with something new added that year—a Jim McConkey week, where better-than-average skiers could improve their powder skiing under the tutelage of the master. There was a Mount Assiniboine tour; six weeks in the Little Yoho; a tour to the Mummery and Freshfield icefields; a tour up onto the Columbia Icefield; and, to finish the season, several weeks of spring skiing at Rogers Pass.

In April, Hans led a ski tour to the Bugaboos, ostensibly to shoot film for the coming year's movie. With him were Linda Crutchfield; Scott and Wayne Henderson, who were ski racers from Banff; and ski instructors Mike Wiegele and Lorne "Oakie" O'Connor. After struggling with their four-wheel-drive truck through the snow and mud of the access road, they unloaded a snowmobile that then pulled the skiers to an abandoned logging camp near the end of the valley. The next morning, they skied up the glacier and set up camp under Marmolata. For a few days it snowed and they waited, full of anticipation, in their tents. Then it cleared and the spectacular Bugaboos emerged from the clouds. In fresh powder and early-morning light, the group ascended higher up the glacier below the south face of Snowpatch Spire to the Pigeon-Howser col. Hans remarked years later, "While we climbed I kept looking around and said this is the place." He had, at last, found the place where helicopter skiing might work.

Two months later, Hans was hired to assist a Japanese team, the Kansei Gakuin University Expedition, in their ascent of the east ridge of Mount Logan. Unfortunately, after walking and skiing the Kaskawulsh Glacier route to base camp, Hans stepped into a hole and twisted his knee so badly that he had to be evacuated by air to Whitehorse. While recuperating in Banff, he remained busy organizing his Canadian Mountain Seminars. This year, six weeks of climbing instruction, including a rock-climbing course and several basic, intermediate and advanced mountaineering courses, were offered at Lac des Arcs, at Lake O'Hara and in the Bugaboos.

Hans's film for the winter of 1964–1965 was called *Adventure Bound*. In his brochure, Hans listed 53 lecture dates, both to major cities such as New York, Chicago, Seattle, Montreal and Toronto, and to smaller venues such as Dawson Creek, Jasper and Golden. From October 2 until February 19, Hans was on the road, driving all night to reach the next presentation. Hans recalled years later that he even did a little barnstorming: "I would go to Seattle for instance, and rent the Palomar Theatre ... I got some posters printed, got somebody to help me put up the posters, got the local ticket office to sell the tickets, sent a mailing to the Seattle Mountaineers and then I came back the day before the show."

Adventure Bound was one of his best movies. Hans begins with a few scenes from his brief Mount Logan adventure with the Japanese team the previous spring: "Each step takes them further away from what we regard as safety, the haven of civilization. And yet by evening, completely cut off from any other human beings, they sit happily around their campfire. They have once more freed themselves from a world stifled by meaningless conventions, riled with corruption and reeking with hypocrisy."

Soon he gets to the skiing. "Skiing as an adventurous sport has given man the means to visibly express his desire to free himself from the drudgery of everyday life." Hans shows scenes of the World Professional Ski Championships held at Heavenly Valley, California, featuring legendary skiers of the time such as Christian Pravda, Stein Erickson, Pepi Gramshammer, Adrian Duvillard and Othmar Schneider.

The heart of the film is his Bugaboo adventure. "After three hours' walking which was beautiful beyond belief and seemed like a dream, we arrived at the Pigeon-Howser col, right in the heart of the Bugaboo Spires. Everyone is overwhelmed and enraptured by the sights we see." Around them, the view of the spires is indeed spectacular.

On the screen Hans then introduces his friend Mike Wiegele. In those days, he and Mike were especially close and Mike appeared in all Hans's movies. Unfortunately, their friendship would later fall apart, but in 1964 Mike was one of the stars of Hans's productions:

Mike takes his skiing more seriously than anything else he does. He is a dedicated ski instructor and goes to any trouble to perfect and improve his skiing. Opinions about ski instructors vary across the scale of human behaviour—from the gigolo playboy, lady-killer type to the uninspiring, dull man of the middle, to the sincere, devoted instructor who can turn his good intentions into reality and give you the feeling that your skiing is a personal concern of his and that you have benefited greatly from his instructions. Mike is a wonderful combination; I have spent many months with him and don't remember any time when he didn't have a smile for you. Any situation is fun for Mike, and yet as a ski instructor he gives 100 per cent interest and devotion to your skiing problem, even though he is a great hit with the ladies and seldom misses an opportunity.

At the end of Part One, Hans eloquently bids farewell to the Bugaboos: "Soon our ski tracks on those glistening slopes will have been drifted over by the ever-shifting snows. Our joyous shouts have long since vanished into the blue sky above, and a great silence settles once more over those mountains, broken only by an occasional rumbling avalanche, the creaking of the glacier and the howling of the winds which sweep over those glaciers with each new storm."

In Part Two, Hans returns to the Bugaboos in the summer and climbs Snowpatch Spire. He likely climbed the mountain on two occasions to get all the footage he required. On his first outing, he was climbing with Leo, Mike, Dick Lofthouse and a young German woman, Lilo Schmid. As they set off up the steep, blank granite of the spire, the most difficult in the range, Hans cracks one of

In the 1960s, Hans Gmoser was North America's mountain idol

his funnier jokes: "Lilo, who had never climbed on granite before, was as nervous as a royal guard with a squirrel running up his pant leg."

Dick does most of the leading, but on occasion Hans goes ahead, giving the camera to Leo. They must have only got halfway up the climb by day's end, for the cast of climbers suddenly changes. Mike and Dick disappear and Franz takes their place. The images of Franz leading the Wiessner Traverse and the Vein Pitch are excellent considering how hard it was for Hans to move around on the vertical terrain. After the summit, a series of spectacular rappels takes them back down to the base of the mountain, from where they run to their campsite for food and drink.

Overnight it snowed, and Hans comments:

> [In the morning] it looked almost like winter, and were we ever glad that we had done our climb. Now it would be out of the question. Who knows, winter might have set in for good and it won't be long before the deep snow blanket will have silenced the rushing creeks and waterfalls, and the Bugaboos will pierce the clear winter sky in their frozen splendour, while the skiers climb up those snow flanks, bound for new adventures. They come back, time and time again. It is almost like a ritual, a religion. There is no tangible benefit from all those adventurous journeys into the mountains. The thrills are as short and as fleeting as a jump through the air, a quick turn in the powder. It is the memories which stay with us, like a light glowing in the background when everything else around us has become grey and dreary. These memories linger on and in times of need they can make our hearts leap just as high and as far as the spirit of

adventure makes these people leap on their skis now.

For almost a decade, Hans had travelled North America with his films, inspiring jaded audiences who were looking for something new and exciting. He had also led a number of remarkable expeditions where he had been an enormously energetic and hard-working leader. It must be remembered, however, that through his lectures, it was Hans who got the recognition and savoured the fruits of success, his teammates largely forgotten. According to one of them, "We were all Hans' donkeys."

Despite his success, at the end of it all, Hans was as poor as he had been at the start. He had nothing to show for all his hard work except a few pairs of skis, a climbing rope and his tattered knickers. The next phase in his life would change all that.

PART FOUR

Heli-skiing Takes Off

1965-1991

"I couldn't see this kind of weekend operation making much sense. I felt then that there must be people out there to pay one hundred bucks a day to get that kind of skiing, but where are they and how do you organize it."

The First Year, 1965

The world changed for Hans in the spring of 1965. Helicopter-assisted skiing, something that he had toyed with for two years, literally took off. The success that he had struggled so long to achieve would soon become a reality, but it would not be easy. Years later, Gmoser wrote:

Here on the Bugaboo Glacier I had found the place where a trip such as Brookie had proposed would be possible. On the way to the Bugaboos we spent one night in an abandoned lumber camp near the foot of Bugaboo Glacier. With a little effort, this camp would provide adequate housing for our guests. Since this area was neither a national nor a provincial park, we could fly the helicopter at will. With the helicopter stationed at the lumber camp, we could fly when the weather was good; and when the weather was poor, we could climb the mountains with skins on our skis as we had always done. I had no concerns about the quality of the skiing. One week of ski touring and my summer knowledge of the area convinced me that this would be, by far, the best skiing any of us had ever experienced.

In his 1964–1965 brochure, Hans offered the complete selection of ski tours that he had offered in previous years, plus two weeks of helicopter skiing in the Bugaboos. One week would be reserved for Brooks Dodge and his group, and he hoped to interest enough clients for another week. The announcement reads: "For the first time we are organizing ski touring weeks where we use helicopters for the uphill transportation in Canada's most spectacular ski country. Depending on the number of participants, each person will get anywhere from 7 to 12 trips on the helicopter during this week. Each trip will enable them to make a 3 to 5 mile downhill run. On days when the weather does not permit flying, regular ski tours will be arranged. All inclusive cost, party of 15 $203 each, party of 10 $266 each."

The first commercial helicopter ski week began in the Bugaboos on April 4, 1965, with six of Gmoser's long-time clients: Bob Sutherland, Lloyd Nixon, Inga Thompson, Dieter von Hennig, Erling Lunde and Ed Sutton. Jim Davies was again the pilot of the Bell 47 G-1 helicopter, Franz was base camp manager and Emily Flender, from Cambridge, Massachusetts, the cook.

Dieter von Hennig described that first week:

Hans met us in Banff, from whence we drove in various cars to the logging road that accessed the Bugaboos. We then switched to the Nodwell, a tracked all terrain vehicle, which better negotiated the muddy road. I recall passing a trapper's cabin where we saw beaver skins hanging out to dry. We stayed in an unused sawmill camp, composed of cookhouse, where we ate our meals, and which

*On the way to the Bugaboos in April 1965. Dieter von Hennig on left,
Inga Thompson on right, Hans in light-coloured jacket in back
and Franz Dopf in dark sweater with back to camera.*

*The helicopter arriving to drop off skiers on
the Bugaboo Glacier on the first morning*

In the dining room at the Bugaboo sawmill. Hans on left in white shirt and Franz across from him in dark sweater. Ann and Brooks Dodge on right.

Emily Flender was the cook in 1965

also contained a couple of bunk rooms for Hans, Jim Davies the helicopter pilot, and Emily Flender the cook. The others slept in small individual cabins, with plywood sides. Hans pointed to one and said Lloyd Nixon and I should take that one. I could barely open the door, as the cabin was full of snow. First I thought it was a joke. But we were assigned another, or the snow was shoveled out, according to Lloyd. Hans would wake us in the morning by coming in the cabin to light a fire in the small wood-burning stove. We slept on iron bedsteads in our own sleeping bags.

On the first day of skiing, they flew high on the Bugaboo Glacier and had a superb run down to the valley. The next day, they skied partway down the Vowell Glacier but were unwilling to risk descending into the valley in case there were problems with the helicopter and it could not pick them up. Later in the week, unable to fly high due to weather, they skied south-facing corn slopes on a lower peak via a run that came to be known as Sauce Alley.

During the second week, 12 members of Brooks Dodge's group from the Chamois Ski Club of Boston and the Wildcat Mountain Ski Club of Pinkham Notch made their way to the Bugaboos. They were Judy Allen, Ken and Tom Boll, Roger Cameron, Carl Dahl, Brooks and Ann Dodge, Charlie Gibson, Bill Nichols, Jan Philip, Munro Proctor and Jim Schenck. Gmoser wrote: "We drove our guests 28 miles along a very poor and partially snow-covered logging road from the small town of Brisco to the Bugaboos. With Brookie Dodge's first group that trip took from 5:00 in the afternoon until 2:00 the next morning. Numerous times we were stuck in the mud, got rained upon and pushed the vehicles for a good part of the way. It wasn't too long before one of those early guests took me aside and said, 'Why don't you charge another $30 and fly us in and out.'"

Hans described how it all worked:

> The routine is every day as follows. Assuming that we have a group of 16 skiers they will be broken up into two parties of eight. While everybody eats breakfast the pilot warms up the helicopter and as soon as this is done the first two are lifted to the top of their run. In short order the other six are brought up and then this party will begin to ski down. In the meantime group number two is flown up. When this is done the first group is already waiting in another valley to fly to the top of their next run and during that time group number two follows their ski tracks on the first run. In this manner we make anywhere from two to four runs, by which time it is 1 or 2 pm. We all now return to the lumber camp and rest for tomorrow's skiing.

The risks of helicopter skiing were soon made abundantly clear. In the middle of the second week, the helicopter crashed while landing at the top of Sauce Alley. Jim had flown up with Hans and one client and was landing on the flat mountaintop when the landing gear sunk into deep snow. The helicopter tipped, the rotor struck the ground and the machine rapidly beat itself to death. The three men managed to get out safely before the helicopter started to burn, and the flames were extinguished quickly, but the helicopter was a complete writeoff. Jim made a trip to Golden to find another helicopter to finish the week. In spite of this setback, the two weeks were deemed a great success, and Hans immediately began planning the next year's heli-ski adventure and a future lodge in the valley.

The last week in April, Hans was guiding in the Little Yoho when he finally met his match: Margaret Grace MacGougan from Calgary, who was a few days short of her

The first group of heli-skiers in 1965 on the Bugaboo Glacier.
Left to right: Inga Thompson, Franz Dopf, Erling Lunde,
Lloyd Nixon, Hans Gmoser, Bob Sutherland and Ed Sutton.

Jim Davies fuelling up the helicopter in 1965

The helicopter that crashed during the second week of heli-skiing in 1965

20th birthday. She and her brother Don had wanted to ski tour onto the Wapta Icefield with a youth hostel group, but her father, Dr. Keir MacGougan, worried about the safety of that plan and offered to pay for them both to join Hans's ski-touring group at the Stanley Mitchell hut.

In the words of McConkey, Hans was "all gaga" over Margaret. She was pretty, intelligent and adventurous and came from a good family. She had fallen in love with the mountains and was out with the youth hostel group every weekend, carrying a heavy pack and breaking trail through deep snow with the guys. Most importantly, she was just as strong-willed and determined as Hans. The fact that she was 13 years younger than him didn't seem to make much difference. Margaret, on the other hand, says that she was oblivious to Hans that first week. It seems hard to imagine. Hans was, after all, handsome, charming, romantic and famous. According to Margaret, Hans was intrigued because she didn't pay any attention to him at all.

After her ski week with Hans, Margaret returned the following week to the Little Yoho with three of her Calgary friends: Connie Wilcock, Charlie Locke and Bernd Kohlfurst, who later changed his name to Jonn Calvert. The cook, Myrna Collins, was expecting a big group that week, so Margaret volunteered to help in the kitchen. Sometime during that visit the connection between Hans and Margaret was made, for Hans invited her to meet him in the Bugaboos a few weeks later. He was doing a ski traverse along the Purcell Mountains and would reach the Bugaboos after about seven days.

Late in the month, on what would be his last expedition, Hans skied 60 kilometres across the Purcells from Toby Creek near Windermere to the Bugaboos. With him were Jim McConkey and his wife, Glenn; Mike Wiegele; Scott Henderson; and Erwin Tontsch. The trip went well and they had reasonably good weather all the way amongst beautiful glaciated terrain—across the Commander Glacier, past Mount Monica, across the Starbird Glacier, past Eyebrow Peak and along Stockdale Creek and Howser Creek. After five days, they were unable to find their airdropped food cache because of new snow, so the last two days they had little to eat. According to Scott Henderson, they were so hungry that they drank the bacon grease the final morning. To finish the trip, they crossed Phacelia Pass into the headwaters of Bugaboo Creek, where they met Margaret, who with Myrna Collins had made her way in via the old logging road from Brisco.

For a few days they ski toured from a camp on the Bugaboo Glacier, one day making a ski ascent of Anniversary Peak. Hans, of course, filmed all of this for the following year's movie. The team had planned to continue on for another 130 kilometres across the Purcells and Selkirks to Rogers Pass, but according to McConkey, Mike Wiegele broke a ski and the rest of the trip was aborted. Mike, however, had a different story: Hans was so infatuated with Margaret that he decided to end their tour at the Bugaboos. Whatever the reason, the entire group made their way to Brisco and back to Banff, where, on May 29, Hans wrote a letter to the director of British Columbia Lands and Forests, expressing a desire to purchase or lease a small tract of land near the source of Bugaboo Creek "suitable for a ski, mountaineering and hiking resort."

In early June, Hans visited the new ski resort of Whistler, north of Vancouver, where they were just building the first lifts. Hans skied by helicopter high on the mountain; then, after a brief trip to Victoria to see the assistant superintendent of Lands about his resort proposal, he returned to the Rockies to begin his summer guiding program. From late June until early September, Hans ran seven mountain seminars: rock-climbing courses at Lac des Arcs, and mountaineering courses at Lake O'Hara and

Mike Wiegele and Hans (in white cap)
at a camp on the Purcell ski traverse

in the Bugaboos. Margaret cooked all summer for him at these camps. From July 18 to 31, Hans worked for The Alpine Club of Canada at their summer camp at Glacier Lake. Hans was indeed a busy man in 1965. He had guided 300 people on 21 ski tours in the late winter and early spring, and during the summer had guided mountain climbing for almost three months straight. In the middle of all this, Hans continued his negotiations to lease the land in the Bugaboos, learning that he would have to get a release from Stone and Gillis Sawmill Ltd. and from Kicking Horse Lumber Ltd. On October 20, Hans staked 160 acres where he planned to build his resort, and in the following weeks published in the *British Columbia Gazette* and *Golden Star* newspaper notice of his intentions. In November, the plot thickened when he learned that the Ski Club of the Canadian Rockies, which owned the Lake

Louise ski resort, had also expressed interest in building a ski resort at the head of Bugaboo Creek.[1]

That autumn, while preparing to tour North America with his latest film presentation, Hans gave a speech to the Canadian Ski Instructors Alliance. It was pure Hans Gmoser—romantic, passionate and idealistic. Here are some excerpts:

> [The ski tourer] wants of course the thrill of downhill skiing. But he wants this thrill enhanced by the satisfaction derived from the physical exertion needed to get to the top of his run, by the grandeur of the country wherein he skis and by the undisturbed silent mountain atmosphere which is so conducive to profound thought, into a complete

Arriving at the Bugaboos. Jim McConkey on left with shovel sticking out of pack, Margaret MacGougan behind, Hans in white cap and Mike Wiegele at right.

experience. In addition to the somewhat frivolous thrill of dancing down the hill he also seeks the aesthetic values inherent in the mountain country to which the ordinary skier is completely oblivious.

This is perhaps not in keeping with the pace of our modern times. We are today geared for fast and superficial living. Being caught up in this whirl we are no more aware of it than one realizes that you are dizzy as long as you are turning. Therefore most skiers cannot imagine that there could be any fun in skiing if you had to walk up.

… Ski touring takes us onto those mountains and slopes which we always look at from the top of our lifts and wish we were over there instead of here. It gives us the means to manifest our, however hidden and subconscious, desires to explore the distant, the new, the unknown, to be adventurers, to be able to throw the shackles of our physical limitations and to go wherever our fancy urges us to go….

… [I]t is a simple law, you have to put out in order to receive….

I am quite convinced that ski touring will never achieve the same popularity as lift skiing, unless our society will undergo a drastic change and switches its emphasis from materialism to humanism. This seems very unlikely although I deem it most essential to the survival of mankind….

It is my contention that if you offer something worthwhile people will come, no matter how far they have to travel. The important thing is you must provide the type of skiing which they can get nowhere else….

[For] uphill transportation for ski touring we need something with far more versatility and mobility than the convenient types of ski lifts. And the machine to fit the bill is a helicopter.

Hans went on to explain the risks and dangers of heli-skiing, as well as its financial aspects. What is interesting in this speech is that he presented helicopter skiing as an extension of ski touring. He spoke of the need to escape from "fast and superficial living." The downhill run is, as he says, "frivolous"; the essential is the magnificent country that we are privileged to share.

Hans's film for 1965–1966 was called *Roving Skis*. Erwin Tontsch had played a large part in the filming, and once again Jim Tarrant provided the music. The narrative was held together by the footage Hans had shot while traversing the Purcell Mountains in May. As the film progresses, he alternates between images of skiers laden with heavy packs, skiing past majestic mountains, and ski races he had filmed the previous winter at Lake Louise and at Heavenly Valley, California. He also shows images of his ski trip to Whistler and of heli-skiing in the Bugaboos:

> The rapidly whirling blades of the helicopter kicked up the soft powder snow and for a moment it looked as though we were engulfed in a raging blizzard. There was a gentle bump and we had come to rest on a small tabletop-like area. As the swirling snow settled we found ourselves amidst mountain scenery of such magnificence that one could only gasp and stare. Time at such a moment is very precious, though, and so we quickly got out, unloaded our skis, and the helicopter lifted up and literally peeled over the steep edge. For a moment we could hear the high-pitched whine as the helicopter just dropped with the blades in autorotation; then the noise of the engine cut in, and with a deep, steady hum we could see the helicopter fly out along the valley where a large, clear area indicated the site of our base camp.

Up here it was silent now. The early-morning sun was barely noticeable in the cold mountain air at 10,000 feet. Ten minutes earlier we had just stepped from the breakfast table in our lumber camp into the helicopter, and in a short, spectacular flight he lifted us 5000 feet up onto this peak.

There is also footage of skiing up Anniversary Peak and of Hans and Margaret sharing a summit kiss: "In old European tradition all the girls have to be kissed when they arrive on the top. I even got one from this pretty girl and this was the beginning of the end for my gay bachelor days."

The film ends with an ascent of the *Red Shirt* route on Yamnuska. Leo, dressed in a bright red shirt, is the star of the film and is shown leading a client from Seattle, Bob Albrecht, up the climb. The footage is remarkable, Erwin shooting long shots of the "flies on the wall" and Hans shooting close-ups of the action. The route ends with the famous exposed traverse rightward around a pillar, then up to the top. "Leo now starts the last lead. His shoelace has just come untied, and nonchalantly he bends down to tie it up again. Continuing on this long traverse, he makes the most spectacular moves of the whole climb." Just a few moments later, Hans traversed out to the corner and Leo took a photo that would become one of the most famous images ever of Hans Gmoser.

Hans showed the film to over 50 audiences throughout North America. Margaret, who at the time was studying sociology at the University of Western Ontario, joined Hans for part of his road trip in the eastern United States. She remembered, "My parents did not know about this. They were not too happy that I was going with Hans, since he was 13 years older than me and had 'a reputation with the girls' through the ACC."

Hans Gmoser leads the final pitch on the Red Shirt route on Yamnuska

Years of Rapid Growth

In the spring of 1966, Hans increased Bugaboo helicopter skiing to six weeks, operating from March 20 to April 30, at a cost of $240/week for the 70 individuals who had signed up. Jim Davies was again the pilot, flying a turbocharged Bell 47G-3 B1 helicopter owned by Bullock Helicopters. Myrna Collins was the cook; Bob Geber, a young skier and climber originally from Germany, assisted with the guiding; and Lloyd "Kiwi" Gallagher, who had just arrived in Banff the year before from New Zealand, was hired to keep the snowmobiles running and to help Myrna with camp chores.

Based once again in the sawmill, the little band led a rustic life and the guests would often help with the chores, mainly chopping wood. After a day of skiing, they would roast in the sauna, drinking a few beers. In the evening, Hans would play his zither and entertain the guests with lovely Austrian folk songs such as *"Bergvagabunden"* ("Mountain Vagabonds"). Then it was early to bed. Hans would lie there in the dark, a candle by his head, reading, always improving his English and his knowledge of the world.

For the first few years, Hans and his guests stayed close to home and, as it would take Jim about 75 minutes to get ten people to the top, skied only two or three runs a day. A favourite was the Bugaboo run, down Bugaboo Glacier right to the forest. Sometimes they skied a run called Bay Street, near the headwaters of Bugaboo Creek, which would achieve notoriety years later. If the weather was good, they skied high on the glaciers: from the Snowpatch-Pigeon col down to the Bugaboo-Snowpatch col, then on down the steep face below; or from the Pigeon-Howser col down the Vowell Glacier. One year, Jim landed right on the top of Mount Conrad and the guests enjoyed a 1500-metre descent down the Conrad Glacier. On the bad-weather days, a regular choice was the nearby Sauce Alley, from the bottom of which the snowmobile would pull them along the road, back to the sawmill.

Hans remembered years later, "Jim and I would consult the four sheets of the 1:50,000 topo maps of the Bugaboos, that we had tacked onto the back door of the cook shack to see where we might fly to today. There were vast snowfields, particularly to the west. It all looked very inviting. Once in the air I would point to a peak and Jim would either nod his head or point to another peak. If we both nodded our heads at the same peak this was where he would land."

Back in Calgary, Elfi Grillmair had been running the office since the spring of 1961. However, with three young children to care for, she found that the workload was just getting too great for her, so she asked Hans to find someone

Setting off from Brisco for the Bugaboos in 1966.
Sitting on fence at left are Alan and Doug Stewart.
In the back of the truck on the right are Ann and Brooks Dodge.

Myrna Collins and Kiwi Gallagher do the laundry

else. In May of 1966, Gertie Hartefeld took over the duties from her home in Banff.

Hans was the last of his close group to marry, Philippe having married a Frenchwoman, Mireille Le Bars, in 1960. Keir MacGougan, Margaret's dad, was not in favour of the marriage. Barb MacGougan, Margaret's younger sister, recalls listening through the door while her father hollered, "You will marry that man over my dead body." So Margaret waited until she was 21 and her father could do nothing about it. Hans and Margaret were married on May 28, 1966, in St. Paul's Presbyterian Church in Banff. Leo was the best man, and Carol Patton the maid of honour; the bridesmaids were Barb and Linda Tigner. Mike Wiegele and Margaret's brother Don were the ushers.[2] It was an old Austrian tradition for the male friends of the groom to "steal the bride" and take her drinking in the local bars during the reception. It was then the best man's job to find the bride before the bar bills, for which he was responsible, got too high. After sending a telegram to Leo from the CPR station, the men took Margaret to the Tom Tom Lounge in the Mountainholme Lodge, where they all had a good party. Eventually, Leo found them and they returned to the Timberline Hotel, where the wedding reception was in progress. According to Margaret, "My grandmother was horrified that I was missing my wedding party and had been out with the men in the bars. The groom is supposed to enjoy his last freedom during this time and dance with all the pretty girls." In marrying Hans, she had broken the mould: "He was a foreigner with an accent and not a doctor. My whole family, including an uncle and grandfather and grandmother, were all medical."

After the wedding, Hans and Margaret set up housekeeping in a small, simple home in Harvie Heights near Canmore that Hans had been renting from the Hartefelds. Later that year, they would buy the house, and it would be their home for 40 years. It was in a quiet location. Across the road from the house, the forest stretched unbroken for many kilometres into the mountains.

Not long after, from June 5 to 19, the ACMG held their first guides' certification course. For two weeks Brian Greenwood, who was running the course, and the four aspirants climbed in the Banff area. Then, according to Hans, who was technical chairman of the ACMG, "Brian simply left me with the candidates, gave me no notes nor any explanation as to how they had performed, and took off. The candidates all felt that they had passed. So I marched them up to the administration building, went into the licensing office and declared that all four had passed the guides' exam. All four then received their guides' badges."

Brian Greenwood had a completely different version of events. In a 1996 interview, he recalled:

> We decided to run a guides' course. I think Peter Fuhrmann and Leo Grillmair were going to be the instructors. I set it all up at the Alpine Club, bought all the food and made all the arrangements. I thought I planned the course pretty well. We went climbing and had a few lessons indoors. I arranged for some Alpine Club Calgary people to come out towards the end of the course to do a climb. That all worked smoothly. I arranged for Walter Perren and Hans and Bob Hind to come out and be an examining committee. But Walter Perren was the only one that ever showed up. At the beginning of the course Leo and Peter both couldn't make it. So I was left. I thought, "Well, I'll do it myself." I thought it went quite well.

This misunderstanding would intensify the rivalry that was developing between Hans and Brian and widen the split that was growing in the mountain community between the Brits and the continental Europeans.

In late June, Ruedi Gertsch, a Swiss aspirant mountain guide and top ski racer, showed up in Banff. Seeing a poster in Monod's sports shop, he walked over to John and Gertie's house; after a brief chat with Fritz Jungener, who phoned Hans, Ruedi was hired. The next day, he was guiding at Lake O'Hara. Ruedi would go on to be Hans's lead guide and play a major role in creating Hans's heli-ski operation.

That summer, Margaret once again cooked for Hans at his climbing camps; then, in the autumn, she rented a basement suite in Calgary and continued her university studies

HANS GMOSER

Presents in Person

HIGH ROAD TO SKIING

A COLOR SKI AND MOUNTAIN ADVENTURE FILM

towards her degree. Meanwhile, Hans put together another film and hit the road. For the 1966–1967 season, the show was called *High Road to Skiing*. It begins with shots of the Canadian Alpine Ski Team working out at Notre Dame College in Nelson, BC, followed by a long sequence of ski -racing at the du Maurier International Ski Race at Mount Norquay near Banff. To end Part One, there is the mandatory heli-skiing, leavened with repeated images of Kiwi cartwheeling in deep powder snow and surfacing with a smile. Lloyd had climbed extensively in New Zealand, but at that time he was a novice skier. Eventually, he would master the sport and become an accomplished heli-ski guide.

During a ski-mountaineering sequence in Part Two, there is the requisite Gmoser idealistic philosophy:

> Even though there are thousands of people who go to the mountains, who camp, who look for the life in the out-of-doors, they do not realize that in order to fully experience the mountains one has to deprive oneself of the comforts we have at home. Instead they take more junk and gadgets into the wilds than they have at home.

St. Dionysius Church in Traun

The Lambacher hut

The Spitzmauer, seen from the Prielschutzhaus

The Dachstein, seen over the Auseer area. In 1948 Hans wrote
of this view: "Lucky is the person who can witness all of this."

The Wilder Kaiser from the Stripsenjoch

Photo: Chic Scott

The Grossglockner, seen from Heiligenblut

Approaching Yamnuska along the 1A Highway

Lizzie Rummel's cabin near Mount Assiniboine

*Mount Assiniboine seen from near
Lizzie Rummel's cabin on Sunburst Lake*

Photo: Chic Scott

Mount Assiniboine in winter from Mount Assiniboine Lodge

Ski touring above the Little Yoho Valley.
On the left, The Vice President; on the right, The President;
and between them, the President Glacier.

The Finger, just west of Banff

Calgary
Route

Direttissima

Yamnuska

Grillmair
Chimneys

Photo: Lloyd Gallagher archives

Mount Robson's south face towers 3000 metres above the valley.

Mount Blackburn, reflected in Willow Lake

Mount Alberta

Modern climbers on the summit ridge of Mount Alberta

Brussels Peak

With phonographs and transistor radios, they shatter the melodious silence of nature and then perhaps wonder why those days in the mountains leave them so empty. To those who come pure and simple with eyes and ears open, the mountains are a constant source of wonderment. They are ever-changing. Now in a cold, forbidding beauty, so distant, yet somehow tempting—then in friendly, warm sunlight, inviting you to enjoy yourself on the warm, clear rocks on the smooth, shining glaciers; and then again unreal as a picture for you to behold just with your eyes. And this in a way is the essence of the mountain experience which the real mountaineer treasures so much.

The final 15 minutes of the film feature Mike Wiegele and Bob Albrecht climbing the north face of Anniversary Peak. Then Hans wraps it up with some spectacular shots of skiing amongst the Bugaboo Spires. "Here the High Road to Skiing takes us through a part of our earth where man can take a brief pause from his blind rush for more, better, higher, faster, bigger, richer—and let himself be awed by nature in its purest state, whose wilderness knows more order and peace than man's most sophisticated civilizations."

To young skiers and climbers around North America, these words were music to the ears. The schedule printed in his brochure for 1966–1967 reveals that Hans showed this film at 47 venues across the continent. According to the brochure, Hans began to market his adventures for the first time under the name Canadian Mountain Holidays. The address given is Box 583, Banff, Alberta. CMH had come to Banff.

In the spring of 1967, heli-skiing continued to grow. That year, ten weeks were offered; there were 150 guests, and the cost of a ski week had risen to $270. There were even four weeks when there were two groups, Bob Geber leading the second group. Kiwi kept the snowmobiles running and acted as tail guide, which meant carrying the pack with the lunch food, a rope and other emergency equipment. To move them around, pilot Jim Davies had a new helicopter, an Alouette II with the Artouste jet engine. It was a much more powerful machine, with a climb rate of 150 metres per minute. If he flew with only a third of a tank of fuel and removed the battery after the engine was running, he could carry four passengers; otherwise, he could take only three.

CMH experienced its first serious skiing accident that year. While skiing a steep and icy pitch of frozen corn snow, Emily Flender, the cook from the first season, who had returned as a guest, slipped and careened at great speed down the slope into a tree, resulting in a double compound fracture of the lower leg. Jim flew back to the sawmill, where he picked up doctor Paul Rondo. Rondo had to leap three metres from the hovering machine and then cut down a tree before Jim could land and pick up Emily. They put her in a stretcher on the outside of the helicopter and back in camp transferred her to the inside of the machine. Then Jim flew straight to the General Hospital in Calgary. Because the Alouette helicopter had shorter rotor blades, he could just squeeze into the gap at the emergency entrance, which shocked a few people. Sadly, Emily's skiing days were finished.

Flying helicopters in those early years was a dicey profession, and there were several incidents, fortunately none of them fatal. One evening, while Jim was flying by himself out to the highway, the fuel control failed, the red light came on and Jim had no choice but to slowly settle the machine into the trees. Jim remembered, "It was very noisy." Luckily, the helicopter stayed upright and the rotor blades remained intact. In deep snow, Jim walked

11 kilometres out to the road. When he returned a few days later, in another machine with an aircraft engineer, they had to follow Jim's footprints in the snow to find the downed aircraft. After the engineer had repaired the fuel control and installed a new tail rotor, Jim cut down the surrounding trees, got into the damaged aircraft, started it up and flew it out.

On February 15, 1967, Hans finally cleared the legal hurdles and received approval for a 21-year lease on ten acres of land where he could build his lodge and on 2,000 acres in reserve for development, with easements for lift lines. The folks in Victoria could not really get their heads around the kind of operation he was running. What he wanted, and would spend years working to acquire, was tenure to hundreds of square kilometres in the surrounding mountains for skiing.

Now that Hans had his land for his lodge in the Bugaboos, he needed the money to build it. For years, when he was in Calgary, he had been visiting his friend Jack MacKenzie, an oil industry businessman with whom he had shared a number of climbing and skiing adventures. Jack and his partner, Charles Barlow, had often said to Hans, "When you want to build a lodge come and see us." To raise the $100,000 that the lodge was going to cost, they proposed that they would put up $25,000 in equity, and Hans and Leo would put up $15,000. The key element of the proposal was that Hans would raise a minimum of $60,000 through what they called "skier's loans." They sold for $5,000 apiece, paid 6 per cent interest and enabled the owner of the loan to take a free helicopter ski week each year until the loan was repaid. Another benefit of these loans was that the owners got the right to make priority bookings. Hans was able to sell 15 of them with little trouble, and in no time they had the money to build the lodge. Hans considered that the proposal "was very fair to Leo and me, but it also imposed a lot of discipline. We had never had to handle money and all of a sudden people give you $100,000 and it's very easy to blow the money and have nothing to show for it." Hans was largely a self-taught individual. Over the years, he had taught himself to ski, to climb, to be a guide, to speak and write eloquent English and to be a filmmaker. He was now teaching himself to be a businessman. Bugaboo Helicopter Skiing Ltd., the company that would own the lodge, was incorporated on May 23, 1967. The shareholders were Hans and Leo, through their company, Rocky Mountain Guides Limited;[3] Jack Mackenzie and his wife, Sheila; and Charles Barlow and his wife, Geraldine.

Hans and his three close mountain friends were all reunited for the lodge construction. Philippe was, of course, the architect, reworking plans he had already drawn up for a lodge in the Little Yoho. (In 1963, Hans had investigated the idea of building a ski lodge not far from the Stanley Mitchell hut and had requested Philippe's help. The idea was ultimately shelved, but the plans were still there, waiting to be used.) Franz was the general contractor, and Leo the project manager. First, they spent three weeks fixing the road so that they could get big trucks to the site. The lodge was actually built by a bunch of Canadian cowboys from the Columbia Valley. Franz remembered years later, "In the floor there were more nails bent over than driven in straight." One of the thorniest issues was whether there would be indoor plumbing. Hans remembered, "I didn't think an outhouse was any hardship. It worked perfectly well. I thought it makes things a lot simpler. You don't have to have all this plumbing inside the building. You just have a couple of nice little outhouses." Hans was overruled and indoor plumbing was installed. The guests, however, slept in bunk beds in communal rooms and had to walk down stairs to

Bugaboo Lodge under construction

the toilets. Hans recalled years later, "Nancy Greene spent her honeymoon in a 6-bed dorm!"

Hans was not there for much of the summer, as he was guiding for The Alpine Club of Canada at the big Centennial Camp in the Yukon's St. Elias Mountains. Although he led an ascent of Mount Walsh, one of the major peaks in the area, his heart was not in it and after a painful attack of kidney stones, he left early for his construction project at the head of Bugaboo Creek. It was obvious that Hans had little time left for expeditions or new climbs. That part of his life had come to an end. Other people now moved to the fore: in 1964, Lloyd MacKay and Don Vockeroth had put up very difficult new routes on Yamnuska; in 1965, Don Gardner and Charlie Locke traversed the entire

Moraine Lake–Lake Louise horseshoe, climbing 23 peaks over 10,000 feet (3048 metres) in only six and a half days; in 1966, Charlie Locke and Brian Greenwood climbed the north face of Mount Temple; in May 1967, Don Gardner, Charlie Locke, Neil Liske and I skied the complete icefields traverse, which had defeated Hans and his team seven years earlier; in 1967 Don Vockeroth, Ken Baker and Lloyd MacKay climbed the north buttress of Howse Peak; and at Christmas 1967, Don Gardner, Eckhardt Grassman and I made the first winter ascent of Mount Assinboine. Almost all these ascents were made by Canadian-born climbers who were members of the energetic Calgary Mountain Club. At some time, all of us had been inspired by Hans's films and his idealistic commentary.

The 1967 guides' course. Back row, left to right: Don Vockeroth, Ottmar Setzer, Bob Geber, John Gow, Charlie Locke and Bernie Royle. Front row, left to right: Leo Grillmair, Lloyd Gallagher, Hans Gmoser, Peter Fuhrmann and Hans Schwarz.

That summer, the ACMG ran its second guide-training course, and this time Hans was in charge. A large group of individuals received their guide pins that year, including a number of homegrown Canadians: Don Vockeroth, Charlie Locke, John Gow, Bernie Royle and Bernie Schiesser. Royle was killed not long after in a plane crash while scouting for new heli-ski terrain in the Purcells, but the others all went on to have successful mountain careers of their own.

From September 28 to January 16, Hans was on the road with his last movie, *Rendezvous in the Selkirks*, certainly his most mature film in terms of story-telling. It features a complex tale of eight ski instructors and racers travelling to the newly built Fairy Meadow hut in the northern Selkirks, interwoven with the story of their professional lives on the ski slopes.

The stars of the film are his old gang: Mike Wiegele; Scott Henderson; Jim McConkey and his wife, Glenn; Lorne McFadgen; Oakie O'Connor; Rob and Linda (Crutchfeld) Bocock; and Kiwi Gallagher. Although Kiwi is absent from most of the skiing footage, he plays a big part in the film and likely helped Hans with the filming. Hans must have travelled across North America to get shots of Rob and Linda ski instructing in Avila, Quebec; Lorne McFadgen instructing at Talisman in Ontario; Oakie O'Connor at his ski resort on Mount Hood, Oregon; Jim and Glenn skiing deep powder at Tod Mountain (now Sun Peaks); Mike with his ski class at Lake Louise; and Scott Henderson competing on the international race circuit. There are even shots of Rob Bocock at the controls of a DC-8 passenger jet (Rob was also a commercial pilot for Air Canada). And with talent like this, the ski footage is some of Hans's best. The sequences of the eight ski pros all dancing down the slope while the wind whips up snow plumes in the sunlight are magical. In this film, there is none of Hans's trademark philosophy—it is all just good entertainment and eye candy for skiers.

On January 2, 1968, Hans sent off a cheque to the BC government for $1,000 to purchase the ten acres he had leased not long before. He had done the required improvements and now exercised his right to purchase the land. The next month, on February 10, Bugaboo Lodge opened for the first guests.

Leo, who for several years had been largely responsible for keeping the ski-touring program going while Hans managed and led the heli-skiing, took over as lodge manager. During all the years he had been faithfully working for Hans in numerous capacities, he had always retained some plumbing work in Calgary. Now, for the first time, he was committed to full-time guiding work. Margaret, now pregnant, worked that winter at the lodge, and Ruedi Gertsch, who had briefly returned to Switzerland to qualify as a fully certified mountain guide, joined Hans, Leo and Kiwi in performing the guiding duties. In the evening, the guides would serve the guests, then join them for dinner. It was a practice that Hans had learned from Lizzie Rummel and Erling Strom, and he felt that it was beneficial for all concerned.

That year, 13 weeks of heli-skiing were offered, at a cost of $350 per week. Jim Davies, once again, had a new helicopter, a six-passenger Alouette III with a climb rate of 400 metres per minute. And the skiing was once more out of this world. Kiwi Gallagher remembered that in those days they were more aggressive than they are today, regularly skiing the north face run from the summit of Anniversary Peak and the long, steep run north from Northpost Spire.

Hans and Margaret's first son, Conrad Keir Gmoser, was born on May 26, 1968. Margaret remembered, "Hans dropped me off at the Holy Cross Hospital. Husbands weren't allowed in the delivery room in those days. I wasn't very prepared for the birth since I had spent the winter cooking and cleaning at the new Bugaboo Lodge. I had a crash course in breathing during the delivery." Conrad was named after the pioneer Austrian guide Conrad Kain, who was a great role model for Hans.

During the summer months, Canadian Mountain Holidays, as they now marketed themselves, offered 11 weeks of climbing instruction. While Hans would do his share of the guiding, managing the business was taking up more and more of his time. He had just applied to purchase another 30 acres of land on which to store the propane, diesel and jet fuel at a safe distance from the lodge. To help him in this work, he hired a new office manager, Jackie Prins, as the job was becoming too big for Gertie. And soon he had a new office, too, a little hole-in-the-wall room at 132 Banff Avenue in the Mount Royal Hotel. CMH shared a small entranceway with Annie Boon's Hairdressing Salon, and there wasn't enough room to swing the proverbial cat. But it was a base for the rapidly growing business that Hans and his faithful employees were creating. Linda Heywood, who joined Jackie in the office in January of 1969, remembered, "You felt as if you were working with history. We were all riding along on his coattails. He was a pioneer."

On the Labour Day weekend, Leo scored a big coup when he guided Pierre Trudeau up Mount Colin, near Jasper. Trudeau had burst onto the political scene that spring in an outpouring of enthusiasm called Trudeaumania and in June, at the age of 48, had been elected prime minister of Canada. He was the darling of the youth of Canada, a country that had just celebrated its 100th birthday and was feeling new confidence and optimism. Brilliant, energetic and totally unconventional, Trudeau was a man whose idea of a good holiday was paddling a canoe down one of the country's great northern rivers or skiing the slopes of her newest ski resort, at Whistler. Known for his flamboyance, he dated movie stars, wore sandals in the House of Commons and even climbed mountains.

It all came about when one of Leo's clients married Tim Porteous, who was Trudeau's speechwriter and executive assistant. She called Elfi in Calgary to enquire about a guide for the prime minister. Elfi then called Leo and told him of the opportunity. Leo drove from the Bugaboos to Calgary, picked up Elfi and his climbing gear, then continued up to Jasper, where Trudeau invited them to dinner at the Jasper Park Lodge. Leo was shocked when the maître d' did not allow Trudeau into the dining room until he had put on a tie. Leo himself was looking very dapper: Trudeau, who was about the same size as Leo, had loaned him some clothes.

The next morning, the weather was poor, and while they waited for the clouds to clear, Trudeau caught a little catnap in the back of the RCMP vehicle. Fearing that the PM would be cold, Elfi found a blanket for him but was warned by his handlers that he "didn't like to be mothered." Elfi ignored their warnings and knocked on the car window; Trudeau graciously accepted the blanket, thanking her for her concern. Eventually, the weather cleared, and with assistance from Willy Pfisterer, Leo led Trudeau to the top of Mount Colin, a rock peak northeast of town. During the climb, Leo told Trudeau about their wonderful heli-ski operation in the Bugaboos and promised him powder snow and privacy should he ever come.

Enticed by Leo's glowing accounts, Pierre Trudeau came in March to the new lodge for a week of heli-skiing. Bob Geber skied one day with Trudeau and remembered that he was an athlete who skied well. Jim Davies liked the PM because he was low-key and had no airs. At one point during the week, a helicopter arrived at the lodge and in it was an RCMP officer with a briefcase handcuffed to his wrist. Trudeau then sat down at a big table to read and sign papers.

Towards the end of the season, Davies had another close call when three pairs of skis not adequately tied down went through the rotors. He managed to land safely high in the mountains and let his passengers out before nursing the machine down to the valley. A new helicopter, a ten-passenger Bell 204, was brought to the Bugaboos to finish the season. That winter, Davies flew from January 25 to April 11 with only two weeks off.

Back in the Banff office, Jackie and Linda were running the show; but without a telephone connection, there was little communication with the Bugaboos. Hans was always away guiding; only on Saturday, when he came out to Brisco for the weekly changeover, could he phone Linda and check on bookings and supplies.

Business was booming, so Hans began looking around for another location where he could establish a heli-ski operation. The Cariboos were the obvious choice: he had led groups there often and knew the area well. The mountains were heavily glaciated and spectacular, got plenty of snow each winter and, on top of that, were not in any national or provincial park. Gmoser and Gallagher visited the area to scout for runs. It was late in the evening, the weather poor, when Jan Elbe, the pilot, dropped them off on top of a peak. Pointing to a clearing in the valley, Hans suggested that Elbe meet them there, then the two guides started down the slope. According to Gallagher, "The snow was over our thighs. It was big snow and it was avalanche prone ... we started down this run and slides were disappearing everywhere." But they were committed; there was no turning back. They safely made it down and were picked up at the appointed spot just before nightfall. Gallagher continued, "I was uptight all the way down ... so we named our first run in the Cariboos 'Up Tight.'" Not long after, from May 10 to 17, CMH offered one week of heli-skiing in the Cariboos, based at the Valemount Hotel.

Robson Eras Gmoser, Hans and Margaret's second son, was born on June 20, 1969. The oft-told story is that Hans was away climbing Mount Robson at about the time his son was born and it was fortunate that he was not climbing Mount Assiniboine, for then who knows what name the boy would have received.[4]

During the summer, Hans was back in the office working with Linda, Jackie having resigned the previous winter. Linda recalled that Hans was at times a hard man to work for. He had a temper and could swear a blue streak. "You would be blasted against the wall. It could burn at a thousand paces and would reduce you to a pile of ashes. You couldn't cower if he swore—you had to give it back. I certainly had some toe-to-toes with him over the years." However, she also said that Hans was "the most incredible boss I ever had. He was a totally inspirational person to work for. You would think, 'If he can do it I can too.' When prospective clients came into the office looking for a guide, Hans would sweep them away with his passion and love for the mountains."

Speed Bumps

The big job for the summer of 1969 was building an addition to Bugaboo Lodge. Although the addition doubled the size of the lodge, it created space for only three more guests. Most couples now had private rooms, and there were toilets and showers on the top floor. There was no longer any need to traipse down the stairs in the middle of the night. Deep powder snow and long runs amongst the Bugaboo Spires were now combined with deluxe accommodation and gourmet meals. Margaret wrote: "I think initially Hans was surprised that people wanted more luxury.... The continual upgrading of facilities to more luxury perplexed him a bit, but he knew it was important in the end."

In fact, it must have been difficult for a man like Gmoser, raised in hardship, to understand the demands of his blue-blooded clients. And it must have been hard for him at times to keep his opinions to himself. However, Hans seems to have had an affinity for the more successful members of our society. He found those who had made their way to the top by their own efforts very interesting and he felt that he could learn something from them.

Meanwhile, the staff was still housed together in an eight-bunk room. Living at close quarters like this all winter long was tough, so after a while Ruedi moved his stuff down to the sawmill, where he could have a little privacy. Before long, Leo and Jim followed him.

In August of 1969, while construction work was going on at the lodge, Hans very nearly died in a climbing accident. Mountain guide Ferdl Taxbock told the story:

> On the day of Hans' accident we each had a group
> of guests with the goal of climbing the north face of

Marmolata. We had set out from our base at Boulder Camp and roped up before stepping onto Bugaboo Glacier. Hans led the way with his group. He was about 200 metres ahead of me when he reached the bergschrund, where a snow bridge led across onto the rock of Marmolata. I heard Hans yodelling and I looked up to see him standing on the snow bridge. Then he suddenly disappeared before my eyes. I heard shouting from Hans' group and hurried my group along. When I reached them all I could see of Hans was his head, face up; the rest of his body was covered by a huge boulder about the size of a small car. He was able to breathe and talk but was in great pain. After asking him, I gave him an injection of morphine, which in those days we were allowed to carry and administer.

I delegated three guests to go back to Boulder Camp to radio Bugaboo Lodge that we needed a helicopter. To the other guests I gave the task of preparing a helicopter landing-site. I commenced digging Hans out of his prison. I had to be careful not to dig so much around him that the boulder would settle and crush both of us. I dug carefully below him and on both sides of him. With the use of my ice axe I loosened the hard packed snow and then moved the snow away from us. Digging below his knees I could feel only one foot. The other I could not find and I was afraid that it had been severed. Then I reached the end of the boulder and realized that the lower limb was sticking up at a right angle around the edge of the boulder. I cleared enough space to allow his leg to be moved out from under the boulder. I warned Hans that it might hurt, but we would pull him free. I gave him another injection of morphine and several of us pulled Hans out and away from the boulder.

I put a provisionary splint on his fractured leg and arm and covered him with warm clothes. We laid him on a bivy bag and carried him down to the prepared heli-pad. By that time it was getting late and no helicopter had showed up. Leaving some strong clients with Hans, I started with the rest of the group down to Boulder Camp. My plan was to get Leo Grillmair and then return with sleeping bags and food, expecting to spend the night on the glacier. Just after we left for the camp I heard a helicopter. We quickly returned and loaded Hans into the helicopter.

During his ordeal Hans did not wince once or complain of pain, which he must have felt strongly in spite of the morphine. Neither he nor I ever forgot his close call on Marmolata.

Hans had been seriously banged up, suffering a broken tibia, fibula, nose and arm, which required a four-week stay in the Calgary General Hospital. Later, he would admit that his actions that day were the dumbest thing he had ever done in the mountains. There was an obvious safe and easy way over the bergschrund, but he had chosen not to take it. Fortunately, his clients were not injured.

In October, a full-length cast on both his leg and arm, he was on the road with a promotional movie for CMH. He recalled:

I went on this tour which started in central Indiana. I was still in much pain and it was a little tricky driving the car. I had to wear a dark suit for those presentations. Totally exhausted and in much pain after my first lecture, I arrived back at my motel and all I wanted was to lie down and sleep. As I started to undress, though, I couldn't bend down far enough to pull my pant leg off the cast. I was almost ready to call down to front desk to send someone up to help me get my pants off. But then I thought better of it and felt that this would not go over very well in this part of the good ol' U.S.A. Finally I was able to pinch the bottom end of the pant leg between my two crutches and pull them off.

On October 10, he wrote to Gertie: "I just wanted you to know that I really appreciated your looking after me during those days in Banff. It is not so much that one needs the physical help, but I was quite depressed not being able to move around. With Margaret being away I was really lost and thus was so glad that I could be with you. Both of you have been so good to me through all those years. I don't see how I can ever make up for it."

In a second letter, dated November 2, Hans wrote again to Gertie: "In a few hours I will drive up to Chicago to meet Margaret. It will be good to have a couple of weeks to ourselves. This tour is quite relaxing, very little travelling and only the show in the evening. In Banff, even when I go home I take all the problems with me and can hardly be sociable." Later he continued: "I agree Gertie, that I must spend more time with my family. It bothers me too. Maybe in those next two weeks Margaret and I can make some concrete plans for our future."

Margaret recalls, "I was working at the lodge with Conrad as a baby and when pregnant with Robson and then with both of them as babies. It was a very busy and demanding time and Hans only saw them at meals. He was never involved in their care. In that respect we had very traditional Austrian roles with him as provider and me as the homemaker." Nevertheless, despite an almost absent father, it was a glorious time for the kids, playing in the snow in the winter or dangling fish hooks in Bugaboo

The Gmoser family

Creek in the summer. There were only the two of them, so they became close friends. At one time, they even had two pet coyotes, Trixie and Chico. The animals had been raised in Calgary by Fred Blumstengl, the stonemason at the Bugaboos, and when they became adults he had brought them up and released them at the lodge. The boys never petted or fed them, and Margaret was careful to never let them touch the boys. "We just went for walks and they followed us." Unfortunately, someone came to the lodge one autumn when no one was around and shot the animals.

That autumn of 1969, CMH experienced its first financial crisis. They had spent about $100,000 for the lodge expansion, hoping to get financing as they needed it. But the money was not available and they could not pay their bills. Hans had raised some of the cash through another series of skier's loans, but he was still short a significant amount. Finally, they were forced to sell shares in Bugaboo

Helicopter Skiing Ltd. to raise the money. Ben Walsh, a businessman and avid skier from New York, came to the rescue and bought a significant chunk of the company. It was not a solution that Hans liked, but he accepted it and wrote to Gertie: "This way I own less of a stronger company and whatever I had to give up in equity is a fair price for being able to drop a bundle of worries."

A Tiger by the Tail

By the 1969–1970 season, the heli-skiing procedure had been worked out. There would be one guide and nine guests in each group, flying in a Bell 204 helicopter. They would be flown to the top of the run and dropped off, and while they began their descent, the helicopter would fly the second group to the top of the run. Then the helicopter would return with a third and a fourth group. By the time the last group was on its way down the slope, the helicopter would be picking up the first group, who were now at the bottom. Four groups would be rotated through this cycle repeatedly during the day; in this manner, a guest was guaranteed 70,000 vertical feet in a week.

That winter, CMH began using Skadi avalanche beacons to safeguard their clients in the event of burial in an avalanche. To begin with, however, they only bought 12 beacons. According to Gmoser, the thinking at the time was, "Only the first group would need them, because if they got safely down a given slope, it should also be safe for the other three groups." According to Kiwi, the Skadis almost immediately proved their worth. Only three days after CMH began using the devices, a guest was safely dug out of a snow slide.

The experimental heli-ski week offered the previous year in the Cariboos had been so successful that three weeks were offered in April 1970. Ruedi was the guide, Jan Elbe was the pilot and the guests stayed in the Ramakada Motel in Valemount. There were complications, however, because Mike Wiegele, Hans's old friend and the star in many of his movies, also began to offer heli-skiing in the Cariboos. Unfortunately, both groups stayed in the same motel, which made for very awkward dining-room arrangements, the CMH group sitting on one side of the room and the Wiegele group on the other. Hans felt betrayed. He had pioneered heli-skiing and worked out the problems. Mike had been his friend and privy to all the plans and developments, and now he was competing against him. Mike, on the other hand, had looked at the map, had seen all the mountains in British Columbia. and had felt that there was room for more than one operator. Unfortunately, a rivalry developed between the two that would never be resolved.

Meanwhile, the CMH ski-touring program, led by Ruedi and Kiwi, continued: powder ski weeks in February at Rogers Pass; a Mount Assiniboine week; two Little Yoho weeks; glacier ski tours to the Wapta, Mummery and Freshfield icefields; and a ski adventure from the Fairy Meadow hut in the northern Selkirks. But the bread and butter was now the heli-ski weeks from Bugaboo Lodge. Many clients returned again and again: Brooks and Ann Dodge came back every year for 30 years. Chip Fisher, then president of Head Ski Company in Canada, suggested to Hans that CMH recognize those guests who had skied one million vertical feet. Hans was in agreement, and in 1970 Ann and Brooks Dodge and Anne and Joe Jones became the first four to receive this honour—a dark blue blazer with a gold embroidered CMH logo. It was soon felt that these blazers were impractical, and they were replaced by a ski jacket. Within two years, however, CMH had decided to go with a complete ski suit to honour these individuals.

Hans Gmoser was a powerful skier

This idea of the million-foot suit was a great hit and also an outstanding marketing idea that continues to this day.

At around this time, Hans teamed up with Peter Bentley and Westmount Records to produce a 33 rpm record to be played while you exercised. Called *Ski Better With Hans Gmoser, 29 skiing exercises with music for the beginner or advanced skier*, it included a number of jazz tunes to stretch, jump or run to while Hans gave instruction and encouragement. Today, it is humorous to listen to Hans urging:

> *One, two; one, two,*
> *Arms hanging loose by your side,*
> *Run a little to the left,*
> *Run a little to the right,*
> *Don't forget to breathe.*
> *Lift those legs and lift those legs,*
> *Up again and over,*
> *And up again and over.*

Years later, this record was something Hans preferred to forget, but it does show how he was prepared to try almost anything new to promote skiing.

Sometime in 1970, Hans became involved in a plan to climb Mount Everest. Hans recalled how it all came about: "I had a client, Lloyd Carlson, who was a doctor from Toronto and he came to me once and said, 'You should organize an Everest expedition.' The idea of climbing in the Himalaya I found intriguing, but to actually organize an expedition myself I wasn't too keen. But he said, 'There's no problem. There is this guy, Chuck Rathgeb, who has a big construction company, Comstock International, and he'll finance the thing.'.... I said, 'Well if somebody finances it and somebody does all the dirty work, I'll certainly organize the climbing part of it, and put this whole thing together.'"

Gmoser and Rathgeb met, and Rathgeb, who had a penchant for dabbling in high-risk adventure, agreed to provide much of the money required to make the dream a reality. In return, however, he would consider himself the leader. Gmoser continued, "At the time I also knew the Prime Minister and he intervened on our behalf with the foreign ministry so that we would get the permit to climb the mountain." Permission was soon forthcoming to climb Everest in the post-monsoon season of 1975. In early 1971, Hans chose his team, selecting some of the leading Canadian mountaineers of the day: Dick Culbert, Brian Greenwood, Lloyd MacKay, Don Vockeroth, Don Gardner, Ken Baker and me.

One night, during the winter of 1971, Hans and Margaret found themselves chatting with Bish McGill, a surgeon from Stowe, Vermont, and his wife, Betty. Margaret mentioned that she was pregnant again, and Bish joked that Hans should get a vasectomy, as three children would be enough. Hans asked Bish a few questions about what a vasectomy would entail, then Bish offered to do it there and then. So they headed off to Hans and Margaret's bedroom, where Bish pulled out his black bag with the sharp instruments. Margaret was the nurse, and for a sterile field she simply tore a hole in the middle of a paper napkin. The work done, Hans went skiing the next day. Unfortunately, Margaret later miscarried and there was no third child.

That winter, CMH introduced another new area: the Monashees. For two weeks, Ruedi Gertsch was the guide and the group stayed at the McGregor Hotel in Revelstoke. In the Cariboos, CMH now offered six weeks of heli-skiing. CMH was on the move, snapping up new areas. Hans was being continually pushed by holders of skier's loans to open up new areas, and by some partners to make a profit. Consequently, in 1972 he experimented with an immense Sikorsky 58 helicopter that took 18 passengers plus the guide. Hans and Ruedi Gertsch gathered with 36 loan holders in Revelstoke. Roy Webster was the pilot, and according to Gertsch he did a magnificent job. Plagued by bad weather in Revelstoke, they moved on to Golden, where visibility was a little better. On one flight, all 19 pairs of skis shifted, everybody rushed to grab them and the helicopter wheeled in the sky, but the pilot managed to stay in control. In the end, it was decided that the machine and the group of 18 guests were just too big to manage.

By now, Hans realized that more formal training in snow science was necessary for his guides, and that winter he brought in Swiss-Canadian snow expert Peter Schaerer to the Bugaboos. It was the beginning of a sophisticated program of snow-stability evaluation that CMH would develop for its operation. The ACMG, which provided the initial training for all CMH guides, also began a snow-science curriculum for its courses. Despite the new programs, luck ran out that winter for Ben Walsh,

Hans meets Pierre Trudeau at the Calgary airport

the New York businessman who had bailed Hans out in 1969. While skiing with a group near Revelstoke, he was carried down by an avalanche and struck a tree, breaking his neck. He would struggle the rest of his life to regain partial mobility.

On July 28, 1972, Hans experienced one of the greatest honours of his guiding career and one of his greatest responsibilities, when he led Prime Minister Pierre Trudeau up Bugaboo Spire. This is not an easy peak, particularly for an inexperienced climber who has not yet developed a head for heights. At one point on the climb the exposure is extreme—a 700-metre drop right below your feet. But Trudeau was a fit and adventurous man and he did fine on the climb. Hans, however, did not fare so well. Early in the day, his knee locked, a piece of cartilage likely caught in the joint, and he had to force it unlocked before continuing the climb, in much pain.

Hans, in lead, and Pierre Trudeau set off to climb Bugaboo Spire

Gmoser, who supported the Conservatives, and Trudeau, who was the leader of the Liberal Party in Canada, had very different political views and adjusted the conversation accordingly. But there was no doubt that they had a mutual respect for the other's toughness and achievements. At the end of the day, back at Bugaboo Lodge, the Prime Minister wrote in Hans's guide's book: "To Hans G. with a thousand thanks for helping me to discover a new part of Canada—and of myself."

At about this time, CMH built a trail over the high alplands from Bugaboo Lodge to the Vowell Creek drainage. Old-time American climber Fred Beckey, who had pioneered new routes in the area for over 20 years, took offense at the red paint marks that had been brushed on rocks along the trail, and on October 25 wrote to Hans with his criticism. It must have hit a nerve, for on November 17 Hans wrote back to Fred:

> I read your letter and my first reaction was "Go piss up a rope." On reading it again there was at least one argument although my view is 180 degrees opposed, namely that "The wilderness terrain is more important than the people using it." Before I get into this, let me clearly state my position.
>
> I caused the trail to be built and did considerable work on it myself. I also wanted the trail well marked with paint, although not as profusely as it was done.
>
> It is one thing, Fred, to entertain lofty ideas apart from the realities of the world we happen to live in and it is another to accept these realities and try to live with them within the confines of your conscience. The latter I find poses the real challenge and involves you in very rewarding endeavors.

There was a time when I too shunned the world of our society, its aggressiveness, its competitiveness, its people, and sought refuge in the mountains, but since most of us have a need to accomplish something, to constantly measure ourselves against something (you should know this more than anybody else), the mountains being among them, climbing them in this selfish fashion soon became nothing more than a toxicant with the need for it growing ever stronger and in spite of the harsh discipline imposed by the mountains and the elements, this society of "idealistic" climbers is infested with the same malign traits of

Three of North America's greatest climbers during the 1950s and 1960s. Hans Gmoser at left, Brian Greenwood in back and Fred Beckey at right.

man, hate, vanity, jealousy, aggression, selfishness, and what makes it really impossible to stomach is that you bastards are so fucking righteous about it all. Give me the rest of the world any day with all its lies, corruption, pollution, poverty, stupidity, wars, crime, filthy noisy cities, there at least is less pretence here and Fred, it is here, on this side of the fence where you have to start cleaning up the manure. There are too many people in the world today and there is no power in the world that can consign these people to any given space or likewise deny them access to other areas like the ones you claim to be more important than these people.

Fred, the challenge that faces us today is to find the means to let the greatest number of people enjoy these beautiful lands with the least amount of damage to these lands but the extravagance of drawing boundaries and declaring vast tracts of wilderness off limits, except for a few self chosen, we can no longer afford.

When you consider that world population is expected to grow in numbers as much in the next 30 years as it has in the last 1,970 years, then whether we like it or not, we must realize that the days are gone when you can just walk at random over the alplands and pitch your tent wherever you find a nice spot convenient for you and expect that you and your group are the only ones in the area. In order to provide at least some measure of outdoor experience to the billions who have begun to tear down the prison walls of their poverty, we have to build trails, huts, so that these people will at least only destroy a minimal area of wilderness while enjoying all of it and this is the approach I have taken unilaterally in building these trails in the Bugaboos.

From the letter it appears that Hans's views extolling the virtues of "the vagabonds of the mountains" had changed since 1965. Some would say that Hans had turned his back on the romantic idealism that had sustained him for so many years. But Hans was into the heli-ski business up to his ears and there was no turning back. He had dozens of employees with families who were depending on him, and he had business partners to answer to as well. This was simply Hans's defensive and self-justifying reply to Fred's attack. Although Hans wrote of providing "some measure of outdoor experience to the billions who have begun to tear down the prison walls of their poverty," what CMH was in fact providing was a deluxe outdoor experience to the wealthy members of our society.

During the winter of 1972–1973, Kiwi took over the operation in the Cariboos and Ruedi ran the Monashees operation from the Mica Village Motel. According to Gertsch, "It was a new frontier. It was something totally new. There was no one who could give us any guidance— we had to figure it out ourselves." Hans was subject to increasing pressure and was spending more time in the office. According to Gertsch, it was "really hard on Hans those years. The pressure. The way the business took off." Hans was forced to hire more guides: Peter Schlunegger, a friend of Ruedi's and a fellow Swiss guide from Wengen; and Sepp Renner, a Swiss guide from Andermatt. Two years later, Sepp would join the family by marrying Margaret's sister, Barb. At about this time, Hans's old friend Frank Stark joined the growing ranks of heli-ski guides. Stark had seriously injured himself in a car accident in 1961 and had left the mountain world for a time. He had come back to work for CMH in 1968 as the maintenance man in the Bugaboos, and was now ready to resume guiding again.

Meanwhile, others were leaving the business. In early 1972, after eight seasons flying in the Bugaboos, Jim Davies

The Bugaboo guides in the early 1970s (from left to right):
Herb Bleuer, Leo Grillmair, Kiwi Gallagher, Hans Gmoser, Ruedi Gertsch,
Peter Schlunegger, Sepp Renner, Frank Stark and Ernst Buehler

left to start his own business based in Banff. He had done a remarkable job of pioneering the techniques required for mountain flying day after day in all kinds of weather. Linda Heywood left CMH in the summer of 1973. Back in 1969, she had been not much more than 20 years old when Hans had made her office manager. In those days, Hans was away guiding most of the winter and she had run the office, aided by Frances Kelly, who had started with CMH at about the same time. To replace Linda, Hans hired Pat Lever, who would stay with the company for over 30 years, much of the time as Hans's executive assistant.

In 1973, the name Rocky Mountain Guides Limited was legally changed to Canadian Mountain Holidays Ltd., a name that would become synonymous with powder skiing. In the brochure that year, the CMH management is listed as Leo Grillmair, manager, Bugaboos; Lloyd Gallagher, manager, Cariboos; Ruedi Gertsch, chief guide; and Hans Gmoser, janitor. Despite the stress that Hans was experiencing, he had not yet lost his sense of humour.

Hans, however, did lose his sense of humour later that winter when he learned that the Mount Everest Expedition, slated for autumn 1975, had been cancelled by the Canadian government. Shocked and angered, Gmoser flew to Ottawa to see what could be done, but it was hopeless: the permit was already gone, snapped up by Chris Bonington for his now famous South West Face expedition. It has never been clarified why the Canadian government cancelled the expedition without even asking Gmoser's opinion. It is known that Hans was considering a scheme whereby team members would train high on Mount Logan, then fly directly to Kathmandu, where we would be airlifted by helicopter to base camp, thus arriving already acclimatized. The scheme would be expensive, and the bill would have to be footed by the Canadian military, who would be called upon to provide the logistics. In later years, Hans could still give no explanation for the government's actions, and no doubt his relationship with Trudeau was damaged by the unexplained cancellation.

The First Fatality and a New Lodge

On February 17, 1974, tragedy struck in the Cariboos. Given the large groups skiing steep slopes of deep powder snow day after day, all winter, it was only a matter of time before someone would die in an avalanche. What is surprising is that it took almost ten years before it happened.

Because of bad weather, several groups were forced to ski the same slope on Mica Mountain. Many times that day they had skied the run, and it was considered safe. Ruedi was leading the first group and had reached the bottom, where he was awaiting the others. Kiwi was leading a second group and had pulled to the side partway down the 1000-metre incline. Franz Frank, a guide from Switzerland, brought a third group in from the top. One guest, 44-year-old Geoffrey Taylor from Montreal, requested that he might go ahead, stop and then film the others coming down. Frank agreed, and as they skied towards the camera, the slope released. It went big, about 300 metres across the crown of the avalanche.

Six skiers from the third group, including Taylor and Frank, were carried away by the slide. Kiwi and one member of his group were also swept away and carried through the trees at the bottom of the slope. Kiwi was on top when the snow settled, but he was crippled, the ligaments in his knee torn. Ruedi took over the rescue, aided by Mike Wiegele, who had been skiing nearby. It was late in the day and they rushed to find everyone before dark. According to Kiwi, the rescue scene was chaotic. Back in the motel that night, Ruedi and Kiwi struggled to be sure they had found everyone. Finally, Ruedi got the guest list and went room to room, accounting for everyone. In the end, there was one fatality—Geoffrey Taylor, the man with the camera—and two people with serious injuries. It was a shocking start to the winter.

Despite the tragedy, business continued to grow in the Cariboos, and Hans decided that this was where he wanted to build his second lodge. Philippe was once again the architect, and Kiwi, a mechanic and guide by trade, became the project manager, although he had no experience with large construction projects. Hans had an uncanny ability to assess people, then he would give them a responsible job and just trust them to get on with it. He expected the best in people and he usually got it. Even though he was sparing in his praise and rarely said thank you, all of his employees remembered the few times when he had complimented them on a job well done. It was a cherished memory.

Kiwi's first job during the summer of 1973 had been to build the road and bridges to the lodge site. He had gone first to Vancouver, where he had purchased a D6 Cat that was delivered to Valemount. The truck driver had shown him how to start the machine, then Kiwi had spent the rest of the summer pushing dirt and boulders around and pouring the concrete for the basement of the lodge. The lodge was composed of precast concrete built in Edmonton by CANA Construction and was trucked to the site in the summer of 1974. Many people helped Kiwi with the construction of the lodge, including Ernst Buehler, Nicole Laliberté, Hermann Frank and even the boss himself, Hans Gmoser. It was a muddy job and there were lots of mosquitoes that year. The lodge opened for guests in December of 1974.

Hans lost his most senior guide after the ski season of 1973–1974, when Ruedi decided to go it alone. It had been a wonderful eight years working for Hans, but there was opportunity and room for more heli-ski operations. Ruedi had always liked the Dogtooth Range in the Purcell Mountains west of Golden, so that year he started his own company, Purcell Helicopter Skiing Ltd. Meanwhile, in the Cariboos, the problem that had festered for five years was relieved when Mike Wiegele moved his operation 85 kilometres down Highway #5 to Blue River. Hans, however, continued to operate a heli-ski service now from the Sarak Motel in Valemount, in addition to the new Cariboo Lodge. At about the same time, the CMH office moved into a much larger space on Bear Street in Banff.

In 1975, another ugly little dispute that had simmered between Gmoser and Wiegele since 1972 seemed to have been laid to rest. Mike's company was called Cariboo Helicopter Skiing Ltd. and he objected to Hans advertising that he offered Cariboo Helicopter Skiing. Hans's lawyers countered that the three words "Cariboo," "Helicopter" and "Skiing" were all in the public domain. After an exchange of numerous letters between their respective lawyers, and even the filing of documents in court, the matter seems to have faded. Things were getting sorted out in the emerging world of heli-skiing.

On August 7, 1975, Hans Resch, Hans Gmoser's biological father, died. According to one of Gmoser's closest friends, the key to understanding the man, his incredible drive and his tolerance for pain and hard work, is to appreciate his relationship or lack of relationship with Resch. Although Gmoser's stepfather, Erasmus Hintringer, had been loving and caring, nothing could hide the fact that Gmoser had been disowned by his own biological father. Resch became an alcoholic in later years, and Gmoser, when he rarely spoke of him, would refer to him dismissively as the town drunk.

In the winter of 1975–1976, Hans introduced another destination in the Purcell Mountains for helicopter skiing, which operated from the Panorama ski resort, and brought in Bob Geber as the manager and lead guide. By 1976, CMH's revenues were $2.1 million and 80 people were on the payroll. About 60 per cent of the guests came from the United States, and the rest were split equally between Canada and the rest of the world. In the 1977 brochure there are photos of 27 guides working for Canadian Mountain Holidays. Only one, Pierre Lemire, was actually born in Canada. This exacerbated the rivalry that was growing between the Greenwood team in Calgary and Gmoser and his guides. The British and their Canadian friends were putting up the new routes and exploring new territory, but the Euro guides were getting the glamour and the powder snow. It is not clear whether Hans had an aversion to Canadian-born guides or whether the few of them who existed, and had the skiing and climbing abilities required, had an aversion

Helicopter skiing is the crème de la crème of skiing

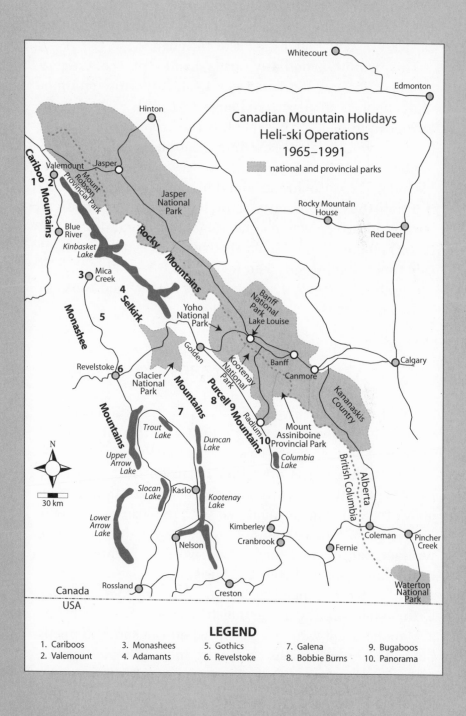

Canadian Mountain Holidays
Heli-ski Operations
1965–1991

national and provincial parks

LEGEND

1. Cariboos
2. Valemount
3. Monashees
4. Adamants
5. Gothics
6. Revelstoke
7. Galena
8. Bobbie Burns
9. Bugaboos
10. Panorama

to Hans and his company. In Calgary, Hans, who had been the darling of the serious climbing community ten years earlier, was now seen by some as the enemy.

This would eventually lead several of the Calgary climbers, led by John Lauchlan, to start their own climbing school as a direct challenge to the ACMG and the European guides. This school, based from the YMCA in Calgary, would later grow into Yamnuska Inc. It would not be until 1979 that Canadian-born guides such as Scott Flavelle, Dave Cochrane and Phil Hein would start to infiltrate the CMH empire. In the 1980s, as more Canadian-born guides received certifications, the dynamics of the ACMG changed and the old rivalry disappeared. At about this time, Greenwood, who had retired from climbing in the mid-1970s, moved to Vancouver Island and took up gardening and winemaking.

Difficult Years

Both 1977 and 1978 were bad years for Hans Gmoser and CMH. The snow came late in 1977 and then it came in buckets. Snow stability was terrible; at the newly established Bobbie Burns operation in an old mining camp, guests actually slept with their beacons on until the slopes above them had been stabilized with explosives. It would have been almost impossible to get through the winter without tragedy, and there were two fatal accidents, one in the Bugaboos and one near Sunshine Village.

Late in the afternoon of March 17, three skiers died on a run called Groovy in the Bugaboos. Carried down by an avalanche, they were all on top when the snow stopped, but as their companions rushed up the hill to aid them, a second avalanche swept down and buried the three under almost five metres of snow. It was 45 minutes before the first victim was dug out and 90 minutes before the last was recovered. It was just too long for survival. Only ten days later, on March 27, a CMH guide was leading a group of 20 guests from Sunshine Village to Citadel Pass, where they were to be flown by helicopter to Mount Assiniboine Lodge. In cloud and heavy snowfall, he ventured onto a steeper slope and triggered an avalanche that rushed down and buried five skiers. Four were found alive, but the fifth was dead.

On top of all this, Hans was wrestling with marital problems. For the previous few years, Margaret had been raising the two boys largely on her own in Harvie Heights. Conrad had started kindergarten in Banff in 1973, and the next year Robson had followed him. Hans, however, was at the lodges, working hard and enjoying the glamorous lifestyle and admiration. It was not the foundation on which to base a successful marriage. Things came to a head in the fall of 1977 when Margaret left him:

> I decided that Hans was totally missing the point of being a father to his sons. I decided to leave the boys with him and I moved to Calgary and enrolled in Henderson Business College in an Executive Secretarial Course, which I completed. Hans hired an older lady [Preb Stritter] to come and look after the boys while he was away and I visited them on weekends. My parents were horrified that I would do this and I got a lot of criticism for leaving my children. I worked at temporary office work during this time in Calgary. During the year we slowly realized that we did have a lot in common. We had to "court" all over again and resolve our differences. We went together and bought a new wedding ring. It had always bothered me that I had to buy my original rings alone because Hans was too busy guiding. He had to do a lot of soul

searching and came to the realization that family and friends mattered more than business. Once we decided to grow old together and be totally honest with each other our relationship was wonderful. I realized that I couldn't change the older Austrian role modelling for the woman and adapted my own way of dealing with that. Hans learned to accept my need for "timeout" when I took my own trips. I needed a break from his more dominant personality.

During this difficult time, Hans visited Philippe and spoke of his problems. He confided that Margaret was the woman he wanted; he was not interested in anyone else. He also admitted, not surprisingly, that losing Margaret would mean failure, and it seems pretty clear that failure was something that Hans could not abide. As it turned out, Hans was the only one of the Austrian trio to remain married to the same woman. Franz was remarried in 1966 to an English woman, Roberta Traill, and Leo was remarried to a Canadian woman, Lynne Seidler, in 1975.

The next winter, on February 11, 1978, CMH was hit by another tragedy. While landing on top of a mountain in the Monashees, the pilot lost control of the helicopter, hit a rock and crashed. Passengers were thrown down the slope over a distance of about 100 metres. The crash then triggered an avalanche that came down and buried them. One passenger, an airline pilot from Germany, managed to dig himself out and started a search. After everyone was located, he took the radio from the guide and struggled through deep snow for two hours to the top of the mountain, where he called for help. Four people died in this incident, including the pilot and guide.

Margaret Gmoser wrote: "All the accidents in CMH were terribly hard for Hans. The results all landed on his shoulders. His primary concern in the operation was

Margaret and Hans skiing

for safety in the field. When we started heli-skiing there were no radios, telephones or avalanche beacons. All of this technology developed along the way. Hans never relaxed when the weather cycles were bad or the snow pack was unstable. His first thing in the morning was to check the weather and he'd worry if there was too much snow or wind. As the operation became larger the load became greater."

Jim Buckingham recently observed, "I was on the very first prototype winter assistant guides' course in the spring of 1974. I was at that time patrol foreman, then in a few years mountain manager at Sunshine Village ski resort. I was in those years taking avalanche courses and doing avalanche control work at Sunshine. There was a debate in the 'avalanche community' whether or not heli-skiing was morally defensible. Some thought it was by its very nature too dangerous."

The final blow came in the spring of 1978. Since 1963, Hans had been running summer climbing courses in the Bugaboos from Boulder Camp, located high above the lodge in the rocky meadows at the base of Snowpatch Spire. He and his guides had worked regularly to improve the trail from the lodge to the camp, had maintained the cleanliness of Boulder Camp and in 1972 had aided in the construction of the Conrad Kain hut. Some climbers took offense at CMH for using a large portion of the hut for commercial purposes. Eventually, BC Provincial Parks[5] required that CMH build its own dining tent and toilet facilities and could only use 22 sleeping spaces in the hut. By then, Hans had had enough, and on May 1, 1978, he wrote to parks officials in Victoria, advising them that CMH would discontinue its climbing school and guiding service at Boulder Camp. It was a disappointing and unpleasant end.

Heli-hiking—The Financial Salvation

During the summer of 1978, Canadian Mountain Holidays finally found a way to keep the employees working year-round and pay the bills for its lodges during the summer months. Hans wrote in *The CMH Story*:

> It was obvious that the lodges we had constructed to date were difficult to amortize with only a winter operation. We had tried various summer programs in the Bugaboos. These ranged from hiking and canoeing, to horseback riding and tennis. The bottom line, however, was that we lost almost as much money in the summer as we made in the winter. We decided to shut everything down in the summer to keep cash drain to a minimum.

In April 1977, I got a phone call from Arthur Tauck, the most respected tour operator in the United States. Arthur had just spent a week with his son skiing at our Cariboo area and thought he could use our lodges in the summer for his sightseeing clientele. I was not very interested. To me, it looked like just another scheme that would cost us money. So I told Arthur that I would think about it and would call him back. I actually forgot about the whole thing. Two weeks later Arthur called me again and wanted to know what I had decided. At that point, I realized that I couldn't get rid of him that easily and gave some thought as to how we could keep his clients occupied at our lodges in the summer. I was actually at a loss and could not come up with any ideas that made sense to me. When I called Arthur and told him so, he said, "Why don't you do the same thing you do in the winter—fly to a few different places, let the people get out, let them enjoy the views and take some short hikes?" It was as if someone had switched on a light. I asked Arthur to come to Banff. I would arrange for a helicopter, invite a few people and we would do a trial run. One of the key players in this whole exercise was Ivor Petrak, Vice-President for the mountain hotels of the Canadian Pacific Railroad. He had to provide additional rooms in his already over-booked hotels so Arthur could develop another tour through the Canadian Rockies, which had Heli-Hiking as its centerpiece. I invited Ivor to come on this trial run. I also invited Lizzie Rummel, who had given me my first job as a young mountain guide at her small lodge at Mt. Assiniboine in 1953.

In July 1977, we set out from Banff by helicopter, flew to Cariboo Lodge and then landed at several of the most scenic locations. Everyone was impressed with the experience and felt it had great potential. Ivor agreed to somehow find the much-needed rooms and Arthur agreed to develop a new tour, including two days of Heli-Hiking from the Cariboo Lodge, and sell it.

In the summer of 1978, Cariboo Lodge was operating at 87% occupancy and Heli-Hiking had become the latest outdoor recreation activity in the mountains of British Columbia. By the summer of 1979, Cariboo Lodge was operating at 100% occupancy and the question was, "Should we run a similar program in the Bugaboos?" Bugaboo Lodge was expanded and renovated and by the summer of 1980 received its first Heli-Hiking guests.

Kiwi Gallagher had played the key role of organizing the Cariboo heli-hiking program, but in the autumn of 1978 he left CMH to create a public-safety program for the newly established Kananaskis Country in the front ranges of the Alberta Rockies. He had been with Hans since 1966; however, now married to Fran Kelly and with a young family, he had chosen to work closer to home in Canmore.

Most of Gmoser's friends agree that Hans began to soften after the traumatic events of 1977 and 1978. He became less demanding and more tolerant of other people's weaknesses. And he also found time to take some holidays. In 1978, he went with Margaret, Philippe and Mireille Delesalle on his first bicycle trip to Europe. They bought bicycles in Lyon, France, then spent almost a month cycling through southeastern France as far as Marseille. It was Margaret who had reintroduced Hans to the bicycle after so many years. On several occasions in the 1970s, she had cycled the Icefields Parkway, once with her sister, Barb, and once with Mireille. She had loved it so much that the Gmosers and Delesalles decided to do a trip together. It was great

*Philippe and Mireille Delesalle and
Margaret and Hans Gmoser cycling in France*

fun, and Hans fell in love with touring all over again. He became an expert mechanic: each night, he would clean and oil his bicycle and do all the repairs himself.

In the late 1970s, Hans had a chance to get the further education he craved, and on January 19, 1979, he graduated from the Smaller Company Management Program at Harvard University, in Cambridge, Massachusetts. He wrote: "I went three years in a row to the Harvard Business School to take some courses. There were usually 90 people in a class, naturally all of them with university degrees and many running a fourth generation family business with gold plated balance sheets, but there I soon realized that some of those people didn't know much more than I did and when we had to solve problems I had also good ideas, ideas the others often didn't have. That gave me a great amount of self confidence, because when I first went there I thought to myself, you better just sit there and listen and keep your mouth shut."

That same January, CMH opened an operation in Revelstoke based from the Regent Inn. According to Bob Geber, it was culture shock for some when CMH moved to Revelstoke, the blue-ribbon ski clientele mingling with the hard-working loggers and miners of the area. On one occasion, Princess Birgitta of Sweden came to town, and after a day of skiing, the guides took her to an exotic dancing show. The lumberjacks and miners stared in disbelief. The next day, they flew to the top of a run near the Jordan River and the princess was amazed when Bob revealed that they had never skied the run before, that this would be the first descent.

By now, the high life of the lodges was wearing thin on Hans, and he often longed for the rustic hut life that he had once known. Bill Putnam, Hans's good friend from the American Alpine Club, had also long wanted a place to call home in the Canadian mountains. In the 1960s, in partnership with The Alpine Club of Canada, he had built the Fairy Meadow hut in the northern Selkirks, but the arrangement had not worked out. With Gmoser, he began to look around for what he called "a home for geriatric alpinists." They eventually found a place they liked in the Battle Range of the southern Selkirks, where with volunteer labour they slowly built a hut. By March 1979, Battle Abbey was ready for occupancy. The skiing and climbing were both first-rate, but Hans used the hut primarily as a place where he could get away from it all and get back to a simpler lifestyle.

Coincidentally, the following season of 1980 was the last one in which CMH offered ski-touring weeks to the Stanley Mitchell hut in the Little Yoho Valley, where it all had begun in the mid-1950s.

A Mature CMH

In December 1981, CMH opened its new Bobbie Burns Lodge in the Purcell Mountains north of the Bugaboos. At about the same time, it terminated its operation at Panorama. It now had six operations in the Columbia and Cariboo mountain ranges of British Columbia—the Bugaboos, the Bobbie Burns, Revelstoke, the Monashees, the Cariboos and Valemount.

Shortly afterwards, Canadian Mountain Holidays went through a period of financial instability. CMH had always swung from financial crisis to financial crisis. According to Charles Barlow, an initial investor and partner since 1967, they would just get a lodge up and running and starting to deliver a profit when Hans would want to start another operation. It finally caught up with him in the financial downturn of the early 1980s. The entire world suffered financial problems; interest rates went through the roof, and bookings dropped. CMH had entered into an agreement to operate an 80-room condominium hotel at Panorama, but the deal went sour and cost CMH dearly. This, combined with the heavy borrowing costs of building the Bobbie Burns Lodge, put CMH into a financial crisis. For the first time, Hans hired a trained accountant to handle the finances.

Evelyn Matthews had grown up in Hamilton, Ontario. She had seen one of Hans's movies in 1964 and "from that day on the only thing I wanted to do was move west and learn how to ski." By 1983, she was a chartered accountant living in Banff when Hans asked her to work for CMH. Over the next few years, the company would resolve its financial problems, and by 1985 it had regained financial stability.

Evelyn felt that Hans was a very astute businessman. He could look at a financial report, digest it for five minutes, then make sound decisions based on it. She also said that he had an incredible ability to think on his feet. He asked people for advice and then just made a decision—usually a good one. In Evelyn's opinion, Hans thrived on stress. It was a positive thing, a catalyst for action.

To counter the stress of running the business, Hans took a yearly cycle trip with Margaret. In 1982, they toured Austria, Italy and Switzerland; then, in August of 1983, they visited Norway with the two boys. Margaret remembered:

> Crown Princess Sonja had been heli-skiing with us and had invited us to stay a night at Skaugum, the official residence. We were met by Sonja's lady in waiting at the airport and driven by car (our bikes in a van) to the residence. Sonja met us at the door. Our boys played Frisbee with the children (Martha Louise and Haakon, who were 13 and 11). We had tea inside and looked at a map of our trip. Later I had my hair done by Sonja's hairdresser, in preparation for an "informal" dinner given by Sonja for 32 of her skiing friends. We had told her that we were travelling by bicycle and that we wouldn't have any fancy clothes. The boys were given a separate room from us and one of them pulled the cord in the bathroom thinking it was a fan and then pulled it a second time when it didn't work. It was actually the call cord for the butler, who came to the door. The informal gathering consisted of ladies in their finery and men in suits. The dining room was immense, with candles, chandeliers and fresh flowers. The cutlery was lined up beside the plates. I had time to tell the boys to copy the person beside them as to which fork or knife to use. Hans and I sat with Princess Sonja and Prince Harald and the boys were far down the table. We

The Norwegian royal family at the Gothics Lodge.
Left to right: Prince Haakon, King Harald, Crown Princess Sonja,
Hans Gmoser and guide Pierre Lemire.

had an incredible meal with three wines and butlers
serving beside every few chairs. Hans showed a heli-
ski film to the guests after the meal.

Other celebrities came skiing during the 1980s, most
notably King Juan Carlos of Spain, who visited the Bobbie
Burns Lodge at Easter of 1984. While he was there, he took
a side trip to Battle Abbey, where Bill Putnam, wearing
a big cowboy hat, welcomed his majesty with the homey
greeting, "Howdy King!"

Shortly after the Norway trip, Conrad went away to
St. Michael's University School in Victoria, BC, and the
next year Robson followed him. Robson at first did not
like being so far from the mountains, but Conrad enjoyed
the freedom, the challenge and the exposure to new ideas.

King Juan Carlos of Spain and Hans Gmoser

In addition, it was a way to escape the influence of his powerful father. Margaret tells the story of Hans visiting Conrad and commenting on his recent haircut. When Conrad revealed the amount he had paid for a stylist to do the job, his father lectured him for not being more frugal with his money. In defiance, Conrad refused to cut his hair for many years and at one time had a ponytail down to his waist. Both boys spent grades 10 to 12 at St. Michael's.

The Dream Fulfilled

After the construction of the Bobbie Burns Lodge, there was no further CMH expansion for several years. Gmoser wrote in *The CMH Story*: "After all the roller coaster experiences, there was a temptation to simply freeze everything at the present size and make the best of the good thing we had going. As the realization of a development freeze sank in with our people, it became obvious that some of our most talented and dedicated people might want to move on if there were no further opportunities available. There were also many guests who suddenly complained that they were not able to get space. The pressure mounted to open yet another area!"

So, in February of 1987, CMH opened the Gothics heli-ski area in the northern Selkirk Mountains, using for accommodation the buildings of a copper mine that had shut down. Demand, however, still continued to outstrip capacity. Hans wrote:

> In the fall of 1988, Mark Kingsbury, who was by now running the day-to-day affairs of CMH, successfully bid on a new Heli-Skiing area called Galena. This area was different because we needed to build a lodge before we could start skiing. This

was something we planned to do within three or four years. At that time we were preoccupied with plans to split the immense Gothics area and to build the Adamant Lodge in the resulting new area. This lodge was scheduled to open in December 1990.

But we needed a new area immediately! Without consulting anyone, I told our reservations people on January 3, 1989, "Go ahead and sell Galena. It will open by the end of December with a new lodge for 44 guests."

Most of Galena was booked before we had even chosen a site for the lodge, much less figured out how it could be done. Bernhard Ehmann agreed to tackle the project. He would build the lodge and be the area manager. Walter Bruns, our construction manager at the time, looked at various alternatives including prefabricating modular units or buying existing modular units. In the end, it was a mix of both. Against all odds and surmounting incredible difficulties, Bernhard and his crew had Galena ready to receive its first guests on December 10, 1989.

Everyone had pitched in to make the project succeed. According to Peter Arbic, as recounted by Peter Lemieux, "On the guides' training week in Galena, I had one of the shittiest jobs: digging holes and pouring concrete for supports for the washers in the guest trailers. And you know, it was all OK because, there in the hole along with me, was the owner of the company."

During the summer of 1989, construction had also begun on Adamant Lodge; on December 15, 1990, it opened its doors. In the summers of 1990 and 1991, CMH, having managed to purchase the Gothics mining camp, finally undertook a major remodelling project to upgrade the facility into a comfortable lodge. And at last, after many years of ex-

Hans and Philippe at work on yet another lodge

perimenting with different helicopters and different-sized groups, CMH had perfected the formula: 44 guests per lodge, skiing in four groups of 11 plus guide, served by one 12-passenger Bell 212 twin-engine helicopter.

Although at the time Barlow was not completely supportive of Hans's expansion plans, he said that in retrospect Hans had done the right thing. Hans was grabbing territory, and by the time he had done it five times no one could compete with CMH. Both Gordon Rathbone, Hans's lawyer for many years, and Marty von Neudegg, marketing manager and legal counsel for CMH, felt that Hans had a European approach to business, whereby the employees and the customers were just as important as the profit generated.

Gmoser himself attributed the impressive growth of CMH to customer loyalty. He wrote: "The strongest driving force behind our rapid expansion was the tremendous amount of support and loyalty our guests bestowed upon us. From the outset, I was amazed at how regularly so many of our guests returned year after year. Before long some of our guests came twice a year, then three times, then four times. They kept bringing their friends, organized groups to fill up whole weeks and actually worked hard to keep all of our places full."

Loyalty is the character trait that more than any other defines Hans Gmoser. If you did him a favour, you would be remembered and ultimately rewarded many times over. All of his friends remark on this. Back in 1982, he finally had the resources to reward all of his long-time friends and supporters. That year, he hosted his first Nostalgia Week in the Bugaboos, where he treated a number of these individuals to a free week of heli-skiing. There were extra guides and slower groups for those who wanted a more leisurely pace. Hans and his old friends gathered to reminisce, and there was an Austrian musical group to

Hans Gmoser, Ethan Compton, Brooks Dodge and
Art Patterson at an early Nostalgia Week reunion

entertain the guests. Hans played his zither and Leo sang. It soon became a tradition that would continue until the 40th anniversary in 2005.

One last essential step in the evolution of Canadian Mountain Holidays took place on November 21, 1988. It had always been a problem that Canadian Mountain Holidays Ltd., the name that everyone knew, was actually Hans and Leo's company, owning shares in the parent company, Bugaboo Helicopter Skiing Ltd. On that date, the two organizations basically switched names, the parent company becoming Canadian Mountain Holidays Inc., while Hans and Leo's company became Bugaboo Helicopter Skiing Inc.

In the late 1980s, the much-deserved honours and tributes arrived. In 1986, Hans was elected an honourary member of The Alpine Club of Canada. On April 29, 1987, at Rideau Hall in Ottawa, Governor General Jeanne Sauvé presented Hans with the Order of Canada. Hans was very proud of this honour and for the rest of his life wore his OC pin on his suit lapel. In November 1989, Hans received two awards: he was elected to the Honour Roll of Canadian Skiing and also received the Summit of Excellence Award at the Banff Mountain Film Festival.

By 1991, CMH was operating nine heli-ski areas, with a staff of 300, and was welcoming 5,000 skiers each winter and 3,000 hikers each summer. Hans had created a completely new industry that would soon have many imitators around the world. Hans had been in the right place at the right time; jet-helicopter technology was just developing when Hans had begun experimenting with heli-skiing. But Hans was also the right man for the job, possessing an extensive knowledge of the mountains of western Canada, superior guiding skills, plenty of experience, amazing leadership ability and an almost inexhaustible energy. Now, however, it was time for him to step back from the company.

PART FIVE

Elder Statesman
1991–2006

"Looking back, I've had a good interesting life. I had my time in the mountains. I had my time as a businessman. So what more can I ask for?"

Retirement and Disaster

Hans began to withdraw from the day-to-day management of CMH in 1989. In his typical style, he had a well-planned "Phase Out Schedule": over the next three years, he would gradually give up responsibilities and would relinquish all operational duties. He would, however, remain chairman of the board. Mark Kingsbury would become president and CEO of CMH; Evelyn Matthews, the chief financial officer; Walter Bruns, the chief operating officer; and others such as Marty von Neudegg, Jori Guetg and Kobi Wyss would assume more responsibilities.

In a letter to Mark Kingsbury dated May 5, 1990, Hans revealed some of his own management philosophy. Referring to a discussion they had had earlier, he wrote: "I also talked about the importance of setting a good example as the best way to inspire the people working for you. Particularly, an appropriate measure of modesty and humility goes a long way in engendering loyalty among the people around you. Along with that I pointed out the dangers of bestowing favoritism among one's own."

Then Hans wrote of something he considered very important: "As you see now, the work load is enormous

and will get more so. As it does, there is a great temptation to overlook the details or not to be totally exacting
in everything you do. You must, at all costs, resist falling
into this trap. While everything has to be done with speed
and efficiency, it <u>always</u> has to be done <u>thoroughly and
properly</u>. Although you are about to be at the head of a
sizeable enterprise and you must delegate many of your
responsibilities, you must always retain <u>relentless attention
to detail</u>, otherwise it will all run away from you!"

Mark was formally named president and CEO of
Canadian Mountain Holidays on January 7, 1991. Hans
was looking forward to a long and enjoyable retirement.
Unfortunately, disaster struck only two months later. On
March 12, an avalanche on a run called Bay Street in the
Bugaboos killed nine guests. Evelyn recalled years later
that it was "the worst day I ever had." CMH management
stayed at the office all night dealing with media, the
authorities and the next of kin.

A lawsuit was later launched against the guide, Jocelyn
Lang, and CMH for criminal negligence and negligence,
respectively. In 1995 and 1996, Mark, Hans, Marty and
their lawyers spent seven months in the British Columbia
Supreme Court in Vancouver defending the case. CMH
and the entire heli-ski industry were fighting for their
lives. Finally, on September 25, 1996, Madame Justice
Koenigsberg wrote in her disposition:

1. The action against Jocelyn Lang for criminal
   negligence is dismissed.

2. The action against any and all of the defendants
   in negligence is dismissed.

3. The waiver is valid and if there was a finding of
   negligence it would exonerate the defendants
   of liability.

Canadian Mountain Holidays and the individuals concerned were found blameless. They had done everything that could be reasonably expected of them to ensure the safety of their clients. Most critically, the waiver that all guests sign, acknowledging and accepting the risk involved and relinquishing the right to sue, was held to be legal and valid. But it was a terrible way for Hans to end his years at the helm of CMH, and according to one friend, he was bitter. He had put so much energy into safety and still he was hit by tragedy.

Shortly after the Bay Street avalanche, Hans had received a letter from Gordon Gray, the husband of his old girlfriend, Carter Meyer. They were coming to Canada to ski at the Gothics; Carter was frightened by the risk of avalanche and unsure whether to come or not. Hans had reassured them and, when they arrived, skied with them for three or four days to calm Carter down.

New Challenges

In the early years of Hans's retirement, he took on several jobs that kept him busy; it was not his nature to sit around. At the urging of Peter Fuhrmann, the president of The Alpine Club of Canada, Hans put a great deal of effort into fundraising for the club's proposed Alpine Centre at Lake Louise and was instrumental in securing several large donations for the project. Hans and Margaret also undertook a quiet philanthropy of their own, supporting some of their favourite institutions: the Whyte Museum of the Canadian Rockies and the Canadian Ski Museum.

From 1990 to 1996, Hans served as the president of the ACMG, the group he had helped form in 1963. According to Karl Klassen, who was the executive director of the organization during this period, Hans worked on a number of important issues: he established the foundation of the ACMG's liability insurance coverage; he was instrumental in raising the ACMG's credibility in the eyes of government; he supported ongoing revisions to the training and certification program; and he started the negotiations and established the groundwork that eventually saw the ACMG's training and certification courses become a recognized program at Thompson Rivers University in Kamloops, BC.

In 1992, Hans was elected an honourary member of the International Federation of Mountain Guides Associations, and in the spring of 1996 he had the great honour of hosting their general assembly in Banff. From around the world came leading mountain guides to meet and discuss their affairs. Hans was at the centre of it all, and many of the foreign guides were invited to visit CMH lodges to see the mountains of Canada. After retiring as president, Hans was made honourary president of the ACMG.

In January of 1993, Hans received a letter from his old client and business partner Jack MacKenzie. It was a warm and emotional summing-up of their time together:

> In all of this I have a sense of gratitude in having been included in the CMH saga. Being in the mountains was always a thrill for this small town boy from Stettler. And in many of those memories you play an outstanding part. You took me places where I could never have travelled. On at least two occasions you caught me on a tight rope when I slipped and might have pulled us both off (once on the Cory Crack at the very top, and another time on very steep snow on the ridge on the Howser Spire in the Bugaboos). But more than that, you taught me respect for the mountains and for those with whom I travelled. And certainly I learned respect and admiration for you!

*Hans at Bugaboo Lodge in 1996 with renowned
German mountaineer and guide Anderl Heckmair*

As a result of all this, our whole family has been enriched, and I don't mean just in the financial senses. But rather in having been involved with an exciting venture in which excellence has been demonstrated in many ways and over a long period of time. And in all of this you have played the leading part.

Time to Sell

For Hans, it was now becoming time to sell Canadian Mountain Holidays. From the beginning, Jack and Charles had said, "When you sell, we will too." Perhaps Hans was uneasy with his major asset being managed by others, or perhaps it was because there were younger members on the board who had a different approach to running the company. Maybe he just wanted to enjoy the fruits of all that hard work. Whatever it was, Hans eventually sold the business in May 1995, to Alpine Helicopters. The original partners—Hans and Leo, Charles and Geraldine Barlow, Jack and Sheila MacKenzie[1] and Ben Walsh—were still the major shareholders. Bill Putnam owned a small number of shares, and about ten employees, who had taken shares in the company in lieu of annual bonuses, also shared in the proceeds. The selling price was rumoured to be about $15 million. Although he had more lucrative offers, Hans sold to Alpine Helicopters because he felt that the owner, Pat Aldous, would respect the corporate culture he had created, and that was more important to Hans than money.

Hans had complex feelings about heli-skiing towards the end. In an interview on October 15, 1994, writer Phil Dowling asked Hans if he had any regrets. Hans replied:

If I had known when it all started, what it would turn into, and had the perspective I have today, I probably would not have done it. I feel a little bit like the Sorcerer's Apprentice or maybe like Doctor Faust. On the one hand it gave an incredible amount of pleasure to a lot of people, but on the other hand you feed an ego that I find a little distasteful. A lot of people are out there and they forget what I think is really the essence: that with a lot of ease you can get in some very beautiful country. But the beautiful country is lost on them. It's purely pitch and consistency of snow, how fast and how much you can ski, and there is no end, no stage where somebody will say, "I am content, I've had a wonderful time." They're always demanding more, and that I am disappointed about.

Freedom to Enjoy

Hans was now wealthy and free to pursue the pleasures that he had put off for so long. He loved classical music, especially the operas of Mozart and Wagner, and often Hans and Margaret would attend symphony and opera performances in Calgary. A particular favourite was *An Alpine Symphony* by Richard Strauss. Margaret also enjoyed classical music: guitar solos and music from the baroque period. Her favourite music, however, was hits of the day, performed by Elton John, Cat Stevens and Joni Mitchell. Hans, as might be expected, had no interest in popular music.

Hans continued to go on long cycle trips with Margaret and friends such as Philippe and Mireille Delesalle. He fell in love with cycling in Japan and returned 13 times, making many friends in that country. And he returned often to Europe to cycle, Horst Eblen from Germany being a regular companion. In Austria, Hans was considered a local, often joining friends for an evening of traditional music. In his hometown of Traun, he was an honourary member of a semiprofessional group called Haus Musik in which his brother, Walter, played.

Hans was finally able to spend more time with his sons. They made cycling trips to Japan, Norway and Austria together and kayaking trips to the Queen Charlotte Islands. Hans and his brother-in-law, Sepp, took the two young men on a climbing trip to Bolivia. According to Conrad and Robson, their dad let them grow up as they chose. Conrad graduated in 1992 from McGill University with a degree in architecture, but he later became a brewmaster at a Vancouver restaurant. Robson had long wanted to be a guide like his dad and remembers that even as children he

Hans maintained his bicycle in perfect condition.

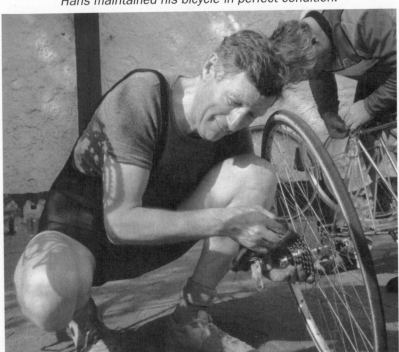

The Gmoser family kayaking in the Queen Charlotte Islands.
Left to right: Hans, Conrad, Margaret and Robson.

and Marco Delesalle, Philippe's son, dreamed of becoming guides. Robson graduated from the University of British Columbia in 1991 with a degree in forest ecology, but he now makes his living as a ski guide.

Hans also took up cross-country skiing. During the winter, on the days when the snow was good, he would ski the Cascade Fire Road near Banff. Margaret wrote: "I think the cross country skiing was an extension of ski touring, which we loved. Hans learned about waxing racing skis from Anders Lenes, who was coaching the Canadian women's team, and we got to know Sharon and Shirley Firth, the twins from Inuvik. Hans loved waxing and tried to learn all the new things from Anders. We entered a few Canadian Ski Marathons with the Delesalles and got our bronze and silver medals for completing the distance." In the early 1990s, Hans and Margaret cross-

Ski touring in Norway in 1993. Left to right:
Hans and Margaret Gmoser, Mireille and Philippe Delesalle.

country skied often in Finland, and in Norway they made a rugged, two-week, hut-to-hut traverse near Lillehammer with the Delesalles.

Hans's niece Sara Renner had grown up playing in the snow at Mount Assiniboine Lodge, which her mother and father, Barb and Sepp, had managed since 1983. During the 1988 Winter Olympics, when the cross-country ski events were held in Canmore, she had fallen in love with the sport. As she became a more accomplished racer, Hans took greater interest in her career and in competitive Nordic skiing. He would faithfully watch her compete in races on the television, even when they took place in the middle of the night, Canadian time. Eventually, she would win World Cup races and Olympic medals.

Mount Louis. The Gmoser Route *follows the dotted line.*

The Gmoser Crack *splits the face of Mount Cory.*

The east ridge of Mount Logan

Photo: Chic Scott

Mount McKinley. The Wickersham Wall is on the right, in shadow.

Photo: Pat McCloskey

Hans Gmoser searching for new horizons in the Cariboo Mountains in 1962

Photo: Fred Lindholm. Courtesy of Canadian Mountain Holidays.

Jim McConkey jumping Jim Davies' airplane in the Cariboos in 1962

Helicopter-assisted skiing in the Cariboos in 1963.
Left to right: Jim McConkey, Bob Smith, Starr Walton,
pilot Russ Timrick, Linda Crutchfield and Hans Gmoser.

*The Bugaboos in winter. Left to right: Marmolata,
Howser Spire (behind), Pigeon Spire (in front),
Snowpatch Spire, Bugaboo Spire.*

The sawmill camp in the Bugaboos in 1967

*Margaret MacGougan arriving in the
Bugaboos in the spring of 1965*

Margaret MacGougan and Hans Gmoser at Lake O'Hara in 1965

Hans and Margaret's wedding at
St. Paul's Presbyterian Church in Banff

The Gmoser family on the front steps of their home in Harvie Heights

Conrad and Robson fishing near Bugaboo Lodge

Helicopter dropping off skiers high in the Cariboos

Snowfall at Galena Lodge

Heli-skiing in the Gothics

Hans Gmoser, the founder of Canadian Mountain Holidays
and of the sport of heli-skiing

*Hans receives his Order of Canada in 1987
from Governor General Jeanne Sauvé.*

Leo and Hans making music at Mount Assiniboine Lodge in 2001

Margaret and Hans

Hans and Margaret travelled extensively around the world. In 1992, 1998 and 1999, they went trekking in Nepal: to the Makalu region, around Manaslu and to the Kanchenjunga region. In 1995, with Margaret, Conrad and Robson, brother Walter and sister-in-law Gretl, he went kayaking in Argentina and Chile. Here, according to guide Steve Smith, Hans had a magical experience when a southern right whale surfaced beside them. Hans, in fact, made many trips in later years with his brother, with whom he grew closer despite their completely different characters—Walter being calm, patient and at peace with himself. Walter had also qualified as an electrician but had chosen to spend his career repairing small motors from his own workshop. His aspirations were modest and he was content with his lot in life. He and his wife, Gretl, raised five children and still live in Traun in the home that Rosa and Erasmus built in about 1951. When Hans visited Austria, this home was his base.

Hans (right) and his brother Walter play their zithers at Battle Abbey

Hans enjoys good times at Cariboo Lodge

Meanwhile, at Bugaboo Lodge, the good times continued. On Ethan Compton's 80th birthday, in April 1997, Margaret and Bish and Betty McGill put on a skit, performing "some surgery with Ethan as the victim. He had complained that as he got older he kept crossing his skis so I [Margaret] had the idea to surgically attach big ski boots to the wrong feet so that his skis couldn't cross. We used power tools, lots of ketchup and vodka in the IV line."

Margaret recalled another skit: "The year of 2000—the millennium problems with computers, clocks, etc.—Bish, Betty, Joan Patterson and I did brain surgery on the oldest heli-ski guide in CMH: Bob Geber. We had to insert a special chip in his brain so that he could function in the new millennium. I had one of the other guides dress up as the cleaning lady with a mop to clean up the operating room after the surgery while Bob was still sedated. Unknown to Bob, I told the cleaning lady to try to fondle Bob to check if he was still alive or a stiff—no pun intended. Of course Bob jumped off the table as though he was on fire, and the guests thought this was a great joke."

The Body Fails

Hans's health was not good in his later years. Perhaps he had just worked his body too hard for too long and it began to let him down. He continued to break bones: a pelvis fracture in 1993 while cross-country skiing, and a hip fracture in 1994 in a fall while cycling. In 1997, he developed prostate cancer and underwent surgery. In 1999, and again in 2000, he underwent surgery for rotator cuff repairs to both his right and left shoulders. He developed disc and facet-joint degeneration and compression fractures of the thoracic spine, which gave him chronic back pain. In later years, he had to wear a back brace when heli-skiing, which did little to help. He also developed chronic obstructive pulmonary disease and had serious difficulty breathing while exercising. Through all of this, however, he still pushed himself. In 2003, with Philippe, he made a month-long cycle trip through Austria, Germany and the Czech Republic, in which they covered 2500 kilometres and climbed 40,000 metres!

Hans did not accept age and his disabilities well. He was constantly looking for the fountain of youth, the magic bullet that would relieve his pains. He took multivitamin pills and Tibetan herbal remedies and, according to Margaret, "seemed to be looking for the answer to aging by changing doctors and trying different things." But there was nothing that would halt the degeneration of his body.

The Suppressed Politician

In his later years, Hans had strong and very right-wing political views. He supported Chilean dictator Augusto Pinochet and opposed Canada's condemnation of the South African apartheid regime. In 2003, he was in favour of the US decision to invade Iraq. On the other hand, he supported the Kyoto Protocol and wrote many times to politicians, asking them to take action on climate change. In view of the nature of the heli-ski industry and its reliance on snow, this is not surprising.

Hans wrote often to the local media, in a style that has been described as "Gmoserian brevity." On January 23, 1988, to the *Banff Crag and Canyon* newspaper, he wrote: "Peering through my salt splattered windshield onto a slimy road, dimly lit by my salt encrusted headlights, I wonder who conceived the idiotic notion that salt on the roads improves winter driving conditions. From my perspective it only makes it worse." On March 18, 1989, he wrote again to the *Banff Crag and Canyon*: "Our government needs to be commended for the swift and decisive action to save us from poisoned Chilean fruit. If our government could act as resolutely to reduce our national debt, we would have something to cheer about."

Hans continued to hate the Liberals and supported both the Reform and Conservative parties, though "not out of belief in what you do, but because your political opponents are even more irresponsible." He often wrote letters to the three levels of government on a variety of issues: tourism; education; subsidies to industry (he was against them); deficit elimination; an airport for the interior of British Columbia; gun control (he supported it); free trade (he supported it); the goods and services tax (he supported it, but at no more than 6 per cent); and trains blowing their whistles near his home in Harvie Heights. In 1988, to Kootenay MLA Anne Edwards, he wrote: "Tourism, like any other industry, should stand on its own feet through vision, diligence and unrelenting commitment to excellence. Anyone in this province not succeeding in the tourism industry is amiss in blaming such failure on the lack of promotional spending by the provincial government. The problems are usually a poorly conceived enterprise, lack of commitment and poor service to the public."

To Preston Manning, leader of the Reform Party, the official opposition in Parliament, he sent the following wise comment in 1997: "We have been spoiled by the overabundance of natural resources in this country. Consequently we use these energy sources as if there was no end to them. Subsequently we have been very slow to develop the skills necessary to building an economy less reliant on natural resource exploitation. What we are doing to our environment in terms of energy consumption and the exploitation of energy sources, borders on insanity."

To Canada's national newspaper, *the Globe and Mail*, he opined in 1999: "If we want young people to find jobs, we have to prepare them for this task. As it is we coddle them for 12 years inside a cocoon, devoid of all reality. There is no discipline, no pressure to perform, no penalty for failure. Being there is good enough! There is strong emphasis on all their rights, little mention of their obligations. Then we turn them loose in a brutal, fiercely competitive world and are indignantly surprised that these people cannot find jobs. They have never been prepared to compete for a job and should they be lucky enough to find a job are ill equipped to acquire specific job skills."

Perhaps Hans's prize letter was written on October 15, 1984, to Greg Stevens, the representative for Harvie Heights in Alberta's provincial government: "Please find enclosed a copy of my 'Notice of Assessment Complaint'. It should be self-explanatory. I thought I had voted for a Conservative Government, not for the Communists. Can you explain to me how a government with your mandate can increase property taxes over 100% in one year and at the same time spend money on ski developments, land developments and activities the government has no business being in and which compete head on with private enterprise. Yours seethingly, Hans Gmoser."

Shunning the Spotlight

After retirement, Hans became the elder statesman of the Bow Valley, working quietly behind the scenes for the well-being of the mountain community. He knew everyone: the successful men of business, the young guides, the leading alpinists, the organizers of clubs and the national and provincial park officials. And he was very successful, for no place in the world has such a together mountain community as the region from Calgary to Revelstoke. Much of this is due to Hans, who realized that we would achieve much more if we worked together than if we argued and competed. In the year 2000, when my book *Pushing the Limits: The Story of Canadian Mountaineering* came out, Brian Greenwood requested that I supply him with four copies for his children and that I ask Hans to sign them for him. Hans very magnanimously wrote in the front of each book: "For Brian, who was always a better climber than me."

Of course, the whole community knew Hans, as he walked the streets of Banff and Canmore with his slightly stooped shoulders and patrician demeanour. Everyone had their story of when they had met Hans and how modest and humble he had been. Most, however, only knew Hans after the success of his heli-skiing operation and not in his

Hans and his granddaughter, Raine

youth, when he was unknown and alone. Hans once said to me, "I spent half my life trying to be recognized and half my life trying to be forgotten."

In 1994, and again in 1996, Hans became a grandfather, to Conrad's two children. Like many ambitious men, he had more time to devote to his grandchildren than he had had for his own children. According to Margaret, "Hans' biggest regret was that he didn't take the time or realize the importance of taking the time to be with his sons when they were young. It's such a rapid developmental time and he missed most of it." But Hans loved being a grandfather to Raine and Wolfie. "He liked to take them skiing—we would take them to Vernon for a few days of ski lessons before Xmas. He enjoyed going to cut the Christmas tree every year and taking them cross-country skiing."

Hans and Margaret continued to live quietly in their modest home in Harvie Heights. Inside the small entrance-way, a collage of family photos hung on the wall. Inter-estingly, there were no images of Hans on his great climbs or with his famous guests. Visitors sat on a small chair to take off outside shoes and put on soft grey felt slippers. The home was unpretentious; Hans and Margaret were not given to showing off their wealth or their exciting lives. Above the fireplace sat an ornate, silver-handled walking stick that Hans had inherited from Lizzie. There were few books or CDs on show. In the dining room, two framed prints hung above the hand-carved wooden table: a picture of Mount Assiniboine in winter and a picture of the Bugaboos in winter, painted by two of our best Canadian artists, Peter Whyte and his wife, Catharine, respectively. An original by Walter J. Phillips also hung on the wall, a painting that Margaret had inherited from her father.

There was always a steady stream of friends passing through the Gmoser home, many of them skiing and cycling companions from Europe, the United States and Japan. Most of them had some connection with CMH: some were old guests, and some worked in their respective countries as agents for the company. The Gmosers just gave them the key to the house and said, "Make yourselves at home."

In the basement was Hans's equipment, waxing and cycle room. Arranged around the room were the skis, boots and bicycles of an active outdoor life. Here he worked intensely, waxing his skis or maintaining his bicycles. And they were good bikes, for Hans was willing to spend money on the highest-quality frames of titanium, steel and carbon made by Seven in the United States.

According to Margaret, Hans was finally happy. "He felt fortunate to be able to follow his dreams in Canada. This country was very good to him. He met such interesting people being a guide. He was proud of what he created, but also happy to let it go so that he could travel and enjoy retirement."

Hans enjoyed a glass of good wine with dinner, but drank little. Often he would split a bottle and decant half for another evening. He rarely watched television unless it was the weather channel, preferring instead to practise the zither every evening. According to Margaret, he did his relaxing while reading in bed before turning out the light.

More and more, Hans avoided the limelight and seemed almost to be embarrassed by all the fuss made over him. Perhaps he even became tired of his own myth. Many people encouraged Hans to write his autobiography, but according to Margaret he would never agree to this. He thought it would be a bit like boasting. For years, The Alpine Club of Canada approached him to be patron of the annual Mountain Guides' Ball, but he always declined the honour. At last, in 2003, along with the rest of the founders of the Association of Canadian Mountain Guides, he allowed himself to be honoured.

Although Hans Gmoser appeared a tough individual, underneath he had an emotional heart. When he spoke of his dear friend Lizzie Rummel, who had passed away in 1980 and with whom he had spent that beautiful winter long ago, he would choke up and come to tears. When he said goodbye to Conrad and Robson after a visit, he would hug them as though it was the last time he would see them. According to Conrad, "He ended up being way more warm and fuzzy than my mom."

In March of 2001, Hans and Leo celebrated the 50th anniversary of their coming to Canada. They decided to honour the occasion by making a ten-day ski trip through the mountains near Banff with their wives, Margaret and Lynne, and old friends Mireille Delesalle and Skip Pessl. And, for some reason, they asked me to join them. Although I wrote a magazine article about the trip afterwards, it certainly wasn't for the publicity that I was included. I was very honoured and enjoyed the tour immensely, for it was something that I could never have afforded myself. We spent three nights at Mount Assiniboine Lodge, a night at Sunshine Village ski resort, two nights at Shadow Lake Lodge, a night at Lake Louise and two nights at Skoki Lodge. We skied with light packs between the lodges, admiring the magnificent scenery and telling stories as we sat drinking steaming tea and eating our sandwiches. At that time, I did not know that Hans had spent so much time skiing this same territory in the 1950s. And he never let on.

At both Mount Assiniboine Lodge and Skoki Lodge, I watched Hans after dinner, "working the room." Although he was not the official host, Hans could not turn off his natural instincts. Over several hours, he went from guest to guest, listening to their stories. He would rarely allude to his own illustrious career, and many of those he talked to likely did not even know who he was. Only later would they find out.

At Mount Assiniboine Lodge in 2001. Left to right:
Hans Gmoser, Chic Scott, Mireille Delesalle, Skip Pessl,
Lynne Grillmair, Margaret Gmoser and Leo Grillmair.

Hans was devastated in May 2001 when Mark Kingsbury, the president of CMH and the man to whom he had passed the reins, died in a motorcycle accident. Hans had great affection and respect for him. Mark's memorial service was a gut-wrenching ordeal, and afterwards Hans decided that when he died there would be no memorial service for him.

Hans continued to receive honours. In 2002, he was elected to the US National Ski Hall of Fame, and that

Hans receiving the Golden Order of Merit of the Republic of Austria at the Landhaus in Linz. Left to right: Dr. Wendelin Ettmayer (Austrian Ambassador to Canada), Hans Gmoser and Landeshauptmann Dr. Joseph Pühringer (Governor of the Province of Upper Austria).

same year he received the Goldene Verdienstzeichen der Republik Österreich (Golden Order of Merit of the Republic of Austria), an award similar to the Order of Canada. In 2004, he was awarded an honourary doctor of law degree. His old friend Nancy Greene, then chancellor of the University College of the Cariboo (today Thompson Rivers University), presided over the ceremony.

Meanwhile, he continued to challenge himself, discovering telemark skiing and resolving to perfect the technique. With newfound friend Sean Booth, who had just undergone knee surgery and needed some encouragement, he visited Mount Norquay and Sunshine Village ski resorts, where he practised the elegant Norwegian turns.

The Last Show

In the spring of 2005, to celebrate 40 years of heli-skiing, Hans hosted the last Nostalgia Weeks at Bugaboo Lodge. He was, in fact, saying goodbye to all his old friends and employees. During the first week, April 9 to 15, his clients from the first season of 1965 were there: Bob Sutherland, Inga Thompson, Lloyd Nixon, Dieter Von Hennig, Brooks and Ann Dodge, Monro Proctor, Judy Allen and Ken and Tom Boll, plus close friends Franz, Philippe, Art Patterson and Ethan Compton. Leo, with whom he had worked for 50 years, shared the hosting duties, and Kiwi was the master of ceremonies.

During the second week, April 16 to 22, Hans invited former employees of Canadian Mountain Holidays: guides Kiwi Gallagher, Peter Schlunegger, Ernst Buehler, Hans Peter Stettler, Ruedi Gertsch, Sepp Renner and Hermann Frank; housekeeper Nicole Laliberté; cooks Hannelore Achenbach, Myrna Frank (Collins) and Lynne Grillmair; secretaries Linda Heywood, Jackie Prins and Fran Gallagher (Kelly); business partners Charles and Geraldine Barlow and Sheila MacKenzie. And his entire family was there, too: Margaret; Conrad and his wife, Leslie Dyer; Robson; brother Walter and his wife, Gretl;

Margaret at the last Nostalgia Week

Kiwi and Hans at the last Nostalgia Week

At the last Nostalgia Week, April 2005.
Left to right: Franz, Hans, Leo and Philippe.

Hans and Leo with Nicole Laliberté,
who worked loyally for CMH for over 30 years

Margaret's sister, Barb; and the two grandchildren, Wolfie and Raine.

Over the years, Hans spent more and more time at Mount Assiniboine Lodge with Barb and Sepp. In February 2006, in order to allow the Renners to attend the Torino Winter Olympics, where their daughter Sara was competing, Hans and Margaret took their place in running the lodge. Hans was very happy shovelling snow and leading guests on ski tours, just as he had done 50 years earlier. On April 10, 1953, Hans had written in his *Tourenbuch*: "I will be happy when my trail leads me back up to the little hut which has become my home on a strange continent."

Hans gave his last public presentation on Tuesday, April 6, 2006, in the Grosvenor Auditorium at the National Geographic Society in Washington, DC. The title of the show was "Heli-Skiing in the Canadian Rockies." In his trademark style, Hans paid tribute to all those pioneers who had laid the foundation for his success. After telling the story of Canadian Mountain Holidays' incredible odyssey from Bugaboo sawmill to empire, he concluded with these words:

> I have no idea what the final judgment will be on my having introduced the helicopter to these mountains, and on having brought thousands of skiers, climbers and hikers year after year. But at this point I am content in knowing that most of those who have come to share these experiences have done so with a great sense of wonderment, gratitude and respect. And those who have worked with me to make it all possible have derived an immense amount of satisfaction and fulfillment in providing this service. I am also content in knowing that I have left this enterprise, its staff and guests, in the hands of people who share my outlook and values, and who will consider it to be the greatest privilege to be able to live and work in such beautiful places.

Hans and Margaret had always loved cycling in Japan. They loved the people, the food, the countryside and the culture. In May, to celebrate their 40th wedding anniversary, they took a cycle trip with Conrad and Leslie and Robson and Olivia Sofer. It was wonderful seeing

Shinsuke Meguro and Hans play their zithers in Japan

old friends, in particular Shinsuke and Tsuyako Meguro, who had befriended them on their first cycle trip in 1985. According to Margaret, Hans and Shinsuke had become like soul brothers because Shinsuke was learning to play the zither. But it was a hard trip physically for Hans; on occasion, Robson and Conrad had to carry his panniers, something Hans hated.

After Japan, Hans flew to Austria to cycle some more and Margaret went to the Queen Charlotte Islands to kayak. Hans was experiencing more back problems and was in such severe pain that both he and Margaret came home early. Hans had CAT and MRI scans done and was waiting to see a specialist. Walking and sitting were painful, but he could cycle comfortably, so he was regularly riding on the Bow Valley Parkway. Hans believed in moving to stay fit and wanted to be strong if he was going to have surgery. On July 3, he set off on his ride to Lake Louise.

At Lake Louise, where the Bow Valley Parkway meets the main highway, Hans stopped. He had pushed himself hard and after 45 kilometres was hot and thirsty. Above him, the runs of the Lake Louise ski resort, where he had first skied in 1954, marked the mountain. After a brief rest, he was on his way again, down the road towards Banff, past Baker Creek, where Al Gaetz had died in the truck accident back in 1953.

The mountains flew by again: across the valley, Mount Temple and the Ten Peaks, and above, on the left, his old friend Castle Mountain. Approaching the scenic viewpoint called Muleshoe, he slowed down. A group of tourists had stopped their cars to look at wildlife. Directly above him in the sunshine rose The Finger and Mount Cory.

It is unclear what happened next, but when several tourists looked over they saw that Hans had fallen from his bicycle and was lying on the ground. When they went to investigate, they found he had stopped breathing. A bystander, who was trained in first aid, breathed for Hans until the ambulance arrived. From Banff, he was flown by helicopter to the Foothills Hospital in Calgary.

Margaret was at home in Harvie Heights with her mother, Peggy, when she received a call from the emergency department at the Banff hospital, telling her that Hans was unconscious and had been flown to Calgary. Linda Heywood came over to take care of Peggy while Margaret drove to the city.

Hans was kept sedated for a day while the doctors did all the tests to determine what had been damaged. When the sedation was eased, it was expected that Hans might be brain-damaged, but he was completely conscious and aware. Because of the ventilator, he was unable to speak, so a method of communication was devised using an alphabet, Hans nodding his head for the letter he wanted. It was soon discovered that he had tremendous discomfort in his mouth from lack of water. This was quickly relieved.

Then he was told the bad news. He had broken his neck at the highest level and was totally paralyzed. The fracture could be repaired, but not the spinal cord injury. He would spend the rest of his life in bed on a ventilator, would develop bedsores and would likely succumb to a pneumonia infection. He could, however, choose a painless exit if he wanted one. For Hans, there was only one choice. At 3 p.m., on July 5, 2006, with Margaret, Conrad and Robson by his side, Hans Gmoser died. According to his wishes, there was no funeral or memorial service. Several weeks later, his ashes were scattered near Sunburst Lake below Mount Assiniboine, where he had found happiness so many years before.

High above, a snow plume hangs from the summit of the great peak, and all around is peace and beauty. The meadows brim with flowers, and at day's end a loon's call echoes across the lake. Then the moon rises in the starry sky. It is a fitting resting place for a romantic mountaineer, and the mountain is a fitting monument.

Notes

PART ONE

1. The city of Linz website: www.linz.at/english.

2. Walter B. Maass, *Country without a Name: Austria under Nazi Rule 1938–45* (New York: Frederick Ungar Publishing Co., 1979).

3. *Ibid.*

4. *Ibid.*

5. Richard Hiscocks, *The Rebirth of Austria* (Toronto: Oxford University Press, 1953).

6. Gordon Brook-Shepherd, *The Austrians: A Thousand-Year Odyssey* (New York: Carrol & Graf Publishers Inc., 1997).

7. *Ibid.*

8. When the author hiked through this valley in the summer of 2007, he was shocked to see the destruction produced by logging operations. Hans would have been saddened indeed to see his cathedral of God destroyed.

9. The Grossglockner road was, and still is, a toll road.

10. We have no word in English like this one. It means comfortable, homey, genial or pleasant.

11. The clerk was probably correct, because at this time Ontario and Quebec would have had far more ski resorts than western Canada.

12. At this time in Europe, climbs were graded in difficulty from I to VI. A Grade II climb would require a rope and on the North American grading scale would be lower-fifth-class climbing. A Grade III climb would be about 5.5, and a Grade VI climb would be about 5.8.

13. Spitzmauer's north pillar is now graded V, but at that time it was a Grade VI climb.

PART TWO

1. The ridge would be climbed ten years later by Brian Greenwood, Don Vockeroth and Phyllis Johnston.

2. Jerry Johnston was born and raised in Banff. During the 1960s and 1970s, he ran the Sunshine Village Ski School. He would go on to found the Canadian Association for Disabled Skiing, for which he would receive the Order of Canada in 2000.

3. Temple Lodge is now a part of the Lake Louise ski resort.

4. Bruno Engler was a Swiss-certified ski instructor but not a Swiss-certified mountain guide.

5. Renate Hick and Sigrid Werte were very adventurous young women indeed. Obsessed with travel, the pair spent a year in England, a year in France and a year in Mexico in the early 1950s. In 1957, after their adventure in the Little Yoho, they travelled by freighter to Japan, where they spent three months, then continued by freighter on to India. Travelling on small motor scooters and sleeping in a tent, they toured India, then walked north to Kathmandu, Nepal, where they made a trek into the Langtang region of the Himalaya. From Bombay, they took a freighter to Egypt, visited Turkey and Greece, then returned to Germany, where Renate would meet Hans again in 1958. Renate eventually married Polish climber Felix Belczyk and settled in Canada.

6. Trima skins were very popular in the 1950s and 1960s. They had three plates attached to the smooth side of the skin, with a groove in them. A pair of holes were drilled at three places in the ski, and three rails inserted and attached to the ski. Then the skin was slid onto the rails in the ski and attached at the tip. They worked very well, but the rails would often bend if one hit a rock.

7. Elfriede Steiner was also a remarkable woman. In 1953, at the age of 22, she set off from Vienna across Europe on a one-horsepower moped (combination motorbike and bicycle). In about a year, she rode across Germany, Denmark, Sweden, Finland and Norway, then back to Denmark, across Holland, Belgium and France, returning to Austria. Shortly afterwards, she set off again across Switzerland, France and Spain. Travelling to Tangiers, she had plans to ride around the Mediterranean, but a close call one night convinced her that this was not a good idea. Elfriede wrote a book about her adventures called *Eine Madchen Sieht Europa*.

8. Fred Crickard went on to become a rear admiral in the Canadian Navy.

PART THREE

1. Blumer and his team assumed that they were making the second ascent of the peak, but, in fact, it may have been the first. An earlier ascent in 1912, by Dora Keen, may have only reached the lower east summit.

2. Hans and his team climbed to the East Peak of Mount Logan (5900 m), which is about 60 metres lower than the main summit.

3. According to the article in the *Canadian Alpine Journal*, the group stopped at the base of the ridge and established an emergency rest camp, then continued the next morning to base camp.

4. A ninth icefield, the Clemenceau, is now included in the traverse.

5. According to Jim, the practice session took place on Johnson Lake near Banff.

6. Jim McConkey's son, Shane, is today one of skiing's extreme risk-takers.

7. Lofthouse was actually born in Windsor, Ontario, but from the age of two grew up in England. He returned to Canada in 1954 at the age of 22.

PART FOUR

1. It appears that the Ski Club of the Canadian Rockies soon abandoned their Bugaboo plans, for Hans never mentions them again.

2. Hans Gmoser was best man at the wedding of Mike and Bonnie Wiegele on October 7, 1967.

3. Leo Grillmair purchased Frank Stark's shares in Rocky Mountain Guides Limited in 1965 and purchased Heinz Kahl's shares the next year, making him Hans's sole partner in the company. Heinz Kahl died of leukemia in January 1967, and Frank Stark died in a plane crash on October 6, 1984.

4. Canadian Mountain Holidays offered an ascent of Mount Robson that summer from July 27 to August 2. Hans led this climb with guides Ruedi Gertsch and Ferdl Taxbock.

5. Bugaboo Glacier Provincial Park and Bugaboo Alpine Recreation Area had been created in and around the Bugaboo Spires in 1969.

PART FIVE

1. Some of the MacKenzie shares had been transferred to their children.

Family Tree

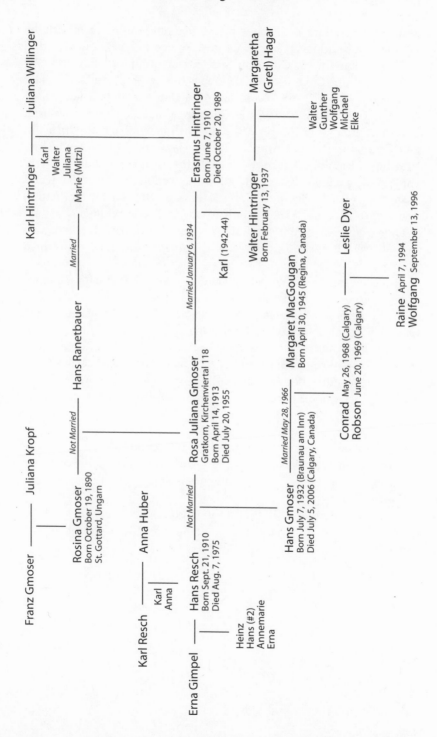

Sources

Much of the content in the book was derived from interviews with the following individuals: Charles Barlow, Renate Belcyzk (Hick), Adolf Bitterlich, Jan Burks, Guy Clarkson, Ethan Compton, Jim and Sue Davies, Philippe Delesalle, Brooks Dodge, Franz Dopf, Pat Duffy, Peter Fuhrmann, Lloyd "Kiwi" Gallagher, Don Gardner, Bob Geber, Ruedi Gertsch, Conrad Gmoser, Hans Gmoser, Margaret Gmoser, Robson Gmoser, Carter Gray (Meyer), Elfriede Grillmair, Elizabeth Grillmair, Leo Grillmair, Lynne Grillmair, Linda Heywood, Walter and Gretl Hintringer, Ralphine Locke, Evelyn Matthews, Jim McConkey, Marty von Neudegg, Lloyd Nixon, Art Patterson, Gordon Rathbone, Sepp and Barb Renner, Isabel Schmidt (Spreat), Steve Smith, Hans Peter Stettler, Bob Sutherland, Jim Tarrant, Keith Webb and Erwin Widmer.

Others shared memories of Hans with me in writing: Dieter von Hennig, Pete Parrish, Skip Pessl, Bill Putnam, Karl Ricker and Inga Thompson.

A special thanks is due to Phil Dowling, who shared with me tapes of his interviews with Hans Gmoser.

Much material of interest is available at the Whyte Museum of the Canadian Rockies, located in Banff, Alberta:

> Hans Gmoser Archives
>> —text (speeches and film commentaries) (M224/1–19)
>> —films (M224/S49/V68)
>> —photos (Accn. 7361—unprocessed)
>
> Chic Scott Archives (M57/S47)
> Catharine Whyte Archives (M36 1314–1316)
> Stanley Mitchell Hut logbook (M200/AC004 M/3)

Hans Gmoser's personal papers—his *Tourenbuch*, expedition journals and personal correspondence—were a rich resource in preparing this biography.

Canadian Mountain Holidays brochures were very helpful in ascertaining dates of events and other facts in the evolution of the company.

Photo Credits

Gmoser Family Archives: frontispiece, 4, 7, 8, 11, 12, 28, 29, 36 (bottom), 62 (bottom), 70 (Clair Brown), 76, 93, 102, 104, 117, 126, 135, 196, 216, 219, 220, 228, 232 (top and bottom), 236 (top and bottom), 246, 250, 256, 257, 267, 270, 273, 289 (P. Wingle), 293, 298, 301, 304 (Alex Pytlowany), 309, 312, 313, 314, 315, 316, 321, 326, 329, 330, 331.

Whyte Museum of the Canadian Rockies: 20, 22, 24, 31, 33, 39, 41, 42, 48, 51, 52, 58 (Elsa Wyatt), 62 (top), 67, 71, 72, 80 (V554/788PA), 89, 90 (P. Delesalle), 91, 95 (V227/5209), 96 (top and bottom), 99, 111, 115, 123 (Clair Brown), 132, 139, 141, 153, 165, 179 (Bruno Engler), 180, 184/85 (P. Delesalle), 189 (Clair Brown), 191, 193, 194, 200, 274, 276.

Hintringer Family Archives: 36 (top), 109, 112 (top and bottom) (P. Delesalle).

Philippe Delesalle: 86, 87, 156, 171, 181, 183.

Lloyd Nixon: 2/3, 231 (top and bottom), 235.

Brad White: 284, 327, 328 (top and bottom).

Canadian Mountain Holidays: 209, 255.

Karl Ricker: 157, 160, 166, 169.

Glenbow Archives: 225 (PA 2351-6).

Franz Dopf: 23, 77, 88, 105, 130, 131.

VÖEST Geschichte Club: 25.

Resch Family Archives: 6.

Renate Belcyzk: 118, 119.

Erwin Tontsch: 239, 240.

Pierre Lemire: 297, 302.

Leo Grillmair: 75, 244.

Lloyd Gallagher: 247.

Alec Pytlowany: 304.

Aileen Harmon: 108.

Bruno Engler: 279.

Leon Blumer: 142.

Roberta Dopf: 47.

Gunti Prinz: 212.

Glen Boles: 128.

Chic Scott: 325.

Pat Duffy: 98.

Brief Bibliography

JOURNAL ARTICLES (CHRONOLOGICAL)

Gmoser, Hans. "Some New Routes." *Canadian Alpine Journal* (*CAJ*), Vol. 37 (1954), p. 108.

Gmoser, Hans. "VI Grade Climbing." *CAJ*, Vol. 39 (1956), p. 89.

Gmoser, Hans. "Mt. Finger." *CAJ*, Vol. 40 (1957), p. 84.

"Mount Edith, Canadian Rockies." *American Alpine Journal* (*AAJ*), Vol. 10, No. 2, Issue 31 (1957), p. 158.

Crickard, F.W. "Sailors Adrift in the Rockies." *CAJ*, Vol. 41 (1958), p. 57.

Gmoser, Hans. "Yamnuska." *CAJ*, Vol. 41 (1958), p. 61.

Spinkova, Sarka. "Mount Robson, 1957." *CAJ*, Vol. 41 (1958), p. 54.

Blumer, Leon. "Mount Blackburn—Second Ascent." *AAJ*, Vol. 11, No. 2, Issue 33 (1959), p. 237.

Spinkova, Sarka. "First Canadian Ascent of Mt. Alberta." *CAJ*, Vol. 42 (1959), p. 45.

Ricker, Karl. "The All Canadian Mt. Logan Expedition." *CAJ*, Vol. 43 (1960), p. 1.

Gmoser, Hans. "High-Level Ski Route from Lake Louise to Jasper." *CAJ*, Vol. 44 (1961), p. 1.

Gmoser, Hans. "How Steep Is Steep." *CAJ*, Vol. 44 (1961), p. 51.

Gmoser, Hans. "Mount Louis." *AAJ*, Vol. 13, No. 1, Issue 36 (1962), p. 237.

Gray, J. K. "The Mummery and Freshfield Glaciers." *CAJ*, Vol. 45 (1962), p. 27.

Gmoser, Hans. "Canadian Mt. McKinley Expedition 1963, First Ascent of the Wickersham Wall." *CAJ*, Vol. 47 (1964), p. 16.

Gmoser, Hans. "Canadian Wickersham Wall Ascent of Mount McKinley." *AAJ*, Vol. 14, No. 1, Issue 38 (1964), p. 43.

Yoshizawa, Ichiro. "Two Japanese Expeditions to Mount Logan's East Ridge." *AAJ*, Vol. 14, No. 2, Issue 39 (1965), p. 435.

Gmoser, Hans. "Neil Brown" (obituary). *CAJ*, Vol. 51 (1968), p. 257.

BOOKS

Donahue, Topher. *Bugaboo Dreams.* Calgary: Rocky Mountain Books, 2008.

Dowling, Phil. *The Mountaineers: Famous Climbers in Canada.* Edmonton: Hurtig, 1979.

Gmoser, Hans (with Neal and Linda Rogers). *25 Years of CMH Heli-Skiing.* Banff: CMH Heli-Skiing, 1991.

Iowa Mountaineers Journal, Twenty-fifth Anniversary Issue, Vol. V, No. 5 (1965).

Jones, Chris. *Climbing in North America.* Berkeley: University of California Press, 1976.

Martel, Lynn. *Route Finding: 40 Years of Canada's Mountain Guiding Association.* Canmore, AB: The Alpine Club of Canada, 2003.

Sandford, R.W. *At the Top: 100 Years of Guiding in Canada.* Canmore, AB: The Alpine Club of Canada and the Association of Canadian Mountain Guides, 1996.

Scott, Chic. *Pushing the Limits: The Story of Canadian Mountaineering.* Calgary: Rocky Mountain Books, 2000.

Scott, Chic. *Summits and Icefields: Alpine Ski Tours in the Canadian Rockies.* Calgary: Rocky Mountain Books, 2003.

Scott, Chic. *Powder Pioneers: Ski Stories from the Canadian Rockies and Columbia Mountains.* Calgary: Rocky Mountain Books, 2005.

Scott, Chic, et al. *The Yam: 50 Years of Climbing on Yamnuska.* Calgary: Rocky Mountain Books, 2003.

Selters, Andy. *Ways to the Sky: A Historical Guide to North American Mountaineering.* Golden, CO: American Alpine Club, 2004.

FILMS

With Skis and Rope (1957–1958)

Vagabonds of the Mountains (1959–1960)

Of Skiers and Mountains (1960–1961)

Deep Powder and Steep Rock (1961–1962)

To the Forbidden Snowfields (1962–1963)

Skis Over McKinley (1963–1964)

Adventure Bound (1964–1965)

Roving Skis (1965–1966)

High Road to Skiing (1966–1967)

Rendezvous in the Selkirks (1967–1968)

Acknowledgements

I would like to thank Margaret, Conrad and Robson Gmoser for offering me the honour of writing this book and for their ongoing support and cooperation. Margaret was always very generous in allowing me free access to Hans's journals, diaries, letters, business papers and corporate documents.

Many others helped me in my task: Walter and Gretl Hintringer and their family, who were so kind and welcoming to me in Austria; Franz and Roberta Dopf, who shared a wonderful adventure at the Prielschutzhaus with me; and Rudi and Sherry Kranabitter, who took excellent care of me in Stubaital. Ferdl Taxbock translated Hans's *Tourenbücher* and very capably led me up the Dachstein and the Grossglockner in Austria.

Special thanks are due to all of Hans's friends who enthusiastically shared their stories with me (see list in "Sources"), in particular Franz Dopf, Leo Grillmair, Philippe Delesalle and Jim Davies.

Once again, the folks at the Whyte Museum of the Canadian Rockies were always patient and helpful: Ted Hart, Don Bourdon, Elizabeth Kundert-Cameron, Lena Goon and D.L. Cameron.

Many people helped by reading the manuscript and providing comments and suggestions: Margaret Gmoser, Jim Davies, Franz Dopf, Leo Grillmair, Philippe Delesalle, Ferdl Taxbock, Ian Mitchell, Kathryn Bridge, Barbara Belyea, Kathy Madill, Jim and Mary Buckingham, Gordon Rathbone and Leslie Taylor.

My sincere thanks to Guy Clarkson and Woody MacPhail, who prepared the superb DVD of Hans Gmoser's films; to Mountain Culture at The Banff Centre, who contributed Woody's time and the authoring of the DVD; to Kelly Stauffer, who contibuted the graphics; and to the Whyte Museum of the Canadian Rockies, who gave permission for the use of the films.

Finally, I must acknowledge the wonderful team of professionals who have transformed my rough manuscript into the book you hold in your hands. For eight months, Gill Daffern and I read, reread, edited, wrote, rewrote and polished the text. It was always a pleasure to work with Gill, and if the book reads well, it is largely due to her hard work. Anne Ryall performed the copy edit and I think very little has escaped her eagle eye and extensive knowledge of grammar, punctuation and spelling. Ken Chow scanned over 500 images and prepared the first draft of the maps. His support for my projects over many years has been incredible. Linda Petras designed the book, and her 35 years of layout experience were always evident. Craig Richards, the Bow Valley's master photographer, did the colour corrections and Geoff Powter designed the striking dust jacket. My sincere thanks to all of you. This book is truly a local effort.

Index